# Left Brain, Right Brain

# Left Brain, Right Brain

## Sally P. Springer
## Georg Deutsch

State University of New York
at Stony Brook

**W. H. FREEMAN AND COMPANY**
San Francisco

*Project Editor:* Judith Wilson

*Copy Editor:* Patricia Herbst

*Designers:* Marie Carluccio and Sharon H. Smith

*Production Coordinator:* Linda Jupiter

*Illustration Coordinator:* Audre Loverde

*Artist:* Sandra McMahon

*Compositor:* Graphic Typesetting Service

*Printer and Binder:* The Maple-Vail Book Manufacturing Group

**Library of Congress Cataloging in Publication Data**

Springer, Sally P   1947-
   Left brain, right brain.

   (A series of books in psychology)
   Bibliography:  p.
   Includes index.
   1.  Cerebral dominance.  2.  Brain—Localization of
functions.  3.  Left and right (Psychology)  I.  Deutsch,
Georg, joint author.  II.  Title.  [DNLM: 1.  Brain—
Physiology.  2.  Laterality—Physiology.  WL 335 S753L]
QP385.5.S67      612′.82        80–25453
ISBN 0–7167–1269–5
ISBN 0–7167–1270–9 (pbk.)

Printed in the United States of America

9  8  7  6  5  4  3  2

*To the memory of*
*Fanny Margulies and Peter Deutsch*

# Contents

# Preface

Assigning functions to specific regions of the brain is a recurring theme in the relatively brief history of human brain research. Nowhere has this been more evident than in the attempt to divide human mental functions along the most obvious physical division of the brain—its separation into a left half and right half. Asymmetries in hemispheric function were first discovered in the nineteenth century by observers noting the differing effects of injury to the left and right halves of the brain. In the ensuing years, clinical investigators continued to document consistencies in the behavioral consequences of such injuries.

Interest in this topic dramatically increased after the split-brain operations of the 1960s and led to an explosion of research seeking to characterize the differences and to explore their implications for human behavior. Considerable attention has also been directed to seeing whether these differences may be related to diverse phenomena such as learning disabilities, psychiatric illness, and variations in cognitive styles among cultures. The topic of functional asymmetry has been controversial for at least two reasons. First, findings have not always been consistent. Investigations designed to answer the same question have sometimes produced conflicting results. Second, the temptation to speculate and draw conclusions well beyond those justified by the data has been great.

This book is an attempt to bring together a great deal of research into the nature of hemispheric asymmetries. We first present basic findings on asymmetry in brain-damaged, split-brain, and normal subjects, and then we consider special topics such as left-handedness, sex differences in brain asymmetry, and the development of asymmetry. In providing an overview of the left brain and right brain, we have tried to separate what is reasonably established as fact from what is purely speculative, without sacrificing the intrigue of either. In addition, we have sought wherever possible to identify potential explanations for inconsistent findings. We have also tried to show how the investigation of hemispheric asymmetry has yielded important insights about brain function in general. Studying the left brain and right brain is, after all, but one approach to brain research. We hope that this book conveys the sense in which it is a fruitful one.

We have written with a relatively broad audience in mind. Our intention was to be as clear as possible without compromising accuracy or understating the complexity of the issues. The text will be useful in a wide range of graduate and undergraduate courses, both basic and applied, dealing with brain–behavior relationships. We feel that it will also interest general readers who would like to learn more about brain asymmetries and wish to go beyond oversimplified or exaggerated popular accounts.

We wish to thank several colleagues and friends for their contributions to the project. Bob Liebert got us started by asking for a reference reviewing the nature of hemispheric differences. When he was told that nothing appropriate was available, he suggested that perhaps it was time to write a book. Alan Rubens, Chuck Hamilton, Phil Bryden, Morris Moscovitch, and Barry Lorinstein each made valuable comments and suggestions on various aspects of the text. Our original, cumbersome title was shortened by Peter Schulman. We would also like to add a special note of thanks to our editor, W. Hayward Rogers, for enthusiastically sharing our belief that this book should be written.

*November 1980*                                                    Sally P. Springer
                                                                   Georg Deutsch

# 1

# A Historical Overview of Clinical Evidence for Brain Asymmetries

In 1836, Marc Dax, an obscure country doctor, read a short paper at a medical society meeting in Montpellier, France. Like most of his contemporaries, Dax was not a frequent contributor to medical conferences. In fact, this paper was to be his first and only scientific presentation.

During his long career as a general practitioner, Dax had seen many patients suffering from loss of speech, known technically as *aphasia,* following damage to the brain. This observation was not new. Cases of sudden, permanent disruption in the ability to speak coherently had been reported by the ancient Greeks. Dax, however, was struck by what appeared to be an association between the loss of speech and the side of the brain where the damage had occurred. In more than 40 patients with aphasia Dax noticed signs of damage to the left half, or hemisphere, of the brain. He was unable to find a single case that involved damage to the right hemisphere alone. In his paper to the medical society, he summarized these observations and presented his conclusions: each half of the brain controls different functions; speech is controlled by the left half.

The paper was an unqualified flop. It aroused virtually no interest among those who heard it and was soon forgotten. Dax died the following year, unaware that he had anticipated one of the most exciting

1

and active areas of scientific inquiry of the second half of the twentieth century—the investigation of the differences between the left brain and the right brain.

· · ·

Although most of us think of the brain as a single structure, it is actually divided into halves. These two parts, or hemispheres, are tightly packed together inside the skull and are linked by several distinct bundles of nerve fibers, which serve as channels of communication between them.

Each hemisphere appears to be approximately a mirror-image of the other, very much in keeping with the general left–right symmetry of the human body. In fact, the control of the body's basic movement and sensation is evenly divided between the two cerebral hemispheres. This is done in a crossed fashion: the left hemisphere controls the right side of the body (right hand, right leg, etc.), and the right hemisphere controls the left side. Figure 1.1 shows this arrangement.*

The left–right physical symmetry of the brain and body does not imply, though, that the right and left sides are equivalent in all respects. We have only to examine the abilities of our two hands to see the beginnings of *asymmetry of function.* Few people are truly ambidextrous; most have a dominant hand. In many instances a person's handedness can be used to predict a great deal about the organization of higher mental functions in her or his brain. In right-handers, for example, it is almost always the case that the hemisphere that controls the dominant hand is also the hemisphere controlling speech.

Differences in the abilities of the two hands are but one reflection of basic asymmetries in the functions of the two cerebral hemispheres. A great deal of evidence has accumulated in recent years showing that the left brain and right brain, though physically symmetrical, are not identical in their capabilities or organization. There is reason to believe that the most complex human mental functions and behaviors are asymmetrically divided between the left brain and right brain.

The earliest and most dramatic evidence of functional asymmetries comes from observations of the behavior of individuals with brain damage. Data of this type are known as clinical data because they are based on the study of patients with brain damage. Marc Dax's insight about the link between damage to the left hemisphere and loss of speech was the first recognition that the two hemispheres have different functions. Other asymmetries have been discovered as well.

For example, in contrast to people who experience speech problems because of damage to the left hemisphere, patients with certain kinds of right-hemisphere damage are much more likely to have per-

---

*A brief overview of neuroanatomy may be found in the Appendix.

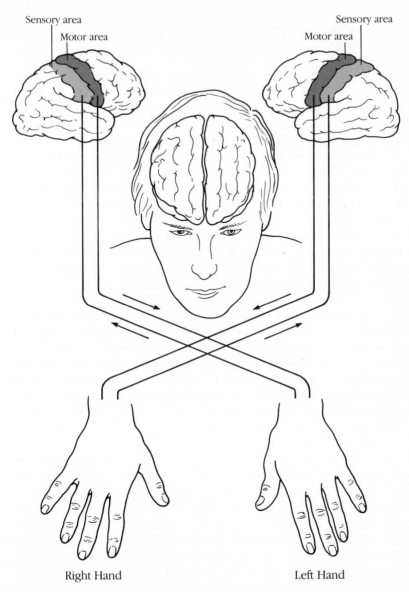

**1.1** Motor control and sensory pathways between the brain and the rest of the body are almost completely crossed. Each hand is primarily served by the cerebral hemisphere on the opposite side.

ceptual and attentional problems. These include serious difficulties in spatial orientation and memory for spatial relationships. For example, a patient may have great difficulty learning his or her way around a new building or may even be disoriented in familiar surroundings. Some right-hemisphere patients have difficulty recognizing familiar faces. Damage to the right hemisphere can also result in a problem called *neglect*. A patient experiencing the neglect syndrome pays no attention to the left side of space and sometimes pays no attention to the left side of his or her body. In many cases the patient will not eat food on the left side of the dinner plate and may refuse to acknowledge a paralyzed left arm as being his or her own. Surprisingly, similar damage to the left hemisphere usually does not produce such severe and long-lasting neglect of the right side of space.

Although clinical data pointing to brain asymmetries have been available for over 100 years, current interest in the left brain and right brain is traceable to recent work involving so-called split-brain patients. For medical reasons, these patients have undergone surgery to cut the cortical pathways that normally connect the cerebral hemispheres. Figure 1.2 shows the corpus callosum, the major pathway involved. To the untrained observer, this radical surgery seems to do little to interfere with the patient's normal functioning. To the inquisitive scientist, however, it affords an unparalleled opportunity to study the abilities of each hemisphere separately within the same head.

Special techniques make it possible to confine detailed sensory information to just one hemisphere. The limiting of stimuli to one hemisphere is often called *lateralization*. One way to accomplish lateralization is to let a blindfolded patient feel an object with one hand only. A split-brain patient who does this with the right hand (which is controlled principally by the left hemisphere) will have no difficulty naming the object. But if the procedure is repeated, this time using the left hand, the patient will be unable to name the object. Apparently, information about the object does not get through to the speech centers located in the left hemisphere. Nevertheless, the patient can easily use his or her left hand to retrieve the object from a number of other objects hidden from sight. A casual onlooker might conclude that the left hand knew and remembered what it held even though the patient did not.

Taking advantage of other techniques that confine visual and auditory information to one hemisphere at a time, researchers have demonstrated significant differences in the capabilities of the two hemispheres in split-brain patients. The left hemisphere has been found to be predominantly involved with analytic processes, especially the production and understanding of language, and it appears to process input in a sequential manner. The right hemisphere appears to be responsible for certain spatial skills and musical abilities and to process information simultaneously and holistically.

Encouraged by dramatic discoveries with brain-damaged patients, investigators have sought ways to study hemispheric differences in neurologically normal subjects. Ideally, one would like to know if the

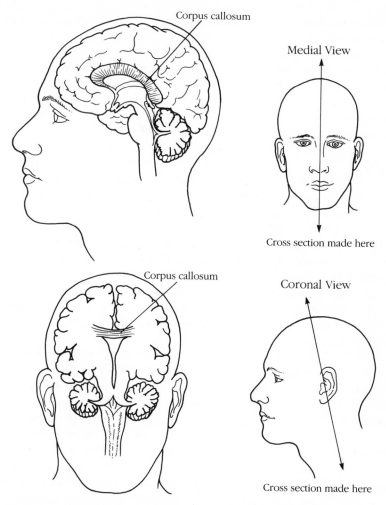

Corpus callosum

Medial View

Cross section made here

Corpus callosum

Coronal View

Cross section made here

**1.2** Two views of the cerebral hemispheres and the corpus callosum, the major nerve-fiber tract connecting them. (After Lindsay and Norman, *Human Information Processing*, p. 442, Academic Press, Inc., 1977.)

differences between the left brain and right brain found in brain-damaged patients have any consequences for the function of the normal brain. Ingenious techniques developed to answer this question have shown that they do.

Taken altogether, this clinical research has generated a great deal of excitement. It is now clear that there are differences in function between the two sides of the brain and that the differences are found in normal subjects as well as in patients. One consequence of these discoveries has been a wealth of speculation about what the asymmetries mean for behavior.

Results of the split-brain studies show that each half of the brain is capable of perceiving, learning, remembering, and feeling independently of the other, but that some differences exist in the way in which each deals with incoming information. Roger Sperry, one of the California Institute of Technology researchers who pioneered much of this work, believes that an independent stream of consciousness resides in each hemisphere of the split-brain patient.[1] He has suggested that the surgical division of the brain divides the mind into two separate realms of consciousness. Such speculation naturally leads to the possibility of dual consciousness in the intact, normal brain under certain conditions.

Other investigators have emphasized the significance of the differences between the hemispheres. It has been claimed that these differences clearly show the traditional dualisms of intellect versus intuition, science versus art, and the logical versus the mysterious. Psychologist Robert Ornstein believes brain research shows that these distinctions are not simply a reflection of culture or philosophy.[2] What used to be a belief in an Eastern versus a Western form of consciousness, he argues, now has a physiological basis in the differences between the two hemispheres.

It has also been suggested that lawyers and artists use different halves of the brain in their work and that the differences between the halves show up in activities not related to their work.[3] Others have extended this idea further and have claimed that everyone may be classified as a right-hemisphere person or as a left-hemisphere person, depending on which hemisphere guides the bulk of an individual's behavior.[4]

Recent interest in brain asymmetries has sparked concern with the general issue of handedness. Studies have shown differences between left-handers and right-handers in the way the brain is organized. What are the consequences, if any, of these differences for intelligence and for creativity? What factors produce left-handedness in the first place? Genes? Experience? Minor brain damage? These and other questions related to handedness have been the subject of intensive study in the last decade.

Various other issues have been related to research in hemispheric asymmetry. Diverse problems such as learning disabilities, stuttering, and schizophrenia have been associated with speculation about the abnormalities in the division of labor between the two hemispheres. Joseph Bogen, a neurosurgeon involved in split-brain research, believes that research on hemispheric differences has important implications for education.[5] He argues that the current emphasis on the acquisition of verbal skills and the development of analytic thought processes neglects the development of important nonverbal abilities. It is, he claims, "starving" one half of the brain and ignoring its potential contribution to the whole person.

From its modest beginnings in 1836, research on the left brain and right brain has gone on to capture the imaginations of scientists and laypersons alike. Few areas of scientific inquiry have generated so much interest from so diverse an audience. This has had both good and bad effects. On the positive side, vast quantities of new data have been collected in a short period of time, and investigators are hard at work considering the implications of their findings for important questions about human behavior.

On the negative side, there is a tendency to interpret every behavioral dichotomy, such as rational versus intuitive and deductive versus imaginative, in terms of the left brain and right brain. This occupational hazard has been named "dichotomania" by some. In addition, the dividing line between fact and fantasy has often been blurred, making it difficult for nonspecialists to know what is speculation and what has been firmly established as fact.

It is undoubtedly the case, however, that important insights into brain function and its relationship to behavior have resulted from the study of the left brain and right brain and that many more important discoveries remain to be made. The goals of this book are to survey the current state of knowledge and to point out the gaps that still exist.

We begin with an account of some of the clinical data that have given rise to current ideas concerning the left brain and right brain.

## Loss of Speech and Right-Sided Weakness: Long Overlooked Evidence of Asymmetry

Anyone who walks through a stroke ward in a hospital cannot help but notice the fairly even division of patients into those with paralyzed left sides and those with paralyzed right sides. A stroke generally involves a stoppage of the blood supply to part of the brain and results in damage to the affected region. Because blood is supplied to each hemisphere separately, strokes usually affect only one-half of the brain. Since each half controls the opposite side of the body, paralysis of the right side indicates a stroke in the left hemisphere and left-sided paralysis indicates a stroke in the right hemisphere.

Throughout the long history of aphasia, the clinical combination of speech disturbances with weakness or paralysis of the right half of the body has been reported again and again. This amounted to a link between loss of speech and damage to the left hemisphere of the brain. The significance of the relationship, however, was not appreciated by the medical community as a whole until the second half of the nineteenth century.

It is perhaps not surprising that this evidence of hemispheric asymmetry was overlooked for so long. Early anatomical studies had shown that the halves of the brain are mirror-images of each other, roughly equal in size and weight. Also, most scientists firmly believed that the brain functions as a whole unit, and thus they were not predisposed to "see" evidence that suggested otherwise.

By the first decades of the nineteenth century, however, serious attention was being given to the idea that particular functions could be assigned to specific regions of the brain. The notion that one could study the role of specific regions became known as the doctrine of *cerebral localization*.

### *The Concept of Cerebral Localization*

Franz Gall, a German anatomist, was the first to propose that the brain is not a uniform mass and that various mental faculties could be localized to different parts of the brain. The faculty of speech, he believed, is located in the frontal lobes, the part of each hemisphere closest to the front of the head. Unfortunately, Gall also claimed that the shape of the skull reflects the underlying brain tissue and that an individual's mental and emotional characteristics could be determined through a careful study of bumps on the head.

In many scientific circles Gall was dismissed as a quack on the grounds that there was no good evidence to show that skull shape could be used reliably to predict anything about the person whose head was being measured. The basic idea that different functions are controlled by different regions within the brain did attract many followers, however. Among them was Jean Baptiste Bouillaud, a French professor of medicine. Bouillaud was so certain Gall had been correct in localizing speech to the frontal lobes that he offered 500 francs (a considerable sum at the time) to anyone who could produce a patient with damage to the frontal lobes that was unaccompanied by loss of speech.[6]

For many years, most scientists quietly aligned themselves with one of the two sides of this issue. One group firmly believed that speech is controlled by the frontal lobes; the other side argued that particular functions could not be localized to specific regions of the brain. At that time there was little in the way of new data to change anyone's mind, and each group held firmly to its position in the absence of compelling evidence to the contrary. It was in this scientific climate that Marc Dax in 1836 presented his work to the medical community in Montpellier. As we have seen, his observations pointing to a special role for the left hemisphere in speech were essentially ignored.

## A Turning Point: The Findings Of Paul Broca

The stalemate ended dramatically in 1861. At a meeting of the Society of Anthropology in Paris, Bouillaud's son-in-law, Ernest Auburtin, repeated Bouillaud's claim that the center controlling speech is to be found in the frontal lobes. His remarks impressed Paul Broca, a young surgeon who was present at the meeting. Just a few days before, an old man suffering from a serious leg infection had been admitted to Broca's service at a local hospital. Although the infection was recent, for many years the patient had suffered from loss of speech as well as from paralysis on one side of his body (hemiplegia).

After the Society of Anthropology meeting, Broca approached Auburtin and suggested that it might be useful for them to examine this patient together. A day or so after they saw him, the old man died and Broca was able to perform a post-mortem examination. It showed quite clearly a region of damaged tissue, or lesion, in part of the left frontal lobe. Broca brought the brain to the next meeting of the anthropological society and told the group of his findings. No one seemed to pay much attention.

Within a few months, Broca again reported to the society that he had observed a similar lesion at autopsy in a second patient suffering from loss of speech. What changes had taken place in the minds of the Society of Anthropology members in the intervening months are not clear, but this time Broca's report was received with great excitement and touched off heated debate and controversy. Broca soon found himself viewed as the chief proponent of cerebral localization of function.

His new evidence did not convince everyone, however. Diehard critics of the concept of localization directed their attacks at him. If speech is localized in the frontal lobes, he was challenged, why don't monkeys with large frontal-brain areas possess the ability to speak? Similarly, how can one account for cases of extensive frontal-lobe damage that do not produce loss of speech?

Even Broca's terminology came under fire. He had been careful to differentiate between (1) loss of speech due to simple paralysis of the muscles used to produce speech and (2) the true loss of speech that he had seen in his patients (he called the latter "aphemia"). One critic, M. Trousseau, claimed that the word "aphemia" was derived from a Greek root meaning "infamous" and was not appropriate in this context. He suggested that "aphasia" was a better term to refer to the loss of speech. Although Broca ably defended his choice of words, investigators had already begun to use Trousseau's terminology, and it has survived to the present day.

Broca was an unwilling participant in the controversy generated by his work. He later stated that his two reports to the Society of Anthropology were simply an attempt to bring to the attention of others a curious fact that he had by chance observed, and that he did not desire to be involved in debates about the localization of speech centers. Despite his protests, Broca continued to figure centrally in the controversy. He went on to collect data from additional cases and was able to pinpoint more precisely the area of the brain involved in instances of speech loss. Figure 1.3 shows the location of this region, which has since become known as Broca's area.

Although his two earliest cases had involved lesions of the frontal lobe of the left hemisphere, Broca did not immediately see the link between speech loss and the *side* of the lesion. For two years, he made no attempt to explain this coincidence. In commenting on other cases showing the same relationship, he noted: "Here are eight cases where the lesion is situated in the posterior portion of the third frontal convolution and a thing most remarkable in all of these patients (is that) the lesion is on the left side. I do not attempt to draw a conclusion and I await new findings."[7]

By 1864, however, Broca had become convinced of the importance of the left hemisphere in speech:

> I have been struck with the fact that in my first aphemics the lesion always lay not only in the same part of the brain but always the same side—the left. Since then, from many postmortems, the lesion was always left sided. One has also seen many aphemics alive, most of them hemiplegic, and always hemiplegic on the right side. Furthermore, one has seen at autopsy lesions on the right side in patients who had shown no aphemia. It seems from all this that the faculty of articulate language is localized in the left hemisphere, or at least that it depends chiefly upon that hemisphere.[8]

This important insight embroiled Broca in yet another controversy, this time over who had priority in the discovery of this fundamental brain asymmetry. Shortly after learning of Broca's work, Gustav Dax, physician–son of Marc Dax, wrote a letter to the medical press claiming that Broca had willfully ignored his father's earlier paper showing that lesions affecting speech always occur in the left half of the brain. Broca replied, protesting that he had never heard of Dax or his work and could find no record of a paper by Dax having been delivered in 1836.

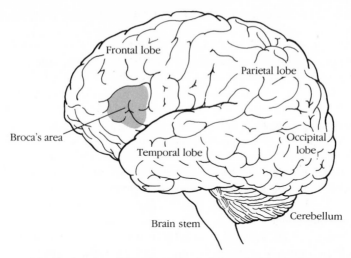

Frontal lobe

Parietal lobe

Broca's area

Temporal lobe

Occipital lobe

Cerebellum

Brain stem

**1.3**  The location of Broca's area in the left cerebral hemisphere.

Meanwhile, Gustav Dax located and proceeded to publish the text of his father's original talk in order to establish the elder Dax's priority.

Historians have disagreed about whether Broca was aware of Marc Dax's work at the time he published his own, and they will probably never resolve this question. Eventually, Broca presented a considerably more impressive argument for the association between aphasia and damage to the left hemisphere than had Dax. Dax's cases lacked verification of the location of damage as well as complete clinical histories. Broca's work, in contrast, contained extensive anatomical findings and information about the nature of the speech problems present.

Broca also went on to consider the relationship between handedness and speech. He suggested that both speech and manual dexterity are attributable to the inborn superiority of the left hemisphere in right-handers. "One can conceive," he speculated, "that there may be a certain number of individuals in whom the natural pre-eminence of the convolutions of the right hemisphere reverses the order of the phenomenon which I have just described."[9] These individuals, of course, are left-handers. Broca's "rule" that the hemisphere controlling speech is on the side opposite to the preferred hand was influential well into the twentieth century.

Broca may be properly credited with being the first person to bring to the attention of the medical community as a whole the asymmetry of the human brain with regard to speech. He was also the first to link that asymmetry with hand preference.

## The Concept of Cerebral Dominance

Within ten years of the publication of Broca's initial observations, the concept now known as *cerebral dominance* began to emerge as the major view of the relationship between the two hemispheres of the brain. In 1864, the great British neurologist John Hughlings Jackson wrote, "Not long ago, few doubted the brain to be double in function as well as physically bilateral; but now that it is certain from the re-searches of Dax, Broca, and others, that damage to one lateral half can make a man entirely speechless, the former view is disrupted."[10]

Later, in 1868, Jackson proposed his idea of the "leading" hemi-sphere—a notion that may be viewed as precursor to the idea of cer-ebral dominance. "The two brains cannot be mere duplicates," he wrote, "if damage to one alone can make a man speechless. For these processes (of speech), of which there are none higher, there must surely be one side which is leading." Jackson further concluded "that in most people the left side of the brain is the leading side—the side of the so-called will, and that the right is the automatic side."[11]

By 1870, other investigators began to realize that many types of language disorders could result from damage to the left hemisphere. Early work concentrating on problems in *producing* speech that re-sulted from injury to the left hemisphere had overlooked the fact that patients frequently had difficulty *understanding* the speech of others. Karl Wernicke, a German neurologist, is credited with showing that damage to the back part of the temporal lobe of the left hemisphere could produce difficulties in understanding speech.

Similarly, problems in reading and writing were identified in some patients and were shown to result from damage to the left hemisphere, not from damage to the right. Clearly, the picture emerging by the end of the nineteenth century was one in which the left hemisphere played a role of great importance in language functions in general and not just in speech per se. It had also become apparent that different kinds of language problems resulted from damage to different areas within the left hemisphere.

Contributing still further evidence to the notion that the left hem-isphere possesses functions not shared by the right was the work of Hugo Liepmann on a disorder known as *apraxia*. Apraxia is generally defined as the inability to perform purposeful movements on com-mand.* An apraxic patient might have no difficulty brushing his or her teeth in the context of a normal bedtime routine, but he or she would be unable to reproduce the same movements when instructed to pre-tend to brush in an unrelated context.

---

*Apraxia and other clinical disorders considered in this chapter are discussed in more detail in the Appendix.

Liepmann had shown that although such deficits are not due to a general inability to understand speech, they are associated with injury to the left hemisphere. He concluded that the left hemisphere controls "purposeful" movements as well as language, but that the specific areas of the left hemisphere involved are different in the two cases.

Taken together, these findings formed the basis of a widely held view of the relationship between the two hemispheres. One hemisphere, usually the left in right-handers, was seen as the director of speech and other higher functions; the right or "minor" hemisphere was without special functions and subordinate to control by the "dominant" left. Although the origin of the phrase is obscure, "cerebral dominance" nicely captures the idea of one half of the brain directing behavior. Although this notion underestimates the role of the right hemisphere, the term "cerebral dominance" is still widely used today.

## The Right Brain:
## The Neglected Hemisphere

Almost as soon as the concept of cerebral dominance became popular, evidence began to appear suggesting that the right or minor hemisphere also possesses specialized abilities. John Hughlings Jackson's notion of the left hemisphere as "leading" was the intellectual grandparent of the idea of dominance. Interestingly, Jackson was also one of the first to consider that an extreme, one-sided view of the way mental functions are localized in the brain was wrong. "If then," he wrote in 1865, "it should be proven by wider experience that the faculty of expression resides in one hemisphere, there is no absurdity in raising the question as to whether perception—its corresponding opposite—may be seated in the other."[12]

This speculation took more concrete form eleven years later when Jackson argued that the lobes at the rear of the brain are the seat of visual ideation or thought, and that "the right posterior lobe is the leading side, the left the more automatic."[13] Jackson based this proposal on his observation of a patient with a tumor in the right hemisphere who experienced difficulty recognizing objects, persons, and places. But like Dax's important insight 40 years earlier, Jackson's idea was way ahead of its time. Although other reports of a similar nature occasionally appeared, for the most part little attention was paid to this evidence. Investigators concerned themselves with localizing various functions within the left hemisphere and essentially ignored the right.

By the 1930s, however, enough data pointing to specialized roles for the right hemisphere had been collected to cause scientists to reconsider the functions of the minor half of the brain.

### Visuo-Spatial Abilities in the
### Right Hemisphere

One important development was the discovery of significant and fairly consistent differences in the way subjects with left-hemisphere damage and right-hemisphere damage performed on standard psychological tests. The tests were originally developed to study and compare normal subjects along dimensions such as verbal ability, appreciation of spatial relationships, and ability to manipulate forms.

The first large-scale effort using these tests to study the effects of brain damage involved over 200 patients and more than 40 different tests—an average of 19 hours of testing per patient.[14] The results of this and subsequent studies were impressive. It was found, as a general rule, that damage to the left or dominant hemisphere resulted in poor performance on the tests that emphasized verbal ability. Although this in itself was not too surprising, it was also found that patients with damage to the right hemisphere did consistently more poorly on non-verbal tests involving the manipulation of geometric figures, puzzle assembly, completion of missing parts of patterns and figures, and other tasks involving form, distance, and space relationships. Two visuo-spatial tests are shown in Figure 1.4.

The most striking evidence for specialized right-hemisphere function came from direct observation of the patients themselves. Profound disturbances in orientation and awareness were seen in patients with right-hemisphere damage. Such patients could be so disoriented in space that they were unable to find their way around a house in which they had lived for many years. Some showed neglect or "hemi-spatial inattention"; they consistently missed objects or events on their left.

Certain *agnosias,* or disturbances in the recognition or perception of familiar information, were also associated with damage to the right hemisphere. Spatial agnosia is a disorientation with respect to locations and spatial relationships. Some right-hemisphere patients have deficits in their ability to comprehend depth and distance relationships or to deal with mental images of maps and forms.

One of the most interesting forms of agnosia is facial agnosia. A patient with this condition is unable to recognize familiar faces and sometimes cannot discriminate between people in general. The deficit is quite specific. Recognition of scenes and objects, for example, may not be impaired. This problem has been found in cases where there was damage to both halves of the brain, although several investigators have argued for the importance of right-hemisphere lesions in this disorder.[15]

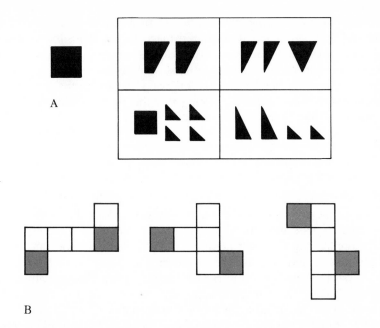

1.4 Visuo-spatial tasks. A. Which of the boxed set(s) can form the square on the outside? B. If you fold these patterns into cubes, in which cube(s) will the dark sides meet at one edge?

## The Role of the Right Hemisphere in Music

Additional evidence pointing to the specialization of the right hemisphere came from the observation that the ability to sing is frequently unaffected in patients suffering from severe speech disturbances. One of the earliest recorded cases of this type was described in 1745:

> . . . he had an attack of a violent illness which resulted in a paralysis of the entire right side of the body and complete loss of speech. He can sing certain hymns, which he had learned before he became ill, as clearly and distinctly as any healthy person. . . . Yet this man is dumb, cannot say a single word except "yes" and has to communicate by making signs with his hand.[16]

Similar cases were reported in the early 1900s, suggesting that the right hemisphere controls singing.

Other evidence consistent with this idea came from clinical reports that damage to the right half of the brain may result in the loss of musical ability, leaving speech unimpaired. This disorder, known as *amusia,* was most frequently reported in professional musicians who suffered from stroke or other brain damage. By the 1930s the medical literature contained many case histories of such people who suffered impairments in various aspects of musical ability after damage to the right hemisphere. Similar reports following damage to the left hemisphere were rarer, again suggesting that the right hemisphere is in some way critically involved in music.[17]

### Why "Discovery" of the Right Brain Took So Long

All this evidence shows that the view of the right hemisphere as the minor or passive hemisphere was inappropriate. Why did most scientists take 70 years after Broca's findings concerning the left hemisphere to recognize that the right hemisphere controls important functions? There may be several reasons for this time lag.

First, it seemed that the right hemisphere was able to withstand greater damage without producing any obvious impairments. Small lesions in particular areas of the left hemisphere drastically affected speech abilities, but comparable damage in the right hemisphere did not appear to cause any serious dysfunction. This disparity was originally interpreted as a sign of the less important role played by the right hemisphere in human behavior. It has been suggested more recently, though, that this difference simply reflects the way processes are organized in the right hemisphere: specific processes are distributed over larger regions of brain tissue in the right half of the brain than in the left half.[18]

The most likely reason for the slow recognition of the importance of the right hemisphere, however, is that disabilities caused by lesions in the right hemisphere were not so easy to analyze and fit into the traditional ideas about brain function. Most damage to the right hemisphere does not abolish any obvious human abilities in an all-or-none fashion; instead, it disturbs behavior in fairly subtle ways. Some of the problems occurring with right-brain damage are not as easy to label as the problems associated with left-hemisphere injury. They often went unnoticed or were masked by more obvious physical disabilities such as those found in most stroke victims.

It is important to keep in mind that the most debilitating effect of a stroke is the paralysis it often causes. The paralysis tends to be the patient's chief complaint or problem. Brain damage that arises from traumas such as accidents or gunshot wounds is also accompanied by complications that make it difficult to weed out subtle intellectual impairments from a host of other problems.

Despite its camouflaged role, the right hemisphere does play a vital part in human behavior. It is now clear that both hemispheres contribute in important ways to complex mental activity while differing in certain ways in their function and organization.

## Handedness and the Hemispheres

It is frequently the case in science that ideas are challenged by new evidence just as they have gained widespread acceptance. We have already seen how an extreme view of cerebral dominance was called into question by new findings dealing with the role of the right hemisphere. In the same way, Broca's "rule" linking aphasia with damage to the hemisphere opposite to the preferred hand was shown to be an oversimplification soon after Broca proposed it.

The rule accounted nicely for the relationship between damage to the left hemisphere and aphasia in right-handers. But left-handers appeared to come in two varieties—those with speech in the hemisphere opposite to their preferred hand (as predicted by Broca) and those with speech in the left hemisphere. The existence of the latter group was discovered through observations of left-handed patients who became aphasic following damage to the left hemisphere. These cases, known as instances of *crossed aphasia,* show rather dramatically that left-handedness is not necessarily the simple converse of right-handedness.[19]

The relationship of handedness to hemispheric asymmetry of function remains one of the most important questions to be resolved in the study of brain organization, and we shall return to it at various points throughout this book.

## Further Insights From the Clinic

To complete our brief account of the contributions of clinical data to the understanding of hemispheric asymmetry of function, two highly specialized neurosurgical procedures developed in the 1930s and 1940s should be mentioned. Both were designed to help the neurosurgeon determine which hemisphere was controlling speech and language function in a given individual about to undergo brain surgery for epilepsy. These procedures have also contributed significantly to our knowledge of hemispheric asymmetry of function in general.

### Direct Electrical Stimulation of the Hemispheres

Epilepsy, a disorder involving abnormal electrical activity generated within the brain, produces reactions that may range from short blackouts lasting a second or two, to full-blown grand mal seizures. During an epileptic attack, the abnormal electrical activity often originates from a specific part of the brain and then spreads to other regions.

In the early 1930s Wilder Penfield and his associates at the Montreal Neurological Institute pioneered the use of surgery to remove the area of the brain where the abnormal activity begins as a treatment for epilepsy in patients who did not respond well to drug therapy. Although the procedure proved to be successful in many instances, surgeons were reluctant to undertake cases requiring the removal of tissue that was close to the parts of the brain controlling speech and language. They wished to avoid these regions to reduce the likelihood that the surgery would merely substitute one debilitating disorder (aphasia) for another (epilepsy). Penfield's own words aptly describe the situation facing him and his colleagues:

> Twenty five years ago we were embarking on the treatment of focal epilepsy by radical surgical excision of abnormal areas of brain. In the beginning it was our practice to refuse radical operation upon the dominant hemisphere unless a lesion lay anteriorly in the frontal lobe or posteriorly in the occipital lobe. Like other neurosurgeons, we feared that removal of cortex in other parts of this hemisphere would produce aphasia. (The) aphasia literature gave no clear guide as to just what might and what might not be removed with impunity.[20]

Clearly, what was required was a method for determining with precision the location of the centers controlling speech and language in a given patient. To meet this need Penfield and his colleagues developed a procedure that involved mapping these areas by using direct electrical stimulation of the brain at the time of surgery.

Direct electrical stimulation of exposed brain tissue was not a new procedure. Preliminary work in the early 1900s had shown that since the brain itself does not contain pain receptors, it is possible for a patient to remain fully conscious while a neurosurgeon removes a flap of skull under local anesthesia and applies small electrical currents directly to the brain surface. The electrode used for the procedure could be moved to stimulate different regions of the brain. Findings had shown that electrical stimulation of specific parts of the brain would cause patients to see, hear, smell, or feel in an elementary sort of way. Stimulation of other regions caused involuntary motor responses such as the movement of an arm or leg. The major contribution made by the Montreal group was the use of direct electrical stimulation as a tool for determining the location of the centers controlling speech and language in a given individual.*

---

*Their work also had important implications for the way in which memories are stored in the brain, although we will not consider them here. The interested reader is directed to *Speech and Brain Mechanisms* by W. Penfield and L. Roberts, a fascinating, well-written account of three decades of research on brain stimulation at the Montreal Neurological Institute.

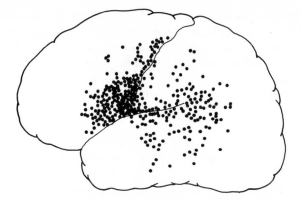

**1.5** Points along the surface of the left hemisphere where electrical stimulation resulted in interference with speech. The interference included total speech arrest, hesitation, slurring, repetition of words, and an inability to name. (From Wilder Penfield and Lamar Roberts, *Speech and Brain-Mechanisms* (Copyright © 1959 by Princeton University Press), Fig. VIII-3, p. 122. Reprinted by permission of Princeton University Press.)

During a typical procedure using direct electrical stimulation to map speech areas, the patient and surgeon are separated by a tent constructed of surgical drapes. A third person, acting as an observer, sits with the patient under the tent. While an electrical current is applied to the regions of the brain normally employed for speech, the patient is unable to speak. This interference is known as *aphasic arrest.*

These areas may be determined by having the observer show the patient a series of pictures and asking the patient to identify each one. The neurosurgeon hears the responses and is able to move the stimulating electrode over the surface of the brain to locate areas that produce interference with naming. Small, sterile squares of paper are dropped on the brain at the point of application of an electrode to provide a record of the areas stimulated and the patient's response. Throughout the procedure the patient is fully conscious but unaware of when and where the electrode will be placed. The mapping takes about 15 minutes, a small amount of time compared to the duration of the surgery itself, which may last several hours. Figure 1.5 maps the points on the left hemisphere where stimulation has resulted in speech disturbance.

Aphasic arrest following the stimulation of a particular part of the brain is a sure sign that the region is part of the speech area of the language-specialized hemisphere. Penfield notes that aphasic arrest never follows from the stimulation of sites within the non-language-specialized half of the brain.

Several hundred patients have undergone direct electrical stimulation of the brain at the Montreal Neurological Institute, and the data obtained have proved to be of great theoretical as well as clinical value in localizing functions within a hemisphere. Another test, known as the Wada test after its inventor, Juhn Wada, has been very valuable in localizing functions across hemispheres.

### The Wada Test:
### Anesthetizing a Hemisphere

The Wada test temporarily anesthetizes one hemisphere at a time on separate days before surgery so that the neurosurgeon can see which side of the brain normally controls the ability to speak.[21] The first step in the Wada test is the insertion of a small tube into the carotid artery on one side of the patient's neck. The tube permits the neurosurgeon to inject the drug sodium amytal into that artery at a later time. The carotid artery on each side brings blood to the hemisphere on the same side as the artery. Thus, sodium amytal injected into the right artery is carried to the right hemisphere. The drug itself is a barbiturate, chemically similar to the ingredients used in sleeping pills. However, because of the way it is administered in the Wada test, it puts only half of the brain to sleep at a time.

Moments before the drug is injected, the fully conscious patient lies flat on his or her back and is asked to count backward from 100 by threes. The patient is also asked to keep both arms raised in the air while counting. The drug is then slowly injected through the tube in the carotid artery. Within seconds of the injection, dramatic results occur.

First, the arm opposite to the side of the injection falls limp. Since each half of the brain controls the opposite side of the body, the falling arm tells the neurosurgeon that the drug has reached the proper hemisphere and has taken effect. Second, the patient generally stops counting, either for a few seconds or for the duration of the drug's effect, depending on which hemisphere is affected. If the drug is injected on the same side as the hemisphere controlling speech, the patient remains speechless for two to five minutes, depending on the dose administered. If it is injected on the other side, the patient generally resumes counting within a few seconds and can answer questions with little difficulty while the drug is still inactivating the other half of the brain.

The Wada test, like direct electrical stimulation, has been very useful in determining which hemisphere controls speech and language in patients about to undergo surgery in areas of the brain that might control speech. Both procedures have also given investigators valuable information about the relationship of handedness to hemispheric asymmetry and the effects of early damage on asymmetry.

For example, from this work it has been determined that over 95 percent of all right-handers without any history of early brain damage have speech and language controlled by the left hemisphere. The remainder have speech controlled by the right hemisphere. Contrary to Broca's rule, a majority of left-handers also show left-hemisphere speech; the percentage (about 70 percent) is smaller, though, in left-handers than in right-handers. Roughly 15 percent of left-handers have speech in the right hemisphere, and 15 percent or so show evidence of speech control in both hemispheres (bilateral speech control).[22]

Data have also been collected using the Wada technique in patients who were known to have had some damage to the left hemisphere early in life. These patients show a much higher incidence of right-hemisphere or bilateral speech: 70 percent of the left-handers and 19 percent of the right-handers fall into one or the other of these categories. This evidence points to the adaptability of the brain and to the limited value of handedness per se as an index of brain organization, particularly in left-handers.

## The Limitations of Clinical Data

We will conclude this chapter with some remarks about the old and still controversial issue of localizing function to particular areas of the brain. Clinical observations of brain-damaged patients have formed the foundation of most of our ideas relating human behavior to brain function. The interpretation of these observations, however, has always been fraught with difficulty and subject to a great deal of criticism. The basic problem is that there is no simple way to relate the function of a piece of destroyed brain tissue to the disabilities a patient seems to incur as a result of the damage.

The oldest idea was to say simply that whatever a patient couldn't do was normally controlled by the area of the brain that was damaged. If a person had a particular lesion and couldn't see, for example, then the damaged area was said to control vision. If someone had a lesion in a different region and couldn't understand spoken language, then the area involved was said to be responsible for speech comprehension.

That approach has turned out to be much too simplistic. For one thing, most of the processes neatly labeled as visual perception, speech production, voluntary movement, or memory are really the result of many complex cerebral interactions. Whether they are diffusely spread over large areas of the brain or are limited to particular regions appears to be determined by which function we are studying, how precisely we are defining it, and how successfully we are able to limit our tests to what we assume they are testing. Just about any fairly limited damage to the brain is likely to interfere with only a step or phase of some larger process. It is also likely to interfere with more than one process. It is not unusual to see damage to a specific area of the brain result in deficits in a number of different functions.

A rough analogy may be useful here. Imagine trying to figure out the function of different components in a radio by removing them and seeing how their removal affects the performance of the radio. The task would be a very difficult one indeed. Similarly, the knowledge we gain about the role of particular brain regions from the effects of brain damage is tentative and most useful in combination with knowledge of brain function obtained in other ways.

Another major problem in deducing brain function from clinical data is the fact that the brain tends to adjust its operations as best it can in the presence of damage. We can't assume that the remaining intact areas of a damaged brain are operating as they would in a normal brain. It is not as though a piece is missing but everything else is working as it was before. In most cases of brain damage there is some recovery of function over time, sometimes fairly dramatic recovery. The recovery can involve changes in the undamaged areas and is a tribute to the adaptability of the brain. This plasticity is a fascinating and obviously very useful feature, but it complicates the efforts of those who are trying to deduce brain function from clinical data.

For these reasons, other ways to study the functions of the left brain and right brain have been sought. Other approaches are necessary both to corroborate brain-damage data and to add whatever knowledge can be gleaned from techniques that do not depend on great intrusions into normal functioning. We shall examine some of these approaches in the following chapters.

## In Summary

Notions about the role of the two cerebral hemispheres have ranged from the idea that the whole brain is involved in every function, to the belief that the left half is the dominant part, to the current idea that both hemispheres contribute to behavior in important ways through their specialized capabilities. Clinical evidence, despite its limitations, has yielded a sizable body of information about the left brain and right brain. Damage to one hemisphere leads to disabilities different from those arising from damage to the other hemisphere. These differences strongly suggest that each hemisphere contributes certain specialized functions to overall human behavior. Moreover, within each hemisphere there is some specialization, since damage in certain locations can be quite selective in the way it affects behavior.

The clinical data presented in this chapter are just part of the picture that has emerged about specialization within the brain. We will now consider how other approaches have led and are leading to additional insights into the workings of the left brain, the right brain, and the two together.

# 2

# Split-Brain Research

In 1940, an article appeared in a scientific journal describing experiments on the spread of epileptic discharge from one hemisphere to the other in the brains of monkeys.[1] The author concluded that the spread occurred largely or entirely by way of the corpus callosum, the largest of several *commissures,* or bands of nerve fiber connecting regions of the left brain with similar areas of the right brain. Earlier, other investigators had observed that damage to the corpus callosum from a tumor or other problem sometimes reduced the incidence of seizures in human epileptics.[2] Together, these findings paved the way for a new treatment for patients with epilepsy that could not be controlled in other ways—the split-brain operation.

Split-brain surgery, or *commissurotomy,* involves surgically cutting some of the fibers that connect the two cerebral hemispheres. The first such operations to relieve epilepsy were performed in the early 1940s on approximately two-dozen patients. The patients subsequently gave scientists their first opportunity to study systematically the role of the corpus callosum in humans, a role that had been speculated on for decades.

The corpus callosum was a puzzle for researchers who expected to find functions commensurate with its large size and strategic location within the brain. Animal research, however, had shown the consequences of split-brain surgery on a healthy organism to be minimal.

The behavior of split-brain monkeys, for example, appeared indistinguishable from what it was before the operation. The apparent absence of any noticeable changes following commissurotomy led some scientists to suggest facetiously that the corpus callosum's only function was to hold the halves of the brain together to keep them from sagging.

Speculations on the philosophical implications of split-brain surgery go back to the nineteenth century and the writings of Gustav Fechner, considered by many to be the father of experimental psychology. Fechner considered consciousness to be an attribute of the cerebral hemispheres, and he believed that continuity of the brain was an essential condition for unity of consciousness. If it were possible to divide the brain through the middle, he speculated, something like the duplication of a human being would result. "The two cerebral hemispheres," he wrote, "while beginning with the same moods, predispositions, knowledge, and memories, indeed the same consciousness generally, will thereafter develop differently according to the external relations into which each will enter."[3] Fechner considered this "thought experiment" involving separation of the hemispheres impossible to achieve in reality.

Fechner's views concerning the nature of consciousness did not go unchallenged. William McDougall, a founder of the British Psychological Society, argued strongly against the position that unity of consciousness depends on the continuity of the nervous system. To make his point, McDougall volunteered to have his corpus callosum cut if he ever got an incurable disease. He apparently wanted to show that his personality would not be split and that his consciousness would remain unitary.

McDougall never got the opportunity to put his ideas to the test, but the surgery Fechner thought an impossibility took place for the first time almost a century later. The issues these men raised have been among those explored by scientists seeking a fuller understanding of the corpus callosum through the study of split-brain patients.

## Cutting 200 Million Nerve Fibers:
## A Search for Consequences

### The First Split-Brain Operations on Humans

William Van Wagenen, a Rochester, New York, neurosurgeon, performed the first split-brain operations on humans in the early 1940s. Postsurgical testing by an investigator named Andrew Akelaitis showed surprisingly little in the way of deficits in perceptual and motor abilities.[4] The operation seemed to have had no effect on everyday behavior.

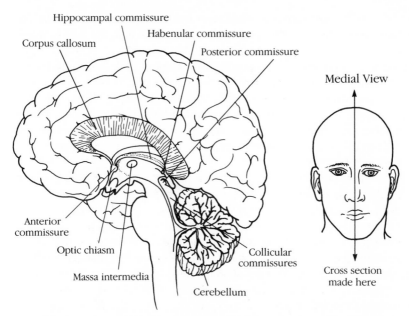

Hippocampal commissure

Habenular commissure

Corpus callosum

Posterior commissure

Medial View

Anterior commissure

Optic chiasm

Collicular commissures

Cross section made here

Massa intermedia

Cerebellum

**2.1** The major interhemispheric commissures. This is a sectional view of the right half of the brain as seen from the midline. (From "The Great Cerebral Commissure," by R. W. Sperry. Copyright © 1964 by Scientific American, Inc. All rights reserved.)

Unfortunately, however, for some patients the surgery seemed to do little to alleviate the condition responsible for the surgery in the first place. Success in relieving seizures seemed to vary greatly from patient to patient.

In retrospect, this variability seems attributable to two causes: (1) individual differences in the nature of the epilepsy in the patients and (2) variations in the actual surgical procedures used with each patient. Figure 2.1 shows the corpus callosum and the adjacent smaller commissures. Van Wagenen's operations varied considerably but usually included sectioning of the forward (anterior) half of the corpus callosum. In two patients, he also sectioned a separate fiber band known as the anterior commissure.

At the time, the importance of these factors was not known, and Van Wagenen soon discontinued the commissurotomy procedure in cases of intractable epilepsy. Clearly, it was not producing the dramatic results he had hoped for. Despite these discouraging results, other investigators continued to study the functions of the corpus callosum in animals. A decade later, in the early 1950s, Ronald Myers and Roger Sperry made some remarkable discoveries that marked a turning point in efforts to study this enigmatic structure.

Myers and Sperry showed that visual information presented to one hemisphere in a cat with its corpus callosum cut would not be available to the other hemisphere.[5] In most higher animals the visual system is arranged so that each eye normally projects to both hemispheres. But by cutting into the optic-nerve crossing called the chiasm, experimenters can limit where each eye sends its information. When this cut is made, the remaining fibers in the optic nerve transmit information to the hemisphere on the same side. Visual input to the left eye is sent only to the left hemisphere, and input to the right eye projects only to the right hemisphere.

Myers performed this operation on cats and subsequently taught the animals a visual discrimination task with one eye patched. A discrimination task involves, for example, teaching an animal to press a lever when it sees a circle but not to press it when a square is presented. Even if this training is done with one eye covered, a normal cat can perform the task later with either eye. Myers found that cats with the optic chiasm cut were also able to perform the task with either eye when tested after the one-eyed training. However, when he cut the corpus callosum in addition to the optic chiasm, the results were dramatically different.

The cat trained with one eye open and one eye patched would learn to do a task well; but when the patch was switched to the other eye, the cat was unable to do the task at all. In fact, it had to be taught the same task over again, taking just as long to learn it as it had the first time. Myers and Sperry concluded that cutting the corpus callosum had kept information going into one hemisphere isolated from the other hemisphere. They had, in effect, trained only half of a brain. Figure 2.2 schematically illustrates the different conditions of their experiment.

These findings, as well as some further studies, led two neurosurgeons working near the California Institute of Technology to reconsider the use of split-brain surgery as a treatment for intractable epilepsy in human beings. The surgeons, Philip Vogel and Joseph Bogen, reasoned that some of the earlier work with human patients had failed because the disconnection between the cerebral hemispheres was not complete. As we have mentioned, Van Wagenen's operations varied considerably from patient to patient. Some parts of the corpus callosum as well as several smaller commissures were usually not included in his operations, and these remaining fibers may have connected the hemispheres sufficiently to mask the effects of the fibers that were cut. On the basis of this logic, coupled with new animal data showing no ill effects from the surgery, Bogen and Vogel performed a complete commissurotomy on the first of what was to be a new series of two-dozen patients suffering from intractable epilepsy.

Bogen and Vogel's reasoning proved to be correct. In some of the cases, the medical benefits of the surgery even appeared to exceed

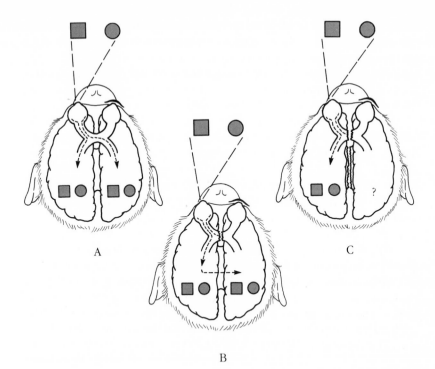

**2.2** Split-brain experiment with animals. In a normal situation, both eyes and both hemispheres see the stimuli. Experimental conditions alter this in the following ways. A. When one eye is patched, the other eye still sends informatin to both hemispheres. B. When one eye is patched and the optic chiasm is cut, the visual information still gets to both hemispheres by way of the corpus callosum. C. When one eye is patched and both the optic chiasm and corpus callosum are cut, only one hemisphere receives visual information.

expectations. In striking contrast to its consequences for seizure activity, the operation appeared to leave patients unchanged in personality, intelligence, and behavior in general, just as had been the case with Van Wagenen's patients. More extensive and ingenious testing by Michael Gazzaniga and Roger Sperry, however, soon revealed a more complex story.

### *Testing for the Effects of Disconnecting Left From Right*

Patient N.G., a California housewife, sits in front of a screen with a small black dot in the center. She is asked to look directly at the dot. When the experimenter is sure she is doing so, a picture of a cup is flashed briefly to the right of the dot. N.G. reports that she has seen a cup. Again she is asked to fix her gaze on the dot. This time, a picture of a spoon is flashed to the left of the dot. She is asked what she saw. She replies, "No, nothing." She is then asked to reach under the screen with her left hand and to select, by touch only, from among several items the one object that is the same as the one she has just seen. Her left hand palpates each object and then holds up the spoon. When asked what she is holding, she says "pencil."

Once again the patient is asked to fixate the dot on the screen. A picture of a nude woman is flashed to the left of the dot. N.G.'s face blushes a little, and she begins to giggle. She is asked what she saw. She says, "Nothing, just a flash of light," and giggles again, covering her mouth with her hand. "Why are you laughing, then?" the investigator inquires. "Oh, doctor, you have some machine!" she replies.

·   ·   ·

The procedure just described and illustrated in Figure 2.3 is frequently used in studies with split-brain patients. The patient sits in front of a tachistoscope, a device that allows the investigator to control precisely the duration for which a picture or pattern is presented on a screen. The presentations are kept brief, about one- or two-tenths of a second (from 100 to 200 milliseconds) so that the patient doesn't have time to move his or her eyes away from the fixation point while the picture is still on the screen.* This procedure is necessary to ensure that visual information is presented initially to one hemisphere only. Stimuli presented to one hemisphere are said to be lateralized.

The design of the human nervous system is such that each cerebral hemisphere receives information primarily from the opposite half of the body. This contralateral rule applies to vision and hearing as well as to body movement and touch (somatosensory) sensation, although the situation in vision and hearing is more complex.

In vision, the contralateral rule applies to the right and left side of one's field of view (visual field), rather than to the right and left eyes per se. When both eyes are fixating a single point, stimuli to the right of fixation are registered in the left half of the brain; the right half of the brain processes everything occurring to the left of fixation. This split and crossover of visual information results from the manner in which the nerve fibers from corresponding regions of both eyes are divided between the cerebral hemispheres. Figure 2.4 shows both the optics and the neural wiring involved.

In animal studies, as we have seen, visual information can be directed to one hemisphere by cutting the optic chiasm so that the remaining fibers in the optic nerve are those transmitting information to the hemisphere on the same side as the eye. This allows experimenters to present a stimulus easily to either hemisphere alone by simply presenting the stimulus to the appropriate eye. The procedure

**2.3** The basic testing arrangement used to lateralize visual and tactile information and allow tactile responses.

is used only with animals, however, because cutting the chiasm substantially reduces peripheral vision, eliminates binocular depth perception, and plays no part in the rationale for the split-brain operation on humans. For these reasons, investigators wishing to transmit visual information to one hemisphere at a time in a human split-brain patient must do so through a combination of controlling the patient's fixation and presenting information to one side of space.

With this as background, let's return to an analysis of the tests administered to patient N.G. In those tests, the patient saw the left half

---

*The rapid eye movements that occur when gaze is shifted from one point to another are known as saccadic eye movements or saccades. Although once started saccades are extremely rapid, they take about 200 milliseconds to initiate with the eye at rest. If a stimulus is presented for a duration less than 200 milliseconds, the stimulus is no longer present by the time an eye movement can occur.

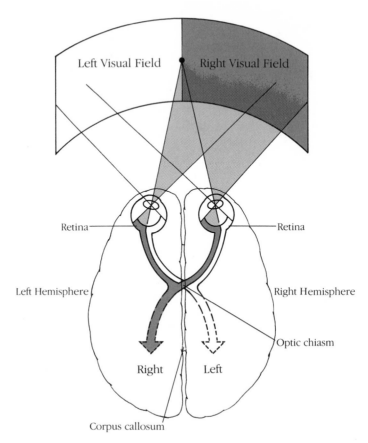

2.4 Visual pathways to the hemispheres. When fixating a point, each eye sees both visual fields but sends information about the right visual field only to the left hemisphere and information about the left visual field only to the right hemisphere. This crossover and split is a result of the manner in which the nerve fibers leading from the retina divide at the back of each eye. The visual areas of the left and right hemisphere normally communicate through the corpus callosum. If the callosum is cut and the eyes and head are kept from moving, each hemisphere can see only half of the visual world.

of the screen (everything to the left of the fixation point) with the right side of her brain and everything to the right with her left hemisphere. The split in her brain prevented the normal interchange of information between the two sides that would have occurred before her surgery. In effect, each side of her brain was blind to what the other side was seeing, a state of affairs dramatically brought out by the additional fact that only one hemisphere controls speech.

As a consequence, the patient reported perfectly well any stimuli falling in the right visual field (projecting to the verbal left hemisphere) although she was unable to tell anything about what was flashed in her left visual field (sent to the mute right hemisphere). The fact that she "saw" stimuli in the left visual field is amply demonstrated by the ability of her left hand (basically controlled by the right brain) to select the spoon from among several objects hidden from view. It is also demonstrated by her emotional reaction to the nude picture, despite her claim not to have seen anything.[6]

The patient's response to the nude picture is particularly interesting. She seemed puzzled by her own reactions to what had appeared. Her right hemisphere saw the picture and processed it sufficiently to evoke a general, nonverbal reaction—the giggling and the blushing. The left hemisphere, meanwhile, did not "know" what the right had seen, although its comment about "some machine" seems to be a sign that it was aware of the bodily reactions induced by the right hemisphere. It is very common for the verbal left hemisphere to try to make sense of what has occurred in testing situations where information is presented to the right hemisphere. As a result, the left brain sometimes comes out with erroneous and often elaborate rationalizations based on partial cues.

## Cross Cuing

As the study of split-brain patients continued, certain inconsistencies in the findings began to occur with greater and greater frequency. Patients previously unable to identify verbally objects held out of sight in the left hand began to name some items. Some pictures flashed in the left visual field (to the right hemisphere) were also correctly identified verbally. One interpretation of these results is that over time the right hemisphere of the patients acquired the ability to talk. Another is that information was being transmitted between the hemispheres by way of pathways other than those that were cut.

Although these were interesting and exciting possibilities, Michael Gazzaniga and Steven Hillyard were able to pinpoint a much simpler explanation for their findings.[7] They coined the term *cross cuing* to refer to patients' attempts to use whatever cues are available to make information accessible to both hemispheres. Cross cuing is most obvious in the simple case where patients are given an object to hold and identify with their left hand, which is out of their line of vision and thus disconnected from the verbal left hemisphere. If, for example, the left hand is given a comb or a toothbrush to feel, the patient will often stroke the brush or the surface of the comb. The patient will then immediately identify the object because the left hemisphere hears the tell-tale sounds.

Cross cuing provides a way for one hemisphere to provide the other with information about what it is experiencing. The direct chan-nels of information transfer are eliminated by the surgery, leaving the patient with indirect cues as the only means of interhemispheric com-munication in most instances. Cross cuing can often be quite subtle, testing the ingenuity of investigators seeking to eliminate it from the experimental situation.

A good example of this is the patient who was able to indicate verbally whether 0 or 1 had been flashed to either hemisphere. The same patient was unable to identify verbally pictures of objects flashed to the right hemisphere, nor was he able to identify most objects held in his left hand. This suggested that he lacked the ability to speak from the right hemisphere. Instead, the investigators proposed that cross cuing was involved when the patient reported the numbers flashed to the right hemisphere. They hypothesized that the left hemisphere would begin counting "subvocally" after a presentation to the left visual field, and that these signals were picked up by the right hemisphere. When the correct number was reached, the right hemisphere would signal the left to stop and report that digit out loud.

To test this idea, the patient was presented with an expanded version of the task; the digits 2, 3, 5, and 8 were added without his knowledge. At first the subject was very surprised when a new number was presented. His response to the first unexpected number presented to the right hemisphere was, "I beg your pardon." With a little practice, however, he was able to give the correct answer for all the numbers presented to the right hemisphere, but with hesitation when the number was high. In contrast, responses to the same digits presented in the right visual field (to the left hemisphere) were quite prompt.

These findings fit well with the idea that the left hemisphere began counting subvocally after a digit was presented to the right hemisphere. The larger the number of potential digits, the longer the list of numbers the left hemisphere would have to go through before reaching the correct one.

Cross cuing is generally not a conscious attempt by the patient to trick the investigator. Instead, it is a natural tendency by an organism to use whatever information it has to make sense of what is going on. This tendency, in fact, contributes further insight into why the common, every-day behavior of split-brain patients seems so unaffected by the surgery.

Careful testing procedures that prevent cross cuing, however, can lead to striking "disconnection" effects of the sort described in patient N.G. In these situations, the patient is unable to tell what picture was flashed to the right hemisphere, although the left hand can point to the correct object. If blindfolded, the patient can't verbally identify an object held in the left hand, but can select (with that hand) other objects related to it (such as a book of matches after having held a cigarette).

To an observer unfamiliar with the patient's surgical history, these findings give the impression that the left arm has a mind of its own. They are less mysterious when we realize that the split-brain operation has disconnected the patient's right hemisphere from the centers in the left hemisphere that control speech. The left hand is thus the primary means through which the right hemisphere can communicate with the outside world.

## Everyday Behavior After Split-Brain Surgery

It is natural to wonder what evidence of disconnection effects there is in the everyday behavior of split-brain patients. A few bizarre instances have been described by both patients and onlookers and are frequently mentioned in popular articles on split-brain research. One patient, for example, described the time he found his left hand struggling against his right when he tried to put his pants on in the morning. One hand was pulling them up while the other hand was pulling them down. In another incident the same patient was angry and forcibly reached for his wife with his left hand while his right hand grabbed the left in an attempt to stop it.[8]

The frequency with which these stories are mentioned makes it easy to forget that they describe rare incidents that are viewed as strange, isolated instances even by the people involved. For the most part, the two sides of the body work in a coordinated fashion. Thus a battery of sophisticated tests specifically designed to identify a commissurotomy patient would be needed for anyone to know the operation had occurred. Much more common are reports of subtle changes in behavior or ability after surgery. Although some of the reported changes have not held up when carefully studied, others do appear to be verifiable consequences of the operation.

Several patients have reported great difficulty learning to associate names with faces after surgery. Verification of this came from a study in which subjects had to learn first names for each of three pictures of young men.[9] This procedure was only incidental to the main purpose of the study, but it proved to be a major stumbling block for the subjects. The investigators reported that subjects eventually learned the name–face associations by isolating some unique feature in each picture (for example, "Dick has glasses.") rather than by associating the name with the face as a whole. This suggests that the deficit in the ability to associate names and faces may be due to the disconnection of the verbal naming functions of the left side of the brain from the facial recognition abilities of the right side.

Deficits in the ability to solve geometrical problems have been anecdotally linked to the absence of the corpus callosum. Patient L.B., a high school student with a considerably above-average IQ, was transferred out of geometry into a class in general math after he experienced inordinate difficulty with the course. Another report told of a college student who had exceptional difficulty with geometry despite average grades in other courses. Research with split-brain patients studying the ability of each hemisphere to match two- and three-dimensional forms on the basis of common geometrical features showed the right hemisphere to be markedly superior, especially on the most difficult matches.[10] Thus, as in the previous example, the patient's deficits may be the result of the disconnection of the speaking left hemisphere from the right-hemisphere regions specialized for such tasks.

Another complaint of some split-brain patients is that they no longer dream. Since dreaming is primarily a visual imaging process, investigators have speculated that it might be the responsibility of the right half of the brain. The operation would serve to disconnect this aspect of the patient's mental life from the speaking left hemisphere and would result in verbal reports that the patient does not dream.

This idea, however, has not been confirmed by further research. Split-brain patients were monitored for brain-wave activity while sleeping and were awakened whenever the record indicated they were dreaming. They were then asked to describe the dream they had just been having. In contrast to the prediction that they would be unable to do so, the patients provided the experimenters with descriptions of their dreams.[11]

Other anecdotal evidence has pointed to poorer memory after surgery. These reports were apparently supported by a study of memory abilities in which several split-brain patients were compared with other epilepsy patients and were found to have poorer scores on a variety of memory tests.[12] A major problem with this type of study, though, is that we really do not know much about split-brain patients' preoperative memory abilities. We can compare their performance after surgery with that of epileptic control subjects who have not had surgery, but we have no way of knowing if the memory skills of the split-brain patients before their surgery were really comparable to the memory skills of the control group. Perhaps they had poorer memories to begin with!

The best approach is to compare memory abilities before and after surgery in the same patients. This has been possible with a patient who is part of a new group of split-brain patients operated on by Dr. Donald Wilson of the Dartmouth Medical School. Instead of poorer memory performance after surgery, patient D.H. showed considerably improved memory ability after his operation.[13]

The most likely explanation of this finding is that D.H.'s true abilities were suppressed by drugs and his general condition before surgery. The operation did not miraculously improve his memory; instead, it allowed his true abilities to emerge. In any case, this single-subject study shows that memory deficits do not *necessarily* follow split-brain surgery, and it indicates that further work will be needed to answer the question of whether the operation affects memory and, if so, in what way. It also points to the importance of appropriate controls in studies looking for changes in split-brain patients.

We have seen that a variety of behavioral changes have been attributed to split-brain surgery. Some of them have been verified experimentally. In each instance, the changes are relatively subtle and not of the dramatic nature one might have expected. There are, however, a few striking, fairly reliable effects of the split-brain operation that are short-lived and evident only during the first few days or weeks after surgery. They are known as the acute disconnection syndrome and probably are due to the surgical division of the commissures as well as to the general trauma resulting from the surgeon's having to squeeze or compress the right hemisphere to gain access to the nerve tracts between the hemispheres.

Patients are often mute for a time after surgery, and sometimes they have difficulty controlling the left side of the body, which at first may seem almost paralyzed and then works very awkwardly. As the patient recovers use of the left hand, competitive movements between the left and right hands sometimes occur. This problem, however, usually passes quickly.

After recovering from the initial shock of major brain surgery, most patients report an improved feeling of well-being. Less than two days after surgery, one young patient was well enough to quip that he had a "splitting headache." Within a few weeks the symptoms of the acute disconnection syndrome subside, making it necessary to use carefully contrived laboratory tests to reveal what had taken place earlier.

## Language Functions in the Hemispheres

Split-brain research has dramatically confirmed that in most persons control of speech is localized to the left hemisphere. We have seen that the typical split-brain patient is unable to identify verbally pictures of common objects flashed in the left visual field (to the right hemisphere), although the patient has no difficulty identifying the same pictures presented in the right visual field (to the left hemisphere). The right hemisphere *knows* what the picture represents, however, for it can guide the left hand to select a similar item from among several objects placed behind a screen out of the subject's sight.

The ability to talk, then, is strongly localized in one hemisphere in the split-brain subject as well as in clinical patients. But what about other language abilities? How well can the right hemisphere understand language, either written or spoken? The earliest split-brain studies to look at these questions flashed printed words to the left or right hemisphere. When simple nouns were presented to the right hemisphere, patients had little difficulty retrieving the corresponding object with the left hand from among several items hidden from view.

Limitations in the ability of the right hemisphere started to appear when verbs such as "smile" were presented. When "smile" was flashed to the left hemisphere, patients typically responded by breaking into a grin. When the same word was presented to the right hemisphere, the patient made no response. Other verbs produced comparable results.[14]

In light of the data with simple nouns, the findings with verbs were surprising. With nouns, the limitations of the right hemisphere appeared to be ones of verbal expression; the right brain showed good comprehension if it could respond nonverbally. With verbs, a different picture seemed to emerge. Since the actions (such as smiling) required by the verbs could be controlled by either side of the brain, differences in the ability of the two hemispheres to *produce* the required movements were not responsible for the results. Instead, there seemed to be a genuine difference in the kind of written material each hemisphere could *understand.*

Considerable effort was spent trying to explain why hemispheric differences would fall along the lines of grammatical distinctions. The most widely accepted interpretation was that verbs are more complex linguistic stimuli and the right hemisphere's inability to deal with them reflects its less advanced linguistic skills.

More recent work has generally confirmed the view that the right hemisphere lacks reading abilities that are the equal of the left hemisphere's. However, this same work suggests that the differences are not along the lines of the noun–verb distinction. The research has been conducted by Eran Zaidel, who has worked extensively with two of the patients in the original California series.

### The Z Lens and a Reexamination of the Right Hemisphere's Language Ability

Zaidel has employed a new method of restricting visual stimuli to one hemisphere. It utilizes a device known as the Z lens, which is illustrated in Figure 2.5.[15] The Z lens is a contact lens that permits the patient to move his or her eyes freely when examining something but at the same

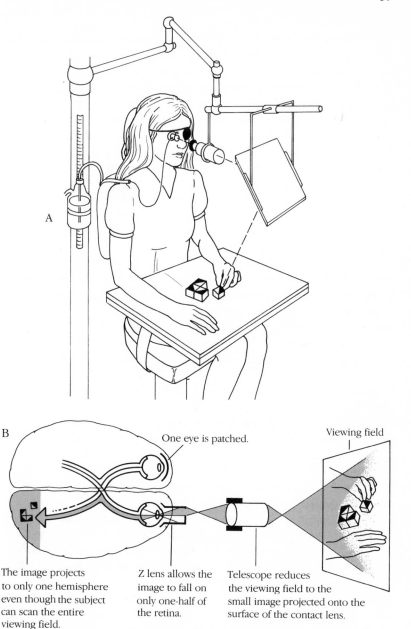

A

B    One eye is patched.    Viewing field

The image projects
to only one hemisphere
even though the subject
can scan the entire
viewing field.

Z lens allows the
image to fall on
only one-half of
the retina.

Telescope reduces
the viewing field to the
small image projected onto the
surface of the contact lens.

**2.5** The Z lens. A. The Z lens setup keeps the patient's field of view lateralized to one hemisphere. B. One eye is patched, and the image is projected to only one-half of the retina of the other eye. (Part A. adapted from E. Zaidel, "Language Comprehension in the Right Hemisphere Following Cerebral Commissurotomy," Fig. 12.2, p. 233. In A. Caramazza and E. Zurif (eds.), *Language Acquisition and Language Breakdown: Parallels and Divergencies,* Fig. 12.2, p. 233. Baltimore, Maryland: The Johns Hopkins University Press, 1978.)

time ensures that only one hemisphere of the patient's brain receives the visual information. The Z lens makes it possible for the subject to view a stimulus for as long as he or she wants, yet allows the investigator to present the stimulus to one hemisphere alone.

Zaidel's strategy was to test the comprehension abilities of each hemisphere by using a variety of stimuli that had been previously used both with children and with aphasic patients. The goal was to obtain data that would allow him to compare the abilities of the right hemisphere of split-brain patients with the right-hemisphere abilities of those two groups for which norms were already available.

In tests of auditory vocabulary, the two split-brain patients heard a single word spoken by the experimenter and then viewed a display of three pictures through the Z lens. The patients' task was to select the picture that corresponded to the word. Since the pathways of the auditory system are arranged so that each ear sends information to both hemispheres, under ordinary conditions it is not possible to tell whether one or both hemispheres have understood a spoken message. The Z lens, however, allowed Zaidel to lateralize the response alternatives to one hemisphere so that he could determine how well each half of the brain matched a spoken word to its written counterpart.

The same procedure was also used with the Token Test, in which the subject is asked to arrange blocks of different shapes and sizes according to verbal instructions such as, "Put the yellow square under the green circle." Again, instructions were delivered orally while the objects to be arranged were viewed through the Z lens. The Token Test is commonly used as a test of damage to left-hemisphere language zones, for it frequently is sensitive to impairments not picked up by other aphasia tests.

Zaidel's work revealed a surprising degree and array of comprehension abilities in the right hemisphere.[16] The pattern of results was complex, though, and it was not possible for Zaidel to make a simple summary statement about the right hemisphere's linguistic "age" or "health." On the vocabulary tests, the right hemisphere generally did at least as well as a normal 10-year-old, although with the Token Test items it experienced difficulty characteristic of aphasic impairments. Zaidel has emphasized that differences between the hemispheres in comprehension ability are somewhat less than had been thought previously. The noun–verb difference found in earlier work, he suggested, may have been an artifact of the method of presenting the stimuli. When the right hemisphere has adequate time to process a verb, as it does with the Z-lens procedure, it appears to do so as well as the left hemisphere.

The language asymmetries we have reviewed so far are those found in "typical" split-brain patients, if it is appropriate to talk of typical patients in view of their varied neurological history. The question of how findings from these patients bear on the division of functions between hemispheres in the normal brain is highlighted when we consider how neurological history can produce dramatic departures from this picture. A case in point is P.S., one of Donald Wilson's patients.

### Case P.S.: Conversing With the Right Hemisphere

P.S., a right-handed male 16 years of age at the time of surgery, has a preoperative history suggesting considerable damage to the left hemisphere early in life. P.S. appears to be unique among the split-brain patients in the extent of his right-hemisphere language ability. He has been extensively studied by Michael Gazzaniga and Joseph LeDoux, who discovered that P.S. was able to spell the names of objects flashed to his right hemisphere by using his left hand to arrange letters selected from a Scrabble set.[17]

P.S.'s ability to "write" with his right hemisphere enabled Gazzaniga and LeDoux to converse with that half of his brain. They would first frame a question in spoken language, asking, for example, "What is your favorite _____ ?" Immediately after, the word "hobby" would be presented in the left or right visual field. P.S. would then answer out loud if the word went to the left hemisphere, or he would spell out "c-a-r" if the word had been presented in the left visual field. This procedure, illustrated in Figure 2.6, has been used to explore various dimensions of the right hemisphere's awareness of the world, an issue to which we will return in Chapter 10.

At first, P.S.'s right hemisphere was able to communicate verbally only by spelling with Scrabble letters, although evidence is accumulating to suggest that P.S. is now speaking with his right hemisphere as well. About three years after surgery, P.S. began to use spoken language to identify words and objects flashed to the right hemisphere. After ruling out cross cuing and inadequate lateralization of stimuli to one hemisphere as possible explanations, Gazzaniga and LeDoux then considered regeneration of the fibers that normally transfer visual information as a basis for P.S.'s newly found ability. Other tests eliminated this explanation as well, providing stronger support that P.S. was indeed "talking" from his right hemisphere. This evidence was elegantly simple.[18]

Words like "cupcake" were presented so that "cup" was to the left of fixation while "cake" fell to the right of fixation. P.S. was able to report that he saw the word "cup" and the word "cake," but he did not spontaneously report seeing "cupcake" the way neurologically normal subjects do under these conditions. More testing is needed before it

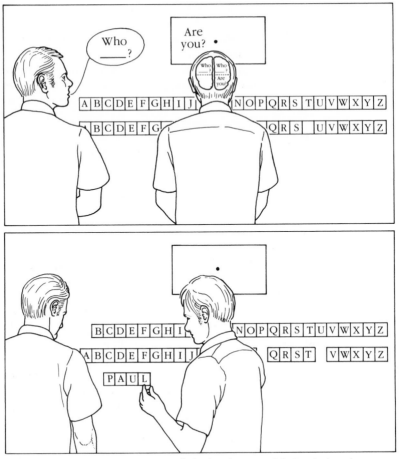

2.6  Patient P.S. can answer questions flashed to the mute right hemisphere by arranging letters with his left hand. (From M. S. Gazzaniga and J. E. LeDoux, *The Integrated Mind,* Fig. 40, p. 144. New York: Plenum Press, 1978.)

will be possible to say definitively that P.S. is now speaking from his right hemisphere, but there is an excellent chance that this is the case.

Although P.S. would represent the first split-brain patient to acquire the ability to speak from the right hemisphere, we should perhaps not be too surprised at this occurrence in light of his history of left-hemisphere damage. For many years, some neurologists have argued that the recovery of language function following severe damage to the language hemisphere is in some cases a result of a process by which the intact hemisphere assumes many of the functions of the damaged one. The intriguing questions are why some people can do this while others cannot, and whether language is learned by the intact hemisphere after the injury or whether it has been present but lying dormant for much of the patient's life. We do not know the answers to these questions.

## Some Cautions About Interpreting Data

Findings with P.S. highlight the importance of considering neurological history when interpreting data from split-brain patients, and they suggest that split-brain data may overestimate the degree of language ability present in the right hemisphere of normal people. Epilepsy affecting the left hemisphere may result in a reorganization of language functions involving the right hemisphere, so that a split-brain patient may show greater right-hemisphere language abilities than would be found in the brains of normal persons without a history of severe epilepsy.

Similar arguments have been made for caution in extending any research finding with split-brain subjects to normal subjects. In many cases it is difficult to know the precise nature of any early brain damage caused by the epilepsy, and it is even more difficult to know what compensations the brain has made as a result. The best way to deal with this problem in interpreting findings is to look for results that appear consistently in all patients, independent of their neurological history. Second best is to study the findings from each patient in the context of his or her neurological background. Some researchers would dismiss split-brain research because of these problems in interpreting results. A better approach, we think, is to continue to learn what we can about the brain from this unique resource, remembering that such research will be but one of several tools needed to complete the picture.

## Visuo-Spatial Functions in the Hemispheres

The older literature on damage to the human brain provided split-brain investigators with good clues about the kinds of tasks likely to be performed better by the right hemisphere. On the basis of split-brain studies, the most general statement that can be made about right-hemisphere specializations is that they are nonlinguistic functions. They seem to involve complex visual and spatial processes.

The perception of part–whole relations, for example, seems to be superior in the right hemisphere. In one task, patients viewed line drawings of geometric shapes that had been cut up and the pieces slightly separated. They then decided which of three solid alternatives felt with one hand out of view was represented by the fragmented figure. The left hand was far superior on this task; the right hand showed chance performance in six out of seven patients.[19]

One of the most dramatic demonstrations of right-hemisphere superiority in visuo-spatial tasks was recorded on film by Gazzaniga and Sperry while they were testing W.J., the first patient of the California series. W.J. was presented with several cubes, each containing two red

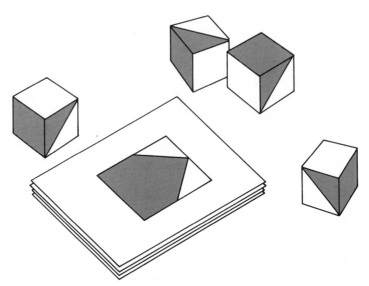

**2.7** Block-design task. The subject is asked to arrange the colored blocks to match the sample pattern.

sides, two white sides, and two sides divided half red and half white along the diagonal. His task was to arrange these blocks to form a square with patterns identical to those shown on a series of cards. Figure 2.7 illustrates the task.

The beginning of the film shows W.J. readily assembling the blocks with his left hand to form a particular pattern. When he tries to form a pattern with his right hand, however, he experiences great difficulty. Slowly and with considerable indecision, the right hand arranges the blocks. At one point, the left hand moves into the picture and begins to assemble the blocks in the correct pattern. It is gently but firmly removed from the table by the investigator, while the right hand continues to fumble unaided by the more skillful left.

Other evidence pointing to right-hemisphere superiority in visuo-spatial ability comes from differences in the abilities of the two hands of the split-brain patient to draw a figure of a cube. Invariably, the left hand produces a better drawing. Examples are shown in Figure 2.8.

What is the basis for the right hemisphere's superior abilities in these visuo-spatial tasks? Two possibilities suggested themselves to investigators. First, the right hemisphere could be dominant for the expression of visual understanding just as the left hemisphere is dominant for the expression of language understanding, although both halves of the brain might be equally skilled in *perceiving* spatial relationships. This view emphasizes an asymmetry in the ability to perform

| | Left hand | Right hand |
|---|---|---|
| Preoperative | | |
| Postoperative | | |

**2.8** Cube drawings before and after commissurotomy. Preoperatively, the patient could draw a cube with either hand. Postoperatively, the right hand performed poorly. The patient was right-handed. (From M. S. Gazzaniga and J. E. Le Doux, *The Integrated Mind,* Fig. 18, p. 52. New York: Plenum Press, 1978.)

the complex motor acts required by the tasks. An alternative interpretation holds that there are true differences in perceptual abilities between the hemispheres.

There is evidence to suggest that both explanations are valid to some extent. True visual differences appear to underlie differential performance of the hemispheres in certain tasks.[20] Asymmetries in other tasks seem to be based on the manipulative component.[21] In the latter cases, asymmetries favoring the right hemisphere are reduced or disappear as the tasks are made purely visual so that the subject does not need to manipulate anything.

## Information Processing in the Two Hemispheres

As research into the specialized functions of the two hemispheres continued, the pattern of results suggested a new way to conceptualize hemispheric differences. Instead of a breakdown based on the type of tasks (for example, verbal or spatial) best performed by each hemisphere, a dichotomy based on different ways of dealing with information in general seemed to emerge.

According to this analysis, the left hemisphere is specialized for language functions, but these specializations are a consequence of the left hemisphere's superior analytic skills, of which language is one manifestation. Similarly, the right hemisphere's superior visuo-spatial performance is derived from its synthetic, holistic manner of dealing with information. What results led to this reanalysis of hemispheric differences? Much of the work was conducted by Jerre Levy and her colleagues working with the California series of patients.

One of the first suggestions that the two hemispheres have different information-processing styles came from a study in which split-brain patients were asked to match small wooden blocks held in the left or right hand with the appropriate two-dimensional representation selected from drawings of blocks shown in opened-up form. Overall, the left hand was considerably better than the right at this task, but the most interesting finding was that the two hemispheres appeared to use different strategies in approaching the problem.

An analysis of errors showed that the patterns the right hand (left hemisphere) found relatively easier to deal with were the patterns that were easy to describe in words but difficult to discriminate visually. For the left hand (right hemisphere) the reverse was true. Specifically, the left hemisphere appeared to make its matches on the basis of verbal descriptions of the properties of the blocks and the two-dimensional patterns. It seemed unable to fold up the two-dimensional representation mentally so that a match could be made on the basis of overall appearance.[22]

Other work has shown that the two hemispheres differ in the kinds of information they pick up from visual stimuli. We will discuss these studies at greater length in a later section of this chapter. For now we need only point out that pictures that can match in either their function (such as cake on a plate and a knife and fork) or their appearance (such as cake on a plate and a hat with a brim) are handled differently by the two hemispheres. See Figure 2.9 for examples of the stimuli. With ambiguous instructions simply to match similar stimuli, the left hemisphere of the split-brain patient matches by function and the right hemisphere matches by appearance.

Levy concluded that the left hemisphere's strategy in dealing with incoming information is best conceptualized as analytic; the right hemisphere appears to process information in a holistic manner.[23] There are other ways to interpret the differences we have just considered, but the analytic–holistic distinction has been the most influential in moving thinking about hemispheric differences away from the verbal–nonverbal dichotomy. The latter is clearly too simplistic to explain all the results found with brain-damaged, split-brain, and (as we shall see in the next chapter) normal subjects.

### The Phenomenon of Visual Completion

Patient N.G. sits in front of a screen. Once again, she is asked to gaze at a spot marked in the middle. A strange picture appears briefly on the screen. It is a split face made up of the left half of one face and the right

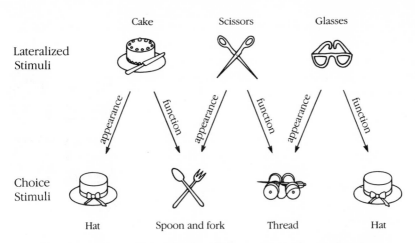

**2.9** Function and appearance matches by split-brain patients. The stimuli in the top row are visually presented to one hemisphere at a time. The patient is instructed to pick the best "match" from the choice stimuli. When the left hemisphere sees the stimuli, it tends to match by function. When the right hemisphere sees the stimuli, it tends to match by appearance. (Adapted from J. Levy and C. Trevarthen, "Metacontrol of Hemispheric Function in Human Split Brain Patients," *Journal of Experimental Psychology*, Fig. 1, p. 302. 1976. Copyright © 1976 by the American Psychological Association. Reprinted by permission.)

half of another, joined down the middle. On the right is half of the face she has been taught to identify as "Dick"; on the left, the face belonging to "Tom." A split stimulus such as this composite is known as a *chimeric figure*. It is named after Chimera, a mythical monster made up of parts of different animals.

N.G. is asked to report what she saw. She says she saw Dick. When questioned further, she denies that there was anything odd about the picture. Later, the same composite picture is flashed on the screen. This time she is asked not to say anything. Instead, she is shown several faces in full view and is asked to point with either hand to the one she saw. This time she points to the picture of Tom.

· · ·

This experiment, shown in Figure 2.10, again shows that each half of the brain is blind to what the other side is seeing. What is particularly striking is that in this split-face study each half of the brain seemed to see a normal, symmetrical face despite the unusual composition of the stimuli. In addition, the patient's report of what she sees differs with the nature of the response she is asked to make. The patient shows no sign of conflict when this occurs.

*Completion,* the tendency for split-brain patients to see as whole

**2.10** Chimeric-stimuli tests with split-brain patients. A. The subject is told that she will see a picture. She is asked to fixate the center of the screen, and then a composite picture is flashed. The subject is asked to identify the picture she saw, either B. verbally or C. by pointing with one hand or the other. Split-brain patients seem unaware that the chimeric stimuli are incomplete or conflicting. When asked to vocalize their answer, they choose the picture from which the right-field half of the composite was made. When asked to point, they choose the picture from which the left-field half was made. (Adapted from J. Levy, C. Trevarthen, and R. W. Sperry, "Perception of Bilateral Chimeric Figures Following Hemispheric Disconnection," *Brain 95,* Fig. 4, p. 68, 1972.)

what are really partial figures falling at the visual midline, was first noted when patients showed the ability to identify accurately a square flashed briefly in the center of the visual field. Since the left half of the square is projected to the right hemisphere and the right half to the left hemisphere, the fact that the patient reported seeing a normal square meant that the left hemisphere had "completed" the partial figure presented to it. The right hemisphere also perceived a normal square, for the left hand would draw a complete figure when the patient was asked to sketch what he saw with that hand.[24] Later studies have shown that chimeric figures such as the composite pictures presented to patient N.G. also give rise to visual completion.

The completion phenomenon is seen in some patients who have unilateral damage to the visual regions of the brain as well as in split-brain patients. It is not well understood in either case, but it is clearly one of the reasons split-brain patients report that the world appears normal. In conjunction with eye movements that bring information to both hemispheres, completion helps bring to visual experience a unity that extends across the visual field.

### The Evidence From Chimeric-Figures Studies

The use of chimeric figures with split-brain patients has advanced the study of how the two hemispheres accomplish their division of labor when the subject is presented with a task. Although we can't be sure that the intact brain works in the same way, it is well worth our time to review what has been learned about the dynamics of hemispheric interaction from split-brain patients.

Jerre Levy and her colleagues have extensively studied chimeric stimuli with the split-brain patients in California. In the first study, they used chimeric faces formed from pictures of three young men.[25] Subjects were told that they would see a picture flashed briefly on a screen and then would be asked to point to the picture seen from among several presented in a display viewed in free vision. Subjects fixated a dot in the center of their visual field and then the chimeric face was flashed for 150 milliseconds to ensure that each half of the face would reach only one hemisphere. Regardless of the hand they used to point with, the patients overwhelmingly selected the face going to the right hemisphere. Double responses, as well as left-hemisphere-only responses, were rare.

This is evidence that the right hemisphere can control the right hand as well as the left hand in a simple pointing task. Up to now, we considered only the crossed, or contralateral, fibers that allow each hemisphere to control the hand opposite to it. However, a much smaller number of same-side, or ipsilateral, fibers allow each hemisphere to exert some control over the hand on the same side of the body. Ipsilateral motor control, though, is generally quite coarse and limited to movements of the whole arm or hand. Fine finger movements require the use of the contralateral hemisphere and generally cannot be controlled by the ipsilateral hemisphere.

In the present task the right hemisphere, better at recognizing faces than the left brain, exercises its primitive ability to control the right hand by using the ipsilateral fibers. When subjects are asked to identify verbally what they saw, however, the error rate goes up and the majority of the responses are to the face that went to the left hemisphere.* When the facial recognition task is set up so that the left hemisphere is forced to play a role (by requiring a verbal response), we get evidence that it can do the task, but it does not do as well as the right hemisphere.

Another study using pictures of common objects (a rose, an eye, and a bee) divided in half to form chimeric stimuli produced almost identical results. When pointing, patients matched the object seen by the right hemisphere. When asked to report verbally what they saw, they gave more left-hemisphere responses. These results extend the generality of the right hemisphere's superior skills in dealing with nonverbal visual stimuli.

### Dominance and Capacity

Levy concluded that two factors are at work in determining the outcome of these tasks.[26] The first is *dominance,* the tendency for one hemisphere to process information and control responding. The other is *capacity,* the ability of a hemisphere to perform a task when the experiment requires it to do so. In the two chimeric-figures studies just considered, the left hemisphere showed the capacity to recognize faces and objects when the subject was required to respond verbally. However, it was not dominant in the task; the overwhelming majority of responses came from the right hemisphere in the manual, free-response situation.

The concepts of dominance and capacity are further illustrated in another chimeric-figures study.[27] This experiment used the rose, eye, and bee stimuli in a task where subjects were instructed to respond on

---

*Most, but not all, verbal responses were to the faces presented to the left hemisphere. A greater-than-chance number of right-hemisphere faces were also reported. The investigators suggest that the right hemisphere may be controlling speech in these instances. A more likely explanation, however, is that lateralization of the inputs was not perfect and that stimuli to the left visual field occasionally reached the left hemisphere.

the basis of phonetic (sound) similarity between the stimulus and choice items. After seeing a chimeric object, they were told to point to the picture that rhymed with what they saw. Toes, a pie, and a key were the choices. In this situation, over 82 percent of the matches were to the item presented to the left hemisphere, regardless of the hand used. In contrast, when subjects were asked to do direct visual matching with the same stimuli, they pointed to the object seen by the right hemisphere.

To see whether the right hemisphere had any capacity at all in this task, the investigators flashed single complete pictures of the rose, bee, and eye in the left visual field and asked the patients to select the figure that rhymed. Performance was at a chance level.

These results are interesting for two reasons. First, they suggest that the right hemisphere lacks the ability to deal with speech at a phonetic or sound level. This finding contrasts with results obtained by Zaidel and the Z lens. Zaidel's work pointed to the apparent ability of the right hemisphere to understand connected speech. Second, Levy's results provide an example in which the left hemisphere is dominant for a task that the right hemisphere appears totally incapable of performing.

## Hemispheric "Disposition": Who Is in Charge Here Anyway?

In the studies we have considered up to now, the hemisphere controlling the response in a free-response situation was always the one with the greater capacity for that particular task. This makes good intuitive sense. If the two hemispheres have unequal abilities in a given situation, the superior hemisphere should assume responsibility for responding. More recent work, however, has suggested that this is not always the case and that the hemispheres can differ in their disposition to respond at particular times.

Jerre Levy and Colwyn Trevarthen constructed chimeric figures from drawings of common objects and asked subjects to point to a similar picture from an array viewed in free vision.[28] Objects could match on the basis of their function or on the basis of their appearance. See Figure 2.9 for examples. Functional and appearance matches for stimuli to both the left and the right hemisphere were included among the choices on each trial. This allowed the investigators to see whether each hemisphere had a preferred "mode" for making matches. The investigators hypothesized that functional matches would be best performed by the left hemisphere, and appearance matches would be the specialty of the right.

This prediction was supported by the data from one patient who was given ambiguous instructions to match "similar" objects. Responses to left-hemisphere stimuli were overwhelmingly functional, while responses to right-hemisphere stimuli were on the basis of appearance. The investigators then specifically instructed the same subject and other patients to perform matches on the basis of function or appearance. In general, function instructions elicited function matches to left-hemisphere stimuli, and appearance instructions elicited appearance matches to right-hemisphere items.

A large number of responses, however, deviated from the expected pattern. In some cases, appearance instructions resulted in a response to the right-hemisphere stimulus, but the subject made a function match. Similarly, function instructions sometimes resulted in a response to the left-hemisphere stimulus that was based on appearance. In these cases, the hemisphere appropriate to the instructions responded, but in an "inappropriate" way. The reverse also occurred: the hemisphere inappropriate in terms of the instructions sometimes controlled the response, using the "appropriate" processing strategy. For example, the right hemisphere might respond under function instructions, making its decision on the basis of function; or the left hemisphere might respond under appearance instructions, with the response based on appearance.

These results show that a given hemisphere does not always do the tasks for which it is thought superior, nor in performing a task does it always process information in the manner expected of it. This surprising result led Levy to speculate that "hemispheric activation does not depend on a hemisphere's real aptitude or even on its actual processing strategy on a given occasion, but rather on what it *thinks* it can do."[29]

## Separated Awareness
## and Unifying Mechanisms

Under certain conditions each hemisphere of a split-brain patient appears to function as an independent processor, producing results reminiscent of the behavior of two separate individuals. As Sperry has observed:

> Each hemisphere...has its own...private sensations, perceptions, thought, and ideas all of which are cut off from the corresponding experiences in the opposite hemisphere. Each left and right hemisphere has its own private chain of memories and learning experiences that are inaccessible to recall by the other hemisphere. In many respects each disconnected hemisphere appears to have a separate "mind of its own."[30]

Yet shortly after commissurotomy, most casual observers would not notice anything unusual about most split-brain patients. In fact, a patient who recovered from the operation without complications could probably go through a routine medical checkup a year or two later without giving away his or her surgical history to anyone not already acquainted with it. Speech, language comprehension, personality, and motor coordination are remarkably preserved in patients without a corpus callosum and other commissures.

What keeps the two separate hemispheres acting as a unit during the everyday activities of these patients? A variety of unifying mechanisms, some of which we have already considered, seem to compensate for the absence of the cerebral commissures. Conjugate eye movements, as well as the fact that each eye projects to both hemispheres, play an important role in establishing unity of the visual world. The eye movements initiated by one hemisphere to bring an object into direct view serve to make that information available to the other hemisphere as well. Much of the conflict that would result from having the two hemispheres view different halves of the visual field is thus avoided.

The operation of ipsilateral as well as contralateral fibers in the touch modality was mentioned in the context of the chimeric-figures studies. It provides another means by which each hemisphere is made aware of stimulation from both sides of space. The ipsilateral information is generally incomplete and inadequate to enable a patient to identify verbally an object held in the left hand. However, the ipsilateral pathways do provide partial information.

Still another way information is made available to both hemispheres is by commissures located in the lower regions of the brain. A great deal of the brain below the cortex is not split by the commissurotomy procedure. The human split-brain operation severs the nerve bundles connecting the cortical levels of the brain. These are the major fibers connecting the hemispheres, but other, smaller commissures remain intact. These commissures connect paired structures that are part of the brain stem. They are shown in Figure 2.11.

One such structure, the superior colliculus, is involved in the location of objects and the tracking of their movement. The colliculus is believed to process the "where" aspects of the visual world, as opposed to the "what" or finely detailed aspects of vision. The left and right superior colliculi communicate through the commissures connecting them, so that each hemisphere is provided with information about the location of objects regardless of where they fall in the visual field.

The brain stem is also believed to play a role in the process whereby the two hemispheres share emotional reactions. Emotional changes induced by presenting something to one hemisphere only are thought

54

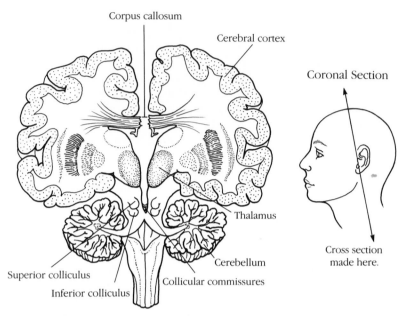

**2.11** Extent of separation of the brain following forebrain commissurotomy. The structures of the midbrain remain connected by the collicular commissures. (From "The Great Cerebral Commissure," by R. W. Sperry. Copyright © 1964 by Scientific American, Inc. All rights reserved.)

to spread partly into the other hemisphere through brain-stem routes. The flow of emotional change is difficult to isolate, however, since emotion involves so many external changes controlled by and accessible to both hemispheres. The overt bodily changes produced by one hemisphere may be read as cues by the other (cross cuing), in addition to the possibility that there is more direct transfer of emotional "tone" between the two cerebral hemispheres through brain-stem commissures.

It remains for future research to assess more carefully the contribution of brain-stem structures and commissures to perception, emotion, and other aspects of human behavior. The split-brain patient, with the phenomenon of her or his apparent unity of mental experience, should serve as a most useful source of this information.

## Partial Commissurotomy

Since the split-brain operations of the early 1960s, several neurosurgeons have attempted to control intractable epilepsy with a procedure less radical than severing all the forebrain commissures. The idea was to limit the surgery to the areas of the corpus callosum and anterior commissure most likely to transmit epileptic discharges in any particular patient. If the source of the epileptic discharges could be localized to some specific region of the brain, they reasoned, then cutting only those fibers connecting that area with the opposite hemisphere should help control the epilepsy.

This was what Van Wagenen had attempted in the first human split-brain operations of the 1940s. His results, however, did not consistently bring relief from the spread of seizures. The success of complete commissurotomy two decades later encouraged neurosurgeons to attempt partial surgical procedures once again. The results have been quite good, from both a medical and a scientific viewpoint. The growing number of subjects with only specific parts of the interhemispheric commissures cut has allowed investigators to study the function of specific regions of the commissures.

One question asked is what kinds of information are transferred across particular regions of the commissures. Gazzaniga and his associates have studied a group of partial-commissurotomy patients operated on by Dr. Donald Wilson to answer this question. Work with these patients has suggested that there is a high degree of specificity of function within the cerebral commissures of humans.

Parts of the front region of the corpus callosum are responsible for somatosensory or touch transfer. The rear third of the corpus callosum, known as the splenium, transfers visual information. Recently, it has been discovered that the anterior commissure also seems to transfer visual information in some but not all patients.[31]

A patient with the front half of the callosum cut will not be able to tell what he or she has in the left hand but will be able to tell what was flashed to the left visual field. The tactile information is not accessible to the verbal left hemisphere, whereas the visual information gets across. A patient with only the back part, or splenium, of the callosum cut may or may not show any sensory disconnection, depending on whether the anterior commissure is capable of transferring visual information in that patient. Tactual identification, in any case, would be normal.

Patients who have undergone partial commissurotomy show interesting capabilities to do visual and tactile matching even though the transfer of one or the other modality is disconnected by the operation. A patient is asked, for example, to hold an object out of sight with his right hand. He then views an object flashed in his left visual field and decides whether they are the same. A patient split either tactually or visually can do this task well. In the first case, the left hemisphere apparently bases the decision on a match of tactual information with the visual information transferred from the right hemisphere. In the second case, the right hemisphere makes the match by comparing visual information with tactile information transferred across the callosum from the left.

Partial commissurotomy has proved itself to be quite effective in alleviating epilepsy in some patients. In addition, the procedure is of considerable interest from a research standpoint. It has helped and will continue to help refine our knowledge about the role of different parts of the interhemispheric fibers and the brain regions they connect. Since the anatomical projections of the fibers are known, one can estimate what regions are connected by the fibers that remain after partial commissurotomy. Patients' abilities and inabilities to perform and transfer lateralized tasks can then give an indication of which parts of the brain are involved in a particular task.

## What Is the Function of the Cerebral Commissures?

We started this chapter with an account of the mystery surrounding the function of the corpus callosum. Are we any nearer now to understanding it? A simple answer would be to say, yes, we know that the cerebral commissures transfer information obtained by one hemisphere over to the other hemisphere. Although this is true, it is not a particularly revealing or complete answer. At the very least, we want to know the nature of the information that is transferred and how it is used by the hemispheres.

Some investigators have suggested that it is primarily sensory information that transfers across the callosum, providing a complete representation of all sensory input in each hemisphere. We do not know, however, that a separate representation of the world in each hemisphere is really necessary. After all, a split-brain animal or human patient does very well in a normal perceptual environment outside of contrived laboratory tests.

Perhaps, then, the corpus callosum transfers more complex, processed information and performs a function other than simply providing a duplicate representation of sensory input. Before we deal further with these issues, however, let's briefly consider the possible basis for asymmetries in human brain function and their consequences. It is likely that an understanding of the role of the cerebral commissures will require an understanding of the nature of hemispheric asymmetry.

### A Model of Brain Asymmetry

It has been postulated that in the course of evolution the functions of the left and right hemispheres began to diverge. Areas in the left hemisphere became more adept at generating rapidly changing motor patterns, such as those involved in fine control of the hands and vocal tract. They also became more skilled at processing the rapidly changing auditory patterns produced by the vocal tract during speech.

Further speculation has led to the idea that the left hemisphere is skilled at sequential processing in general and is therefore the more analytic of the two hemispheres. This analytic mode of information processing is thought to apply to all incoming information, not just to speech. Visual information, for example, would be treated in an analytic manner by being broken up and reorganized in terms of features.

Areas of the right hemisphere, by contrast, became more adept at simultaneously processing the type of information required to perceive spatial patterns and relationships. Its specialties have been claimed to be an outgrowth and elaboration of the processes considered basic to vision and visual memory. Further speculation has led to the idea that the right hemisphere is the more holistic and synthetic of the two in handling all kinds of information.

Although some of these labels describing the functions of the left and right hemispheres are vague and await further work to clarify them, it is clear that differences along these lines do exist. Some investigators have argued that a basic incompatibility between the mechanisms generating these processing styles accounts for their evolutionary development in different hemispheres.

A question that immediately comes to mind is how the two hemispheres share control of behavior in everyday situations. The first possibility investigators have considered is that one hemisphere, usually the left, dominates the control of behavior. The original concept of cerebral dominance was based on this idea. It gained support from early findings with split-brain patients showing that the left hemisphere assumed control of responding in situations where there were simultaneous and different inputs to the two hemispheres. What was overlooked was the fact that these tests generally involved linguistic stimuli (words, for example) and often required a verbal response. Given these conditions, it is not at all surprising to find the language-rich hemisphere "dominating."

An alternative idea, that there is a constant vying for control between the hemispheres, is an outgrowth of subsequent work with split-brain patients. As a wider variety of tasks was employed, including some that could be performed better by the right hemisphere, some interesting results emerged. In the chimeric-figures studies, for example, we have seen that it is not always possible to predict which hemisphere will control a response, despite instructions specifically designed to "engage" one hemisphere. Observations of this sort have led to speculation that there is a delicate balance between the hemispheres, with one or the other taking over depending on the task and other as yet unspecified factors.

Some investigators have suggested that the corpus callosum and other commissures play an important role in achieving interhemispheric harmony in the normal brain, serving to integrate the verbal and spatial modes of thinking into unified behavior. How is this harmony achieved? Is it simply a matter of ensuring that the two hemispheres have the same information available to them, or does it also involve a more complex system of inhibition or suppression of activity in the hemispheres?

### The Commissures as Interhemispheric Integrators

This brings us back to the question of the role of the cerebral commissures. There are no definitive answers yet. At this point, the role of the callosum and other commissures can perhaps best be seen as that of a conduit through which the hemispheres exchange information and perhaps handle the problems associated with conflicts among independent processing units. Because the commissures are simply bundles of nerve fibers, they cannot in and of themselves *control* anything. But they can serve as channels through which synchronization of hemispheric function occurs and duplication or competition of effort is prevented.

Perhaps this integration is accomplished by the callosum's simply serving as a sensory "window," providing a separate and complete representation of all sensory input in each hemisphere. More likely, though, is the possibility that more complex, processed signals normally traverse the commissures, informing each hemisphere about events in the other and, to an extent, controlling their respective operations. This would allow the whole brain to supersede individual hemispheric competencies.

Early in the course of evolution and the development of bisymmetric bodily organization, the continuous transmission of sensory information from one side to the other may have been the one essential function of interhemispheric pathways. It seems likely, however, that with the development of asymmetries in brain function, the role of these pathways became more profound.

If this is the case, why do we not see evidence of serious problems in split-brain patients? We have previously discussed at least part of the answer, including the fact that the hemispheric disconnection in these patients is never really complete. Another possibility is that the role of the commissures is most important in the early developmental period following birth. Severing them later in life may not be overly critical because hemispheric differences and interhemispheric relationships have already been established.

What would happen if the cerebral commissures were severed at birth? Although there are no cases of split-brain surgery performed in infants, reports of several cases of a congenital absence of the callosum might provide insight into its role in development.[32] Unfortunately, these cases are difficult to interpret. It is impossible to know whether any impairments are the result of the absence of the commissures or simply other manifestations of the development problem that resulted in agenesis in the first place.*

## In Summary

Our review of data from split-brain subjects has led us to the conclusion that hemispheric specialization is not an all-or-none phenomenon but rather falls on a continuum. Recent work with split-brain patients has revealed that each hemisphere is capable of handling many kinds of tasks but often differs from the other in both approach and efficiency. Almost any human behavior or higher mental function, however, clearly involves more than the actual specialties of either hemisphere and utilizes what is common to both hemispheres.

In research with split-brain subjects, language continues to stand out as the most salient and profound difference between the left brain and the right brain. Some investigators have claimed that all other hemispheric differences are manifestations of the verbal asymmetry.[33] They argue that the region of the left hemisphere that developed specialization for language would no longer be available to handle the processing of spatial information formerly controlled by either half of the brain. The right hemisphere, then, would appear specialized for spatial skills, although its specialization was really a result of the left hemisphere's "deficit" rather than the right hemisphere's "superiority." This argument provides an interesting perspective on the problem of how lateralization developed, although it would be exceedingly difficult to "prove" in the usual sense.

---

*Cases of callosal agenesis without other symptoms are exceedingly rare. The bulk of the evidence suggests that these individuals have language functions distributed more bilaterally than is the case in neurologically normal persons, a finding we would have predicted on the basis of what is known about brain plasticity. It is also observed that persons with callosal agenesis generally fall in the marginally normal IQ range or lower. Although it is tempting to see a causal link between intelligence and the development of the corpus callosum, it is clearly unwarranted to do so from these findings.

# 3

# Studying Asymmetries in the Normal Brain

Fortunately, most people are neurologically normal, having two undamaged hemispheres connected by intact commissures. What does evidence about the left brain and right brain from studies of brain-damaged and split-brain patients tell us about the role of the two hemispheres in the rest of humanity?

We have already considered some of the problems involved in trying to draw conclusions about the normal brain from clinical studies. We have seen how a specific deficit resulting from damage to a particular region of the brain does not necessarily mean that the damaged area once controlled the disrupted function. We noted as well the striking adaptability of the brain, which complicates the interpretation of studies with brain-damaged and split-brain subjects.

Because of these problems, it is not possible to draw firm conclusions about the workings of the normal brain from what we have learned in the brain-damage clinic alone. The clinical work can suggest what to look for, but rigorous conclusions about normal functioning require the confirmation of research with normal brains. The problem is to devise ways of studying the contribution made by each half of the brain to behavior in an intact system.

The investigation of asymmetries in normal subjects has been carried out in several ways. One of the oldest and most extensively used techniques takes advantage of the natural split in human visual pathways. This split neatly divides our visual world into two fields, each of which projects into one hemisphere. By flashing material very briefly to the left or right of the point where a subject is fixating, investigators are able to lateralize inputs—that is, to present them to one hemisphere only. Because of the connections between the hemispheres, this one-sided presentation lasts only a fraction of a second, but it appears to be sufficient to allow investigators to compare the abilities of one hemisphere to those of the other.

Similarly, it has been discovered that simultaneously presenting different auditory information to each ear leads to the initial laterali-zation of auditory stimuli. Information presented to the left ear appears to project first to the right hemisphere, and information presented to the right ear is lateralized to the left hemisphere. This procedure, known as *dichotic listening,* has allowed investigators to study differ-ences and similarities in the way the two hemispheres handle speech as well as other types of auditory information.

More speculative but nevertheless intriguing approaches to the study of asymmetry in normal subjects have involved the careful ob-servation of overt behavior while subjects engage in different tasks. For instance, a person's eye movements to one side or the other have been used to show which hemisphere is more active when the subject is solving a problem or playing a mental game. In another technique, investigators observe the consequences of performing several tasks at the same time. The idea is that the tasks interfering with each other the least are likely to be controlled by different parts of the brain, in some cases perhaps by different hemispheres.

In this chapter we will review data collected from normal subjects with whom such techniques have been used.

## Asymmetry and the Visual System

The investigation of visual asymmetries in normal subjects often resem-bles the testing situations used with split-brain patients. Visual stimuli flashed briefly in the left visual field project first to the right hemisphere; stimuli flashed to the right visual field project initially to the left hem-isphere. In split-brain patients this initial lateralization to one hemi-sphere or the other is maintained because the connections between the hemispheres have been cut. In a normal subject, however, the connec-tions are intact and can transfer information presented to either hemi-sphere. Nevertheless, it was found that differences could be detected in a person's performance on certain tasks, depending on whether the task was presented to the right or left visual field.

*Visual-Field Differences:*
*The Result of Reading Habits*
*or a Sign of Hemispheric Asymmetry?*

In the early 1950s, Mortimer Mishkin and Donald Forgays demonstrated that normal right-handed subjects were better at identifying English words briefly presented to the right of fixation than they were at identifying words flashed in the left visual field. However, when Yiddish words were presented in the same way to subjects who could read Yiddish, a slight advantage in favor of the left visual field was found. The authors concluded that experience with reading produces a "more effective neural organization (which) is developed in the corresponding cerebral hemispheres (left for English, right for Yiddish)." In other words, acquired directional reading habits result in better processing of written English in the right visual field, while Yiddish, a language read from right to left, is processed more accurately in the left visual field.[1]

This explanation enjoyed widespread acceptance for several years, although it did not address the question of why the advantage for the right visual field with English words was considerably greater than that for the left visual field with Yiddish words. A decade later, however, the publication of work with the California split-brain subjects suggested a reason for the lack of parallelism in the size of the visual-field differences.

Split-brain subjects, as we have seen, showed dramatic differences in their ability to report printed English words in the left and right visual fields. Those differences were interpreted as a reflection of the functional differences between the hemispheres for language functions. Perhaps, investigators began to think, the asymmetries found in the split-brain patients contribute to the visual-field differences found in normal subjects as well. Mishkin and Forgays' findings, then, may have been due to two factors operating simultaneously: (1) the biases in favor of one visual field due to acquired reading habits in a particular language *superimposed* on (2) an advantage for the right visual field resulting from differences between the left brain and right brain.

An important test of this two-factor interpretation came from later studies investigating visual-field asymmetries with English or Yiddish words presented vertically to minimize the possible role of directional scanning. With the effects of directional scanning reduced, the two-factor interpretation predicts that the functional differences between the hemispheres should produce a right visual field advantage for both Yiddish and English words. Precisely this result was found.[2]

These findings, as well as a variety of other data that we will consider, lend support to the idea that visual-field differences in normal subjects reflect brain asymmetries in those subjects. This conclusion is an exciting one, for it suggests that differences between the left brain and right brain found in clinical and split-brain subjects have reality for the normal brain as well, and that these differences can actually be studied in normal subjects.

## Why Does Lateralized Presentation Result in Asymmetric Performance?

Before we turn to other evidence supporting the conclusion that visual-field differences reflect brain asymmetries in normal subjects, we should first address a fundamental issue. Even if there are functional differences between the hemispheres in normal subjects, why are they reflected in differences in performance for the two visual fields? Despite the initial lateralization or one-sided presentation, both hemispheres have access to all incoming information. Very brief presentations to one side of fixation ensure that initially a stimulus is directly projected to only one half of the brain, but the connections between the hemispheres can transmit information about the stimulus to the other side almost instantaneously. Why, then, do we find differences in performance between the visual fields?

The answer, apparently, is that the hemisphere receiving stimulus information directly has an advantage over the hemisphere receiving the same information indirectly by way of the cerebral commissures. The reasons for the advantage are not entirely clear, but several possibilities have been suggested.

It is possible that transfer between the hemispheres results in some loss of clarity of information. Figure 3.1 illustrates this possibility schematically. It is also possible that only certain kinds or levels of information pass across the commissures. The dynamics of a fully intact brain may be such that the cross-connections serve more to inhibit the duplication of processing than to transfer raw sensory input.

Despite uncertainty over the exact reason for the advantage, investigators have assumed that information presented to only one visual field is processed most efficiently by the hemisphere that first receives the information. Asymmetries in performance between the visual fields emerge in tasks where the hemispheres do not have equal capacities to begin with. The condition where information is presented directly to the hemisphere specialized for a specific function would be expected to produce better performance—that is, more accurate or faster responding—than one in which information goes first to the other half of the brain.

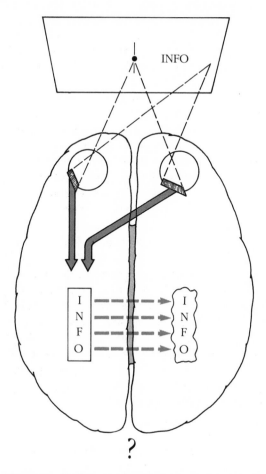

**3.1** The quality of information transferred across the commissures is a complex issue. A hemisphere receiving information indirectly during a lateralized presentation may be at a disadvantage due to any of several possibilities, including time losses, limitations on what aspects of the information are transferred, and inhibitory processes between the hemispheres.

Probably the strongest evidence for this model of visual-field differences in normal subjects is that these differences do seem to reflect hemispheric asymmetries like those uncovered by research on brain-damaged and split-brain patients. While a right visual field advantage is found with normal subjects in a variety of tasks using words and letters, subjects show a left visual field advantage for stimuli that are thought to be handled by the right hemisphere.

For example, several studies have demonstrated that subjects recognize faces presented in the left visual field more quickly than those presented in the right visual field.[3] Other work has shown that subjects are more accurate at remembering the location of dots presented on a card when the material is presented to the right hemisphere initially.[4] These findings provide strong support for the idea that visual-field differences reflect hemispheric differences: the right visual field advantage reflects left-hemisphere specialization for language functions, and the left visual field superiority results from right-hemisphere specialization for the processing of visuo-spatial stimuli.

We should point out, though, that studies using nonverbal stimuli have not produced results as consistent as those found with words or letters. Some studies using nonsense forms and geometric shapes have shown no differences for the two visual fields; other studies have reported differences in performance.[5] For the most part, however, the studies that do obtain differences between fields show the left visual field to be superior. The problem is that many studies that use stimuli believed by investigators to be processed by the right hemisphere do not find any differences between visual fields. This is reminiscent of the problems encountered when investigators started to look for evidence of special right-hemisphere functions in studies with brain-damaged patients. The functions of the right hemisphere proved to be much more elusive than those of the left. A similar picture has emerged in studies with neurologically normal subjects.

## Asymmetry and Audition

Techniques to lateralize auditory information have also been used to study hemispheric differences. Doreen Kimura, working at the Montreal Neurological Institute, noticed that under certain conditions subjects were more accurate at identifying words presented to the right ear than they were at identifying words delivered to the left ear. Kimura was using the dichotic listening procedure, in which subjects listen to two different spoken messages simultaneously, one message to each ear. She wanted to compare the performances of brain-damaged subjects and normal subjects in a task involving an overload of information.

### Dichotic Listening

The stimuli used by Kimura consisted of pairs of spoken digits—for example, "one" and "nine." The members of each pair were aligned for simultaneity of onset and were recorded on separate channels of audio tape. Subjects listened through headphones to trials consisting of three pairs of digits presented in rapid succession. After each trial, the subject was asked to recall as many of the six previously presented digits as possible, in any order.

Kimura found that patients with damage to the left temporal lobe did more poorly than patients with damage to the right temporal lobe; but regardless of where the damage was located, subjects typically reported the digits presented to the right ear more accurately. This right-ear advantage was also found in normal control subjects.[6]

The finding that patients with damage to the left hemisphere performed more poorly overall than patients with damage to the right hemisphere was predictable. The dichotic listening task involves the abilities to understand and produce speech, both of which are primarily left-hemisphere functions that might be disrupted to some extent in patients with damage on the left side. The observation that the ears performed asymmetrically, however, was surprising.

A little anatomy reveals why the asymmetry was unexpected. Unlike the retina, which sends projections contralaterally to the brain from one half of its surface and ipsilaterally from the other half, each ear sends information from all its receptors to both hemispheres. Thus complete information about a stimulus presented to the right ear is represented initially in both hemispheres, and vice versa. Even if speech stimuli could be processed in only one hemisphere, we would not expect to see any evidence of the asymmetry because each ear has direct access to both hemispheres.

### Kimura's Model of Ear Asymmetry

To explain her findings, Kimura noted evidence from animal studies suggesting that the contralateral projections from ear to brain are stronger than the ipsilateral or same-side pathways.[7] She also proposed that when two different stimuli are presented simultaneously to each ear, the difference in the strength of the pathways is exaggerated so that information sent along the ipsilateral route is suppressed. Given these assumptions, it was then possible to explain the right-ear advantage.

Under dichotic presentation conditions, the stimulus to the left ear may reach the left hemisphere in one of two ways—over the suppressed ipsilateral route or over the contralateral pathways to the right hemisphere and then across the cerebral commissures. The stimulus to the right ear, however, has a simpler task. It gains access to the left hemisphere along the contralateral route. Since it is likely to arrive at the left hemisphere for processing in better form than its left-ear counterpart, a small right-ear advantage emerges. Kimura's model is depicted in Figure 3.2.

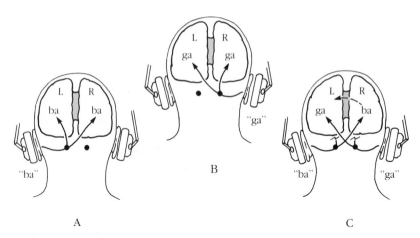

**3.2** Kimura's model of dichotic listening in normal subjects. A. Monaural presentation to the left ear is sent to the right hemisphere by way of contralateral pathways and to the left hemisphere by way of ipsilateral pathways. The subject reports the syllable ("ba") accurately. B. Monaural presentation to the right ear is sent to the left hemisphere by way of contralateral pathways and to the right hemisphere by way of ipsilateral pathways. The subject reports the syllable ("ga") accurately. C. In dichotic presentation, ipsilateral pathways are suppressed, so "ga" goes only to the left (speech) hemisphere and "ba" to the right hemisphere. The syllable "ba" is accessible to the left (speech) hemisphere only through the commissures. As a consequence, "ga" is usually reported more accurately than "ba" (a right-ear advantage).

Some support for Kimura's ideas has come from studies showing that there is basically no difference between the two ears in a subject's ability to detect or identify stimuli presented one at a time. Individual subjects may have hearing losses in one or both ears, but overall when data are collected from large numbers of subjects, the two ears perform similarly.[8] This suggests that ordinarily, without any competition from the contralateral pathways, the ipsilateral fibers are sufficient to produce good performance. This point has been confirmed in work with split-brain subjects.

### Dichotic Listening in Split-Brain Subjects: Testing Some Assumptions

Split-brain patients show a normal pattern of response when speech stimuli are presented to one ear at a time. They can identify words equally well in either ear, just as neurologically intact subjects do. This shows that the ipsilateral path from the left ear to the left hemisphere is functional under conditions of monaural presentation. If, however, speech stimuli are presented dichotically to split-brain subjects, a dramatic, highly exaggerated version of the ear asymmetry found in normals occurs. The typical split-brain patient reports the right-ear items accurately, but the left-ear report is at chance level. In fact, the patients frequently have to be coaxed into guessing about the identity of left-ear items because they report that they hear only one stimulus.[9]

This situation with split-brain patients is consistent with Kimura's model and helps confirm it. With the corpus callosum cut, communication between the hemispheres is disrupted, but both the ipsilateral and the contralateral projections of each ear are left intact (these pathways are subcortical and are not cut during surgery). If, as Kimura suggested, the ipsilateral pathways are suppressed under dichotic stimulation, each ear would send its half of the information to the opposite hemisphere only over the contralateral pathway. The right hemisphere would receive input from the left ear, and the stimulus to the right ear would reach the left hemisphere. Since the right hemisphere is very limited verbally, it would not be able to talk about the word it received from the left ear. At the same time, information about the left-ear word could not "transfer" into the left hemisphere because the corpus callosum was cut. As a result, the left-ear items would not be identified. Figure 3.3 shows how Kimura's model of ear asymmetry would operate in split-brain patients.

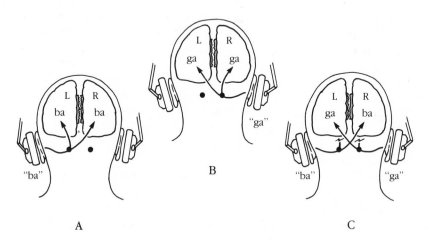

**3.3** Dichotic listening in split-brain subjects. A., B. Monaural presentations operate as they do with normal subjects. Because both ipsilateral and contralateral pathways are unaffected by commissurotomy, the patient can accurately report a signal to either ear. C. In dichotic presentation, the ipsilateral pathways are suppressed (as in normal subjects), but "ba" is not accessible to the left (speech) hemisphere because the commissures are cut. Only "ga" is reported (a complete right-ear advantage).

The split-brain patient is able to report only the right-ear words in a dichotic presentation. If the presentation is not dichotic (that is, if the words go to one ear at a time), both ipsilateral and contralateral pathways do function so that left- as well as right-ear words reach the left hemisphere. The patient can then report words presented to either ear, and the dramatic ear asymmetry disappears.

In summary, simultaneous presentation of different words to both ears of the split-brain subject results in the patient's reporting only the right-ear words. Neither the contralateral nor the ipsilateral auditory pathways are affected by the split-brain operation, lending support to the idea that ipsilateral pathways are suppressed by such dichotic presentation. In normal subjects, the ear asymmetry with dichotic presentation is not as dramatic because information can transfer across the callosum. There is, nevertheless, an advantage for incoming information that does not have to transfer across interhemispheric commissures for processing. This is reflected in a small advantage for right-ear words because they project most directly to the verbal left hemisphere.

### Ear Asymmetry and Results of Sodium Amytal Testing

Other support for Kimura's model comes from the finding that the ear advantage reverses in subjects who have been shown to have speech controlled by the right hemisphere instead of by the left. Patients tested with sodium amytal to determine the hemisphere controlling speech have been given the dichotic listening task to see whether the ear asymmetry is related to hemispheric asymmetry. Those with left-hemisphere speech centers typically show a right-ear advantage; those with right-hemisphere speech show a left-ear advantage.[10] The amytal test allows a direct assessment of speech lateralization without having to infer it from the patients' handedness. Thus in the rare cases of right-handers with right-hemisphere speech, a left-ear advantage would generally be found. These data are very important in establishing the validity of the dichotic listening test as a measure of brain asymmetry.

Finally, research has demonstrated that the ear asymmetry found in a given subject differs as a function of the nature of the stimuli that are presented. A left-ear advantage has been found with stimuli believed to be processed by the right hemisphere—stimuli such as musical chords and melodies. The dichotic listening procedure serves to lateralize auditory inputs in the normal brain in the same way that tachistoscopic presentation lateralizes visual inputs. If an input goes first to the hemisphere specialized for processing it, subjects are more accurate than if the stimulus must be transferred to the other hemisphere. Because two stimuli must be presented at once to produce this lateralization, the dichotic procedure differs from the visual case. This difference, though, appears to be a consequence of anatomical differences between the auditory and the visual systems and does not represent any fundamental difference in the nature of the asymmetries themselves.

## What Has Been Learned From Visual and Auditory Asymmetries?

During the last decade, a great many studies have been conducted using the techniques of dichotic listening and lateralized tachistoscopic presentation with normal subjects. As in the research with split-brain patients, there has been a gradual evolution of ideas about the nature of hemispheric asymmetries as new data suggest different interpretations of earlier work.

### The Verbal—Nonverbal Distinction

Much of the early work on the left brain and right brain in normal subjects led investigators to believe that the two hemispheres differ basically in terms of the types of stimuli they are best prepared to deal with. A typical visual task involved the lateralized presentation of stimuli that the subject was asked to identify. A similar procedure was employed with dichotic stimuli as well: two items were presented simultaneously, and the subject was asked to report what was heard. Sometimes the basic task was modified so that the subject was required to recognize a specific stimulus rather than identify each item, and sometimes the experimenter was primarily interested in how quickly a subject could respond to a stimulus instead of how accurate the response was. Often both speed and accuracy were measured in the same study.

Stimuli were said to show a left-hemisphere advantage if performance was superior when items were presented in the right ear or right visual field. A right-hemisphere advantage was assumed if performance was superior when items were presented in the left ear or left visual field. Differences in performance between sides were quite small—frequently just a few percentage points better in identification or a few milliseconds faster in response. But anywhere from 70 to 90 percent of the right-handed subjects tested in a typical study would show the asymmetry.

Most of the early studies showing a right-side advantage used stimuli that were language related in a very obvious way. Tachistoscopically presented words and even single letters produced a right visual field advantage.[11] Dichotically presented spoken digits and words also resulted in an advantage to the left hemisphere.[12] The advantage, though, was not limited to meaningful spoken utterances.

Studies have shown that nonsense syllables such as "pa" and "ka" also produce a right-ear advantage and that speech played backward produces a right-ear superiority in recognition as well.[13] Backward speech can be produced by reversing the position of the playback and take-up reels on a tape recorder, rewinding, and then playing the tape. The end result sounds like an exotic Scandinavian language. Taken together, these results suggested that stimuli do not have to be meaningful to produce a left-hemisphere advantage but should be language related or verbal in some way.

The picture for the right hemisphere is more difficult to summarize. A wide variety of visual stimuli have produced left visual field or right-hemisphere superiorities. We have mentioned studies that used faces and dot displays as stimuli and obtained a left visual field advantage. The dichotic listening studies that result in a right-hemisphere advantage are also diverse. One of the earliest demonstrated a left-ear superiority in the recognition of melodic excerpts.[14] Two different four-second piano melodies were simultaneously presented on each trial. The subject was asked to indicate which of the four sequentially presented excerpts played immediately after had been members of the pair delivered dichotically. Other studies revealed a left-ear advantage when familiar environmental noises were presented dichotically.[15] In a typical trial the subject would be asked to identify a pair of sounds such as a dog barking and a train whistling.

All these "right-hemisphere" stimuli share the attribute of being nonverbal, and many investigators have argued that the distinction between the functions of the two hemispheres lies along this verbal–nonverbal dimension. In this view, all language-related stimuli are dealt with primarily in the left hemisphere, and the right hemisphere is specialized for handling certain types of nonverbal stimuli. This appears to be a neat, reasonably satisfying summary of the data we have reviewed so far. However, problems that have emerged in more recent work have led researchers to seek another explanation of the fundamental differences between the left brain and right brain.

### The Information-Processing Approach

Consider the following experiment. The subject is given a short list of letters to memorize and then briefly views a familiar object in the left or right visual field. The subject's task is to decide whether the first letter of the name of the object is among the letters in the memorized list. Which visual field would lead to a faster response?

Suppose that the subject viewed single letters instead of pictures and had to decide whether the letter was among those that had been memorized. What could be predicted about the speed of response in this case?

It would be reasonable to expect a left visual field superiority in the first case and a right visual field superiority in the second. Pictures, after all, are nonverbal stimuli, and letters clearly fall in the verbal domain. In fact, the results obtained were the complete reverse. Picture stimuli resulted in faster performance when they were presented to the left hemisphere, and the letters were responded to more quickly when they were projected initially to the right hemisphere.[16] Why?

Studies such as the one just described provide fairly compelling evidence that an analysis of hemispheric differences simply in terms of verbal and nonverbal stimuli is inadequate. What seems to be more important than the nature of the stimulus is what the subject does with the stimulus. In the case of the supposedly nonverbal pictures, the subject was asked to identify each picture and recover the initial letter of its name, a clear-cut language function. The single-letter stimuli, on the other hand, were verbal in nature but in this task did not have to be approached as verbal stimuli. The subject could readily perform the task by matching the mental image of the letter against the images of the set of memorized letters. Theoretically, the subject could do this without ever knowing the name of the letter presented.

This kind of explanation emphasizes the task to be performed by the subject rather than the nature of the stimulus per se. It reflects a shift away from left- and right-hemisphere stimuli to left- and right-hemisphere modes of processing information.

Another study that highlights this information-processing approach to brain asymmetry was one that took advantage of the fact that there are alternate ways for subjects to remember pairs of words. One is to rehearse the words by repeating them out loud or subvocally; a second is to form an image of the two items interacting in some way. For example, faced with the task of remembering "flag" and "chicken," subjects can repeat the words over and over again, or they can form an image of the two words, such as a chicken carrying a flag. (The use of images of this type has been shown to be a very effective memory aid.)

The researchers hypothesized that verbal and imagery strategies would involve different cerebral hemispheres. They proposed that this difference would be tapped by having subjects indicate whether a picture flashed to the left or right visual field corresponded to one of the words previously presented. Results showed that when subjects were told to remember the word pairs by subvocal rehearsal, response time was faster for probes to the right visual field. When subjects were asked to form images of the to-be-remembered pairs, response time was faster for the left visual field. These findings were in keeping with the predictions.[17]

The way a subject approaches a particular task, then, has important consequences for the outcome of studies investigating differential hemispheric involvement. The two studies we have just reviewed directly manipulated the subject's strategy with specific instructions to deal with the stimuli in a certain way. Perhaps the strategies different subjects naturally bring to bear on a particular task can affect the outcome as well.

## Problems in Interpreting Dichotic and Tachistoscopic Studies

Tachistoscopic presentation and dichotic listening studies have served as the basis for much of our current theorizing about the nature of the left brain and right brain in normal subjects. Unfortunately, certain problems prevent them from being the ideal tools investigators would like to have.

One concern is that these behavioral tests typically underestimate the incidence of left-hemisphere speech in right-handers found with sodium amytal (Wada) testing. Studies generally find that approximately 80 percent of right-handed subjects show a right-ear or right visual field advantage for language stimuli; sodium amytal testing, in contrast, indicates that more than 95 percent of right-handed individuals have left-hemisphere language. What causes this discrepancy?

One possibility is that the tests are not a pure measure of brain asymmetry and that other factors are involved. Perhaps individual differences in the neural pathways connecting the eyes and ears to the brain play a role in the outcome of the studies.

The strategies that subjects adopt in these tasks may also contribute in a major way to performance.[18] In dichotic listening, for example, subjects can actively shift their attention to the left- or right-ear stimulus. If the left-ear items are at a disadvantage because of hemispheric asymmetry, some subjects may choose to direct their attention to the weaker ear, thereby producing a smaller right-ear superiority than might be found otherwise. Other subjects, in contrast, may focus their attention on the clearer of the two stimuli on any trial, without trying to identify both of them. These subjects would show a larger right-ear advantage than one would expect. At the present time we do not have any really good way to deal with this potential problem.

We should also note that the discrepancy between the results of

Wada testing and behavioral measures of asymmetry may be due to the possibility that each is tapping a different aspect of functional asymmetry. The Wada test is used to determine the hemisphere that controls speech output. Perhaps tachistoscopic and dichotic listening tasks, which are basically tests of perception and not production, reflect functions that are less lateralized.

Another problem is that visual and dichotic measures of lateralization are not highly correlated with each other. If these tests are measuring the same lateralized functions, it would be reasonable to expect them to produce results that are highly related to each other. Studies that have compared asymmetries in dichotic listening and tachistoscopic tasks in the same subjects have found some degree of relationship, but not a high one.[19] Why? Perhaps these tests are not measuring the same thing after all.

Another concern, one that has implications for the preceding two as well, is that repeated testing of the same subjects does not always produce the same results. A test is reliable to the extent that repeated administrations yield similar results. Some studies have found the reliability of the dichotic listening and tachistoscopic tests to be lower than one might expect.[20] For example, some subjects who when first tested showed a right-ear advantage for dichotically presented speech shifted to a left-ear advantage when tested a week later. Presumably, the organization of an individual's brain is a stable characteristic and does not change over short periods of time. Signs of variability within an individual may mean that the laterality tests are tapping functions, such as the formation of strategies to be used in performing the tasks, which can shift over brief intervals of time.

## Theoretical Considerations Stemming From the Use of Dichotic and Tachistoscopic Tests

Dichotic listening and tachistoscopic studies with normal subjects have raised several interesting theoretical issues. We will briefly mention a few of them here.

### Hemispheric Differences: Absolute or Relative? Large or Small?

The first issue is whether hemispheric differences are absolute or relative. Does a difference in performance between visual fields mean that only one hemisphere is capable of performing the task? Or does it

*The terms *lateralized* and *lateralization* are frequently used to refer to the division of functions between the hemispheres as well as to the restriction of information to one hemisphere.

simply reflect the fact that one hemisphere is better at the task than the other? The typical study with normal subjects does not allow us to tease these alternatives apart because performance in the "inferior" visual field may be the result of either less efficient processing by the non-specialized hemisphere or processing by the specialized hemisphere after transfer of information across the commissures. In either case we would expect the same results—a difference in performance between the two sides.

A related issue is whether the size of the asymmetry found in different subjects can tell us anything about the degree of lateralization for certain functions in particular subjects. We mentioned earlier that a subject's strategies may play a role in determining the size of the asymmetry effects, independent of lateralization per se. Is it also possible that differences in the size of the asymmetry can tell us something about the extent of lateralization? Is a subject with a large right-ear advantage more lateralized than a subject with a smaller right-ear advantage? This intriguing problem has many investigators looking for ways to transform scores reflecting a subject's performance into a meaningful index of lateralization.*

### The Role of Attentional Bias

The last issue we will consider is the absence of general agreement about the basis of the lateral asymmetries found in normal subjects. When we introduced tachistoscopic and dichotic listening work, we argued that asymmetries reflected the initial lateralization of stimulus input to the hemisphere best able to deal with the material. This type of explanation has been characterized as a "wiring" account of the difference because the asymmetries result from the wiring of the nervous system and processing differences between the hemispheres. Information lateralized to the hemisphere *not* specialized for it was at a disadvantage because it had to traverse callosal pathways in order to get to the more appropriate hemisphere. Another, quite different explanation has also been offered for these results.

Marcel Kinsbourne has proposed that asymmetries observed in dichotic listening and tachistoscopic studies reflect covert shifts in attention to one side of space following the activation of one hemi-

---

*The issue of how to compute measures of lateralization from scores on behavioral tests is important and complex. In tests where percent correct is the dependent variable, it is possible to use difference scores (left minus right, or variations thereof) as the index of lateralization. Such scores are not independent of overall performance, however. Some investigators have claimed that a laterality measure should be independent of how well someone does; others have argued that information on overall performance may itself be related to lateralization.

sphere.[21] He argues that the hemisphere specialized for a particular task becomes differentially active, or "primed," when appropriate material is presented to a subject, and that this activation or priming "spills over" to the centers controlling attention to the opposite side of space.

For example, in Kinsbourne's view the right-ear advantage in tasks with dichotically presented speech is a consequence of the activation of the left hemisphere, followed by greater attention to the contralateral or right ear. A left-ear advantage in a dichotic music task would reflect differential right-hemisphere involvement and a concomitant shift of attention to the left side of space.

Kinsbourne's model of asymmetries is similar to the wiring account in that it begins with the assumption that there are basic functional differences between the hemispheres. It differs from the wiring model in its explanation of how hemispheric differences give rise to the performance differences that are studied in behavioral tests.

Kinsbourne's attentional model of asymmetries has received some support from a variety of different studies. In a series of interesting experiments, Kinsbourne and his colleagues showed that tasks not normally showing a visual-field asymmetry could be made to show a right-side advantage if subjects were asked to rehearse subvocally a short list of words while they viewed the laterally presented stimuli.[22] The rehearsal is presumed to activate the left hemisphere and produce a shift in attention to the right side, resulting in more accurate performance in that visual field.

Other evidence consistent with the attentional model comes from studies showing that the context in which stimuli are presented affects the type of asymmetry that is observed. For example, the right-ear advantage in speed of responding to certain dichotically presented syllables becomes a slight left-ear advantage when the subject is required to compare a brief melody presented immediately before each syllable pair with a melody presented immediately after.[23] An attentional view would claim that the musical stimuli "primed" the right hemisphere so that the shift in attention to the left ear would cancel out the shift to the right ear that ordinarily occurs when speech is presented.

We should note, though, that some attempts to replicate and extend work based on the attentional model have not been successful, and few investigators believe it is a complete explanation of asymmetries observed in lateralized testing. At the same time, some researchers question the adequacy of the wiring account of these asymmetries and are inclined to think that both views may play some role in the phenomena we have been considering. Both models can be combined, for example, if we assume that priming one hemisphere serves to facilitate the processing of stimuli that are presented directly to it.[24]

.   .   .

Although there are still many questions to be resolved about inconsistencies, dichotic and tachistoscopic techniques have confirmed that much of the split-brain and clinical data do reflect processes in the normal brain. There is a striking correspondence between many of the hemispheric differences shown in normal subjects through these indirect techniques and the ideas gleaned from the brain-damage clinic by several generations of neurologists and neuropsychologists.

Although the development of thought about the implications of the split-brain data has been similar to the development of ideas about the implications of the normal data, research with normal subjects using dichotic listening and tachistoscopic techniques has made contributions that go beyond the verification of clinical evidence. Many of the contributions are theoretical and help to sharpen the focus of research into laterality by pinpointing important issues.

We turn now to discussions of two other behavioral techniques that have become popular in research with normals.

## Left-Lookers and Right-Lookers

According to poets, the eyes are windows to the soul. To some neuropsychologists, they are windows to the left brain and right brain as well. We are all familiar with the patterns of looking at and away from others that characterize social interaction. A listener will generally look directly at a speaker when asked a question but will look away while answering.

In the course of his practice, clinical psychologist M. E. Day noticed that patients tended consistently to look to the left or to the right when answering questions. On the basis of further work, Day suggested that the direction of these lateral eye movements (LEMs) might be associated with certain personality characteristics.[25] Five years later, psychologist Paul Bakan of Simon Fraser University published data supporting Day's ideas and went on to propose that the eye movements are related to hemispheric asymmetry as well.[26]

### The Direction of Lateral Eye Movements
### The Result of Individual Differences or Question Types?

Bakan's hypothesis was based on the well-established fact that eye movements to one side are controlled by centers in the frontal lobe of the contralateral hemisphere. He suggested that cognitive activity occurring primarily in one hemisphere would trigger eye movements to the opposite side, so that eye movements could be viewed as an index of the relative activity of the two hemispheres in an individual. Accordingly, left-lookers, or persons who typically make eye movements to the left, are those for whom the right hemisphere predominates. Right-lookers are persons who have greater left-hemisphere involvement in overall functioning.

Bakan viewed the direction of lateral eye movements as a stable characteristic of each individual. Later investigations exploring LEMs as an index of hemispheric activity began to consider the role played by the type of question used to elicit eye movements.[27] Questions requiring verbal analysis, it was reasoned, will tend to activate the left hemisphere in most right-handers; questions involving an analysis of spatial relationships will activate the right hemisphere. The differential activation of the halves of the brain would then be reflected in right or left LEMs respectively.

The predicted association between the nature of the question and the direction of eye movement has been reported in many studies. To engage the left hemisphere, subjects have been asked to interpret proverbs, spell words, provide definitions, do simple arithmetic (Solve 144/6 times 4), and solve logical problems (Al is smarter than Sam, and Al is duller than Rick. Who is smartest?). Questions involving visualization (How many edges are there on a cube?), spatial relations (If a person is facing the rising sun, where is south in respect to him?), and musical skills (identifying piano melodies) have been used to activate the right hemisphere. When differences in direction are found, right LEMs predominate in response to questions in the first group, and left LEMs follow questions of the second type.[28]

Gary Schwartz and his colleagues at Yale have also looked at lateral eye movements in response to emotional questions. In addition to verbal and spatial questions of the sort just described, verbal emotional questions (For you, is anger or hate the stronger emotion?) and spatial emotional questions (When you visualize your father's face, what emotion first strikes you?) were studied. Results showed that verbal questions overall produced more right LEMs than did spatial questions, in keeping with earlier work. Emotional questions overall produced more left LEMs. These findings have been taken as support for greater right-hemisphere involvement in the processing of emotional information.[29]

The first studies relating the direction of lateral eye movement to hemispheric asymmetry generated a great deal of excitement. The notion that there were individual differences in *hemisphericity,* the tendency to rely on the processes of one half of the brain, was appealing to many investigators. Lateral eye movements seemed to be a very straightforward, quick, and harmless measure of these differences in normal people.

Later studies indicating that the direction of eye movements is related to the nature of the question posed to the subject had great appeal to those who were interested in studying functional differences between the hemispheres. The work suggested that it is possible to explore the abilities of the left brain and right brain in normals quite directly, without using dichotic listening or tachistoscopic procedures.

For these reasons, LEM research has been very attractive and has generated considerable interest. Important issues that have serious implications for the interpretation of these studies remain unresolved, however. Why have some studies indicated that the tendency to be a left-looker or a right-looker is a stable characteristic of each person, while other studies show that the direction of eye gaze is a function of the type of question posed to the subject? One possible explanation is suggested by the work of Ruben and Raquel Gur, who proposed that factors in the experimental situation may account for these results.[30]

### Eye Movements and the
### Location of the Experimenter

In the earliest work suggesting stable differences in lateral eye movements among subjects, the experimenter typically faced the subject when asking a question and then manually recorded the direction of the eye movement that followed. Later studies frequently employed a camera to video-tape all eye movements, and in these cases the experimenter sat out of view behind the subject or in another room.

Perhaps, the Gurs reasoned, the presence or absence of another person in full view of the subject affects the pattern of eye movements. They postulated that the experimenter-present situation may be more threatening and anxiety provoking and that under these conditions the anxious subject will reveal certain characteristic modes of response: the subject may show greater activation of the hemisphere most compatible with his or her cognitive style, although that hemisphere might not be appropriate for a particular type of question. In the experimenter-absent condition, the level of anxiety would be lower, permitting the differential hemispheric activation to reflect the nature of the question posed to the subject.

A study by Gur and Gur used the same set of questions to compare directly the eye movements that occurred when an experimenter sat in front of the subject with the subject's LEMs when the experimenter was out of sight. The results confirmed their prediction. When the experimenter was facing the subjects, they typically looked to the left or to the right regardless of the nature of the question. When the experimenter was positioned behind the same subjects, their eye movements were linked to the type of question posed.

### Do LEMs Really Measure Brain Activation?

The Gurs' findings point to an important procedural factor that may account for some of the conflicts between studies, but they leave unresolved a major problem. Do lateral eye movements really reflect differential hemispheric activity, or can they be explained in other ways? What exactly is the evidence linking LEMs to hemispheric asymmetry? A recent review of work in this area has noted that the link is an indirect and weak one, based primarily on investigators' conceptions of what constitutes a left-hemisphere or a right-hemisphere question.[31]

Questions requiring an analysis of words or meanings are believed to engage the left hemisphere; questions involving spatial relations or musical skills are considered right-hemisphere tasks. When eye movements in the predicted direction follow these questions, the results are generally seen as supporting the link between eye movements and differential hemispheric activity. The problem, however, is that there is little in the way of direct evidence outside of the eye-movement research itself to support this association.

Especially troublesome is the fact that approximately half of the studies in this area have failed to find the predicted differences. A priori, the questions used in these studies seem just as "left hemisphere" or just as "right hemisphere" as those employed in the studies reporting success. The logical problem of establishing a relationship between eye movements and brain asymmetry becomes somewhat circular if one must define left- or right-hemisphere activity in terms of the questions that produce the expected results.

Unfortunately, we have no eye-movement data on split-brain patients engaged in various tasks, nor do we have any information about eye movements in the presence of direct electrical stimulation. In the absence of independent verification that eye movements are related to differential hemispheric activity, it would be wise to interpret results of LEM studies cautiously. In particular, it may be premature to reach conclusions about brain asymmetries and the processing of other kinds of questions on the basis of the direction of eye movements.

Despite these cautions, the LEM work is interesting and definitely worthy of further study. In certain situations, people do differ in the way they characteristically shift their gaze, and in other situations the pattern of shifts is related to the nature of the questions posed to the subjects. The link between eye movements and brain asymmetry may eventually prove to be a firm one. At the present time, however, it is important to keep its fragility in mind.

## Doing Two Things at Once:
## Mapping Functional Cerebral Space

We all know that certain combinations of tasks are relatively easy to do together and other tasks seem to interfere with each other. For example, many people can listen to music and read simultaneously, although the same people are unable to follow a conversation as they read. Intuitively, it seems as if tasks that call on different areas of the brain show less interference when performed together than tasks that rely on the same general areas. Perhaps, then, it would be possible to study patterns of brain organization in normal subjects by seeing how tasks interfere with each other.

Marcel Kinsbourne has taken precisely this approach in a number of interesting studies investigating what he refers to as "functional cerebral space."[32] He proposes, first, that the distance between brain areas controlling different movements is reflected in the extent to which there is competition or cooperation when several movements are attempted simultaneously. He notes that the two arms are better at performing cooperative movements than is an arm–leg combination but are worse at performing competitive tasks. It then follows, according to Kinsbourne's model, that the brain area controlling an arm is closer to the brain area controlling the other arm than it is to the brain area controlling the leg.

Kinsbourne's studies to map functional cerebral space have concentrated on observing subjects vocalizing and doing something with one of their limbs at the same time. In one of the first studies utilizing this approach, right-handed subjects were asked to balance a dowel rod on their index finger under two conditions—in silence and while repeating short sentences. Results indicated that when the subject was speaking, the right hand could not maintain balance as well or for as long as it could when the subject was silent. This was not the case with the left hand, however, which performed equally well in both conditions.[33]

Although there are no direct connections between the speech control center and any limb control center, Kinsbourne assumed that the control region for speech is closer to the control center for the right arm than to any of the left-arm control centers. This idea is reasonable enough anatomically, in view of the contralateral rule (the right hand is controlled by the left brain) and the fact that the speech area is in the left hemisphere. What is unique about Kinsbourne's work is that his model of functional cerebral space led him to make predictions about interference of speech and dowel balancing that were borne out by the data.

A later study showed that the difficulty of the spoken material affected the degree of disruption in the right hand's performance. More difficult material produced shorter right-hand balancing times than easier material. Left-hand balancing times were unaffected by the difficulty of the verbalization. Interestingly, left-handers showed disruption in the balancing times of both hands under the verbalization condition, in keeping with evidence suggesting that left-handers as a group have less clearly lateralized verbal functions.[34]

Work using this approach has also been extended to split-brain subjects and children. These studies employed a rhythmic tapping task in which subjects were required to tap at a fixed rate with the index finger of one hand. In one condition subjects performed verbal tasks while they tapped; in the control condition the subjects tapped in silence. For both groups, disruption of tapping was greater for the right hand.[35]

The experiments investigating so-called functional cerebral space are clever and quite interesting, although there remain some important reservations about this approach. First, there is no validation of functional space that is independent of the study used to demonstrate it. If two tasks interfere with each other, they are assumed to be closer in functional space than two tasks that interfere less or not at all. Standing by itself, this type of reasoning is too circular for comfort.

Second, phenomena of this type have not proved themselves to be as robust as one might wish: there have been numerous reports of failures to replicate basic findings. The reasons some investigators have been unsuccessful are not clear, but it is obvious that the outcome of these studies is influenced by many factors.

A third problem is that certain reasonable predictions about functional cerebral space have not been confirmed by experimentation. For example, many sources of evidence point to the right hemisphere as playing a crucial role in singing. However, singing does not differentially disrupt left-hand performance in the same way that speaking disrupts right-hand performance. Why doesn't it? We need answers to this as well as to the other questions raised here before we can evaluate the functional cerebral space approach to the study of asymmetry.

## In Summary

In this chapter we have reviewed researchers' efforts to explore hemispheric differences by studying the behavior of normal subjects in special testing situations. This general approach is commonly termed "behavioral" because directly observable behavior is what is being measured. Overall, the data fit well with the picture of hemispheric differences that emerged from studies of brain-damaged and split-brain patients.

In tracing the history of behavioral investigations of laterality in normal subjects, we have seen an increasingly complex picture unfold. We have seen that attentional factors may play a role in producing asymmetry in behavior. It is also clear that differences between the hemispheres go beyond the kinds of stimuli they are best equipped to deal with. As in the research with split-brain patients, we see that basic differences lie in the processing strategies of each hemisphere.

The appeal of work with normal subjects is unmistakable. First, the limitations placed on clinical and split-brain research by the scarcity of subjects are avoided. Second, work with neurologically normal subjects offers the investigators more freedom in the kinds of experiments that can be devised. Third, and perhaps most important, work with normal subjects permits the study of asymmetries in the same system one is ultimately trying to understand—the normal human brain.

# 4

# Activity and Anatomy: Physiological Correlates of Function

Perhaps the most direct way to investigate differences between the hemispheres is to measure the activity of the brain itself. This strategy contrasts with the approaches considered in Chapter 3, where inferences about the brain were drawn from behavior in special testing situations. More direct measurements of brain activity bypass the need for many of the assumptions that are made in behavioral studies. They also make it possible to study special groups of subjects, such as infants or animals, who might not be able to respond in the manner required by behavioral tests.

There are many different ways to measure the brain and its activity. Perhaps the most obvious is to measure the size and shape of the hemispheres themselves. We can also see whether cell differences are present in corresponding regions of the two hemispheres.

The metabolic processes of neurons require that blood bring oxygen to brain tissues and remove waste products. Thus the flow of blood to the two sides of the brain is a useful measure of brain activity. Differences in metabolism involving certain nutrients can be monitored in the brain as well, permitting an even finer analysis of activity on each side. Ultimately, all these processes result in electrical activity that can be recorded from electrodes placed on the scalp. The so-called brain waves recorded at various sites on the head can also be studied for differences within and between hemispheres.

In this chapter we will review evidence using these different measures to study more directly the activity of the left brain and right brain.

## Electrical Activity in the Left Brain and the Right Brain

In 1929, an Austrian psychiatrist named Hans Burger discovered that patterns of electrical activity could be recorded from electrodes placed at various points on the scalp of human beings. These patterns were called the *electroencephalogram (EEG)*, literally meaning "electrical brain writing." Although the EEG is monitored from the scalp, Burger was able to demonstrate that some of the activity it records originates in the brain itself and is not simply due to scalp musculature.

Devices to record the EEG soon became commonplace in clinical settings as investigators demonstrated that brain abnormalities such as epilepsy and tumors are accompanied by distinctive patterns of electrical activity. Its potential as a research tool was also quickly recognized, and innumerable studies looking for EEG correlates of personality, intelligence, and behavior were undertaken.

### Using the EEG to Study Asymmetry

Until the late 1960s, EEG recordings were typically made from electrodes placed at different points along the top of the head or on one side of the head only. It was simply assumed that activity would be identical on the two sides. A few studies, however, did report EEG asymmetries when electrodes were placed on each side. The asymmetries seemed to be related to hand preference but not in any simple way. David Galin and Robert Ornstein of the Langley Porter Neuropsychiatric Institute were two of the first investigators to study these asymmetries in detail and to relate them to the nature of the task performed by the subject while the EEG was being recorded.

The rationale for their approach is nicely stated in this excerpt from one of their papers:

> Although the split brain work has shown that the verbal and spatial cognitive systems can function independently, there are few studies which attempt to evaluate their interaction in normal people. Our opinion is that in most ordinary activities we simply alternate between cognitive modes rather than integrating them.... Therefore, in a subject performing a verbal or a spatial task, we expected to find electrophysiological signs of differences in activity between the appropriate and inappropriate hemispheres.[1]

They recorded EEG activity from symmetrical positions on either side of the head while subjects performed verbal tasks such as writing a letter and spatial tasks such as constructing a memorized geometrical pattern with multicolored blocks. Results were analyzed in terms of the ratio of right-hemisphere EEG power (R) to left-hemisphere EEG power (L). Electroencephalogram power is simply the amount of electrical energy being produced per unit of time. Galin and Ornstein found that the R/L power ratio was significantly greater in the verbal than in the spatial tasks.

They were thus successful in showing a link between the amount of EEG activity in the hemispheres and the type of task performed by a subject. At first glance, though, these results seem to be the precise opposite of what one would predict on the basis of what is known about the relationship between tasks and hemispheres. Letter writing is a left-hemisphere task and should produce relatively more left-hemisphere activity than the task involving the blocks. This "problem" is readily resolved by considering the composition of the EEG activity.

Several different rhythms of activity have been identified as constituents of the EEG record. The first one discovered is also the most famous—the alpha rhythm. Alpha activity is a rhythmic cycling of electrical activity occurring from 8 to 12 times per second. It is the predominant activity present in the EEG when the subject is resting quietly with his or her eyes closed. The other rhythms that are part of the EEG are also identified by Greek letters. Figure 4.1 shows EEG waveforms for five different brain states.

An analysis of Galin and Ornstein's results showed that the predominant rhythm in their EEG records was alpha. Since alpha reflects a resting brain state, *less* alpha activity would be expected to follow *greater* involvement in a particular task. It then follows that the left hemisphere should show relatively less alpha when a subject is performing a language task, in contrast to the amount of alpha activity present when the subject is doing a spatial task like the block-design problem. This is precisely what was found.

### Advantages and Disadvantages of the EEG

Electroencephalographic measures of asymmetry have been popular with many investigators for good reason. Because they do not rely on an overt response from the subject, they can be used to study brain asymmetries in infants, aphasic patients, and other subjects from whom it might be difficult to obtain such responses. In addition, EEG is a continuous measure over time and can be used to study ongoing activity in the brain while the subject performs long, complex tasks.

Although the latter feature of the EEG measure is quite useful in some studies, it poses a problem for others. The EEG is an overall, continuous measure of brain activity. Thus it is difficult to see changes

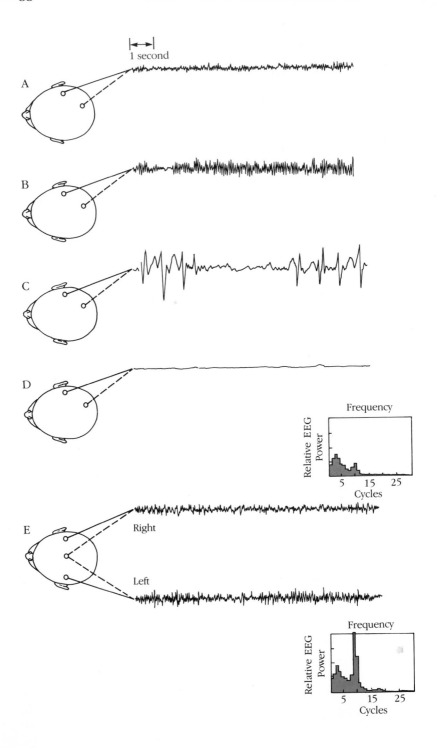

in the EEG that relate to the occurrence of specific stimulus events. In fact, the complex EEG waveforms do not appear to change very much during different kinds of sensory input but rather seem to reflect the general arousal level of the brain.

## The Evoked Potential

A searching analysis of the EEG, however, reveals that specific changes do occur in response to the presentation of a stimulus such as a flash of light. The problem is that these changes are hidden by the overall background activity of the brain. In order to make the change in response to a specific stimulus visible, a computer is used to average the waveform records following repeated presentations of the same stimulus. Electrical activity that is random with respect to the stimulus presentation will tend to be canceled out by this process, while electrical activity occurring in a fixed time relation to the stimulus will emerge as the potential evoked by the stimulus.

Figure 4.2 shows how the evoked potential (EP) emerges from an EEG record by averaging the waveforms that follow successive presentations of the same stimulus. The evoked potential consists of a sequence of positive and negative changes from a baseline and typically lasts about 500 milliseconds after the stimulus ends. Each potential can be analyzed in terms of certain components or parameters such as amplitude or latency (the amount of time from the onset of the stimulus to the onset of the activity).

---

4.1 *(opposite.)* Typical electroencephalograms. The "head" to the left of each record shows the approximate placement of the electrodes. A. At rest with eyes open. B. At rest with eyes shut. The large-magnitude waves occurring at a frequency of from 8 to 12 per second are the alpha waves. C. The dramatic spiking associated with an epileptic seizure. D. "Brain death" or "cerebral death." Even though the patient's heart may be beating, the electrically quiet record shows he or she is clinically dead. E. Simultaneous recording of left and right temporal EEG activity while the subject performs a block-design task. The graph to the right of each hemisphere's record is an analysis of the relative "power" of various frequencies in the EEG waveform. Notice that the left recording contains a greater amount of alpha, evident from 8–12 cycle peak in the frequency graph. During speaking and writing, more alpha is recorded on the right. The degree and direction of asymmetry varies with the task. (Part E. adapted from D. Galin and R. Ornstein, "Lateral Specialization of Cognitive Mode: An EEG Study," *Psychophysiology* 9, Fig. 1, p. 417 (Copyright © 1972, The Society for Psychophysiological Research) and from J. C. Doyle, R. Ornstein, and D. Galin, "Lateral Specialization of Cognitive Mode: II. EEG Frequency Analysis," *Psychophysiology* 11, Fig. 1, p. 571 (Copyright © 1974, The Society for Psychophysical Research). Reprinted with permission from the publisher.)

90

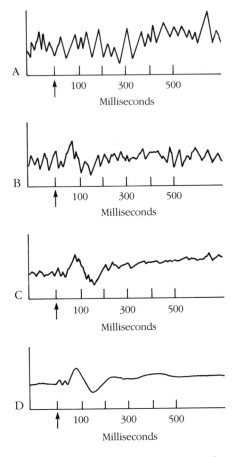

4.2 A single evoked response is seen emerging from the background noise of an EEG after the averaging of the EEG patterns obtained from successive stimulations. The stimulus, an auditory click, occurs at the time indicated by arrow. A. EEG response to a single stimulus. B. Average of 2 responses. C. Average of 16 responses. D. Average of 64 responses.

The nature of the stimulus is one of the factors that affects the precise form of the evoked potential. As a whole, auditory evoked potentials differ from visual evoked potentials, which differ from evoked potentials produced by touch stimulation. In addition, the region of each hemisphere generating maximum activity differs for each type of stimulus. Figure 4.3 shows some representative EPs to stimuli in different modalities.

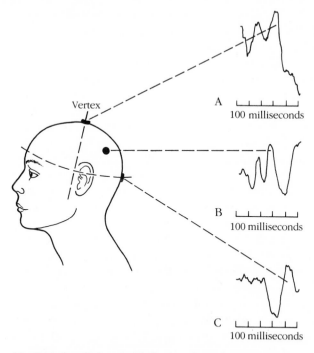

Vertex

A

100 milliseconds

B

100 milliseconds

C

100 milliseconds

4.3 Typical evoked potentials for A. auditory, B. somatosensory, and C. visual stimulation. The dotted lines indicate the approximate location on the scalp from which the most pronounced peaks are recorded. (Adapted from "Human Average Evoked Potentials," Fig. 3.5, p. 114, in *Bioelectric Recording Techniques,* Part B, R. F. Thompson and M. Patterson, eds. New York: Academic Press, 1973.)

Of primary concern to us here is whether the evoked potential generated by a stimulus is the same when recordings are made from equivalent locations on the two sides of the head. Are there differences between the hemispheres in the electrical activity evoked by various stimuli, and, if so, what can such differences tell us about the role of the left brain and right brain in normal subjects?

A number of studies have recorded EPs from each hemisphere while subjects were presented with simple stimuli such as clicks or blank flashes of light.[2] Some of these studies have reported asymmetries in the amplitude or latency of the EP. Of greater interest, however, are the studies in which subjects were presented with more complex stimuli or tasks that presumably engaged the specialized functions of the hemispheres.

In a study by Monte Buschbaum and Paul Fedio of the National Institutes of Health, for example, differences were observed in EPs while subjects viewed verbal and nonverbal stimuli flashed in the left or right visual field.[3] The verbal stimuli were three-letter words; the nonverbal items were nonsense stimuli composed of an artificial alphabet of letters. When recordings were made from the occipital lobes, results showed greater differences between the EPs to the two types of stimuli in the left hemisphere compared to the right.

Asymmetries using auditory stimuli have been reported as well. Psychologist Dennis Molfese has collected extensive data on evoked potentials to speech and nonspeech stimuli.[4] In one study, he found that the amplitude of part of the EP to speech stimuli was greater in the left hemisphere than in the right hemisphere. This difference was seen even when the subject merely listened to the stimuli and did not try to identify them. Nonspeech stimuli, however, produced larger amplitude activity in the right hemisphere.

Several studies have also looked at how asymmetries are affected by the task the subject is performing while the EP is recorded. In one such study, subjects were presented with a sequence of synthetically produced spoken syllables that could differ in initial consonant ("ba" versus "da") or in pitch (high pitch or low pitch).[5] On one half of the trials, subjects were instructed to listen for each occurrence of "ba" regardless of its pitch. On the other half, the subjects were instructed to listen for high-pitched syllables independent of their name.

Evoked potentials to the high-pitched "ba" were recorded from the left and right hemispheres in each case. This procedure enabled the investigators to study the effect of the task performed on EP asymmetry using exactly the same stimuli in the two conditions. The only difference between conditions was the kind of mental activity the subjects had to perform when the stimuli were presented.

Results showed a difference in the EPs produced during the naming and pitch tasks, but only in the left hemisphere. The evoked potentials recorded from the right hemisphere were not different for the two conditions. These findings led the researchers to suggest that there are hemispheric differences in the ability to identify a syllable, but no differences in the ability to determine the pitch of the syllable.

Another study recorded EPs to simple flashes of light while subjects engaged in spatial or linguistic tasks similar to those used by Galin and Ornstein in their EEG work.[6] Electroencephalogram power was also analyzed in this experiment, allowing the investigators to compare EP and EEG as indicators of lateralized mental functions. Results suggested that both EP and EEG reflect asymmetrical brain activity but the EEG measure yields more consistent findings.

## *Electrical Activity and Asymmetry: A Summary*

The initial success of laterality studies using EEG and evoked potentials as measures encouraged many investigators to use this methodology. Unfortunately, some of the newer work has served to confuse rather than clarify the relationship between these measures and hemispheric asymmetry. Attempts to replicate findings have frequently met with failure, and studies that do obtain asymmetries sometimes fail to agree on which aspect of the electrical recording shows the asymmetry. For example, a recent study examining EPs to a light flashed while subjects performed spatial and verbal tasks failed to find any convincing evidence of asymmetry.[7]

Why are so many studies in conflict? A good case has been made for inadequacies in design, conduct, or analysis. The problems range from an unwise selection of the aspects of electrical activity that are measured, to failure to control for individual differences among subjects, to the use of tasks that do not in fact differentially involve the two hemispheres.[8]

These difficulties lead readily to the conclusion that it is premature to advocate without qualification the use of EEG and EP recordings as measures of hemispheric asymmetry. The results are too conflicting. On the hand, amid all the inconsistencies there emerges a body of positive findings that cannot be ignored. The measures have great promise, but that promise is yet to be fully realized.

## Blood Flow in the Hemispheres

The flow of blood through the tissues of the body varies with the metabolism and activity in those tissues. The blood flow, which provides necessary nutrients and removes waste products, turns out to be very sensitive and responsive to minute changes in cellular activity. In fact, changes in the activity in various regions of the brain appear to be reflected in the relative amount of blood flowing through those regions. This discovery has made it possible to identify and study the interaction of various areas of the brain during the ongoing human behavior by measuring the regional changes in blood flow.

Modern techniques of measuring blood flow in an awake and functioning human were developed by Niels Lassen, David Ingvar, and others.[9] They injected a special radioactive isotope (Xenon 133) into the bloodstream leading to the brain and monitored the flow with a battery of detectors arranged near the surface of the head. The low level of gamma radiation emitted by the isotope is not considered harmful and washes out of the bloodstream within 15 minutes. The technique, originally used with patients requiring the test for medical reasons, has since been refined to the point where subjects can breathe a special air–xenon mixture and have their blood flow monitored by placing their head next to a machine housing the special detectors.

The results of a host of studies measuring cerebral blood flow during different kinds of physical and mental activity have been quite impressive. Classic predictions about brain areas involved in psychological functions have been "brought to life." The regions of each hemisphere involved in vision, for example, show increased blood flow if the subject is looking at an object. Speech stimuli increase blood flow in the auditory areas of each side.

Although the most striking patterns of blood flow show differences from front to back across the whole brain, differences between the hemispheres have also been found. Using techniques that permit the study of regional blood flow in the two hemispheres simultaneously, Jarl Risberg compared the blood-flow pattern of right-handed male volunteers during two tasks, one a verbal analogies test and the other a test of perceptual "closure." In the closure task the subjects had to view very sparsely drawn pictures and figure out what they were.[10]

Small but highly significant hemispheric differences in blood flow of about 3 percent were found in the two conditions. As expected, the mean left-hemisphere flow was greater during the verbal analogies task, and the mean right-hemisphere flow was greater during the picture completion task. Risberg was able to measure which regions within each hemisphere contributed the most to interhemispheric blood-flow differences. The largest differences were found in the frontal, frontotemporal, and parietal regions for the verbal tests. In the resting state, differences between corresponding regions of the hemispheres were very small.

Despite the hemispheric differences observed, blood-flow investigators Lassen and Ingvar report that they have been most impressed by the striking similarity in the blood-flow patterns in the two sides even during such highly lateralized activities as speech.[11] Hemispheric differences in activity seem to be much more subtle than the changes that occur in both hemispheres. This suggests that hemispheric differences are but one of several different organizational schemes in the brain. The work on cerebral blood flow shows that complex tasks typically involve increased patterns of activation in many areas of each hemisphere.

## Cerebral Metabolism: Some Measures of the Near Future

Cerebral blood-flow techniques do have some limitations as measures of brain activity. Present-day blood-flow systems do not provide accurate information about the deepest regions of the brain. Most of the observed patterns are at the cortical levels. Techniques are needed so that activity in deeper parts can also be selectively analyzed. Secondly, blood flow is probably not responsive enough to rapid variations in brain activity. For these reasons, more sophisticated techniques allowing direct measures of metabolic activity are being developed.

Cerebral metabolism on a microscopic scale can be monitored by measuring the rate at which radioactively labeled glucose or other nutrients are used by different regions of the brain. The low-level radiation emitted by these substances is measured from various angles about the head and analyzed by computer to obtain the distribution of its source throughout the brain.

It has been shown that the metabolic rate within small regions of the brain changes in a consistent pattern during a specific behavioral activity.[12] Many investigators offer high hopes for the use of such techniques to establish accurate brain–behavior relationships, including the differences and similarities between the two hemispheres. The possibilities seem endless, especially in light of the fact that the techniques offer the ability to monitor the metabolic processes of the brain during active behavior.

## Questions Raised by Techniques
## Measuring Brain Activity

Electrophysiological measures, studies of regional blood flow, and other measures of metabolic processes all offer investigators the opportunity to study relationships between brain activity and behavior. They have been of great value in validating physiologically some of the insights about brain function gleaned from psychological research with brain injured as well as normal subjects.

At the same time, measures of brain activity during behavior have raised some questions about the most exaggerated claims for hemispheric asymmetry. There is little to support the notion that either one or the other hemisphere turns on to perform a specific task all by itself. Each of the measures we have discussed points to the involvement of many areas of the brain in even the simplest task. There are asymmetries in activity between the hemispheres to be sure, but they can be very subtle, a fact that should lead us away from thinking about hemispheric specialization in overly simple terms.

## Anatomical Asymmetries in the Two Hemispheres

A 1968 report by Norman Geschwind and Walter Levitsky demonstrated unequivocal anatomical asymmetries in the two hemispheres of the human brain in the regions important for speech and language.[13] Published in a journal widely read by scientists in a number of different disciplines, their paper generated a great deal of excitement among those interested in hemispheric asymmetry of function.

Geschwind and Levitsky were not the first investigators to notice such asymmetries in the brain, however. Asymmetries had been sporadically reported as far back as the second half of the nineteenth century. In general, at that time the differences were considered trivial and insufficient in size to account for functional differences between the left brain and right brain.

By the late 1960s, however, the time was right to reconsider the possibility that functional asymmetries between hemispheres might have a physical basis on a nonmicroscopic, anatomical level. Since the publication of Geschwind and Levitsky's paper, several other investigators have studied the problem and extended the search for asymmetries to neonates and nonhuman primates as well.

Here we will review the evidence pointing to asymmetries in the adult human brain. We will reserve discussion of work with neonates and nonhuman primates for Chapters 7 and 8, respectively.

### Measuring the Hemispheres

The asymmetry found by Geschwind and Levitsky was in the length of the temporal plane, the upper surface of the region of the temporal lobe behind the auditory cortex. Of the 100 brains measured post-mortem, 65 percent were found to have a longer temporal plane in the left hemisphere than in the right, 11 percent had a longer temporal plane on the right, and the remaining 24 percent showed no difference. On the average the temporal plane was one-third longer on the left than on the right. Figure 4.4 shows the location of this asymmetry.

Although the size of these asymmetries is impressive, most significant is their location. The temporal plane is part of Wernicke's area, a region named after Karl Wernicke, who first noted that damage to the area frequently results in a variety of aphasic symptoms. Geschwind and Levitsky suggested that the asymmetries they observed were compatible with the functional asymmetries believed to be controlled by this region.

Several studies using various procedures to measure the temporal plane have confirmed Geschwind and Levitsky's observations.[14] Direct

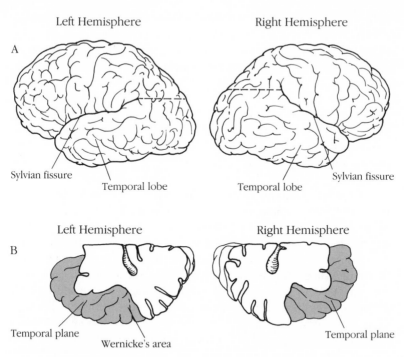

Left Hemisphere | Right Hemisphere

A

Sylvian fissure

Temporal lobe

Sylvian fissure

Temporal lobe

Left Hemisphere | Right Hemisphere

B

Temporal plane

Wernicke's area

Temporal plane

4.4 Anatomical asymmetries in the cortex of the human brain. A. The sylvian fissure, which defines the upper margin of the temporal lobe, rises more steeply on the right side of the brain. B. The temporal plane, which forms the upper surface of the temporal lobe, is usually much larger on he left side. This region in the left hemisphere is considered part of Wernicke's area, a region involved in language. (From "Specializations of the Human Brain," by N. Geschwind. Copyright © 1979 by Scientific American, Inc. All rights reserved.)

measurements on a total of 337 brain specimens (including the 100 brains studied by Geschwind and Levitsky) have been reported. Seventy percent showed asymmetry favoring the left hemisphere in length or area of the temporal plane.

### Measurements in the Living Brain

All the anatomical studies considered up to this point have involved measurements taken from brains examined post-mortem. Other evidence suggests that it is also possible to find asymmetries in the living brain.

One technique takes advantage of the fact that the paths of the large blood vessels in the brain reflect the anatomy of the surrounding brain tissue. In particular, the middle cerebral artery courses through the language-critical region of the temporal lobe. For many years, neurologists have used a procedure known as cerebral angiography to visualize this major blood vessel to determine whether the brain regions surrounding it have been damaged. A dye injected into the internal carotid artery in the neck (the same artery used in the Wada procedure) flows into the middle cerebral artery, making the artery visible when a skull x ray is taken. Marjorie LeMay and her colleagues have evidence suggesting that left–right asymmetries consistent with those found in post-mortem brain measurements may be observed with the angiographic procedure.[15]

A second technique used to measure asymmetry in the living brain is computerized tomography, or CT scan. In a CT scan an x-ray source is revolved in a plane around the head as detectors continuously monitor the intensity of the x-ray beam passed through to the other side. A computer stores this information and then uses it to reconstruct an image of a slice of brain. By simply adjusting the angles through which the x rays pass, the appearance of any slice of the brain is made available. Figure 4.5 shows a representative CT scan. This technique has been used for several years to pinpoint the location of lesions in cases of brain damage. LeMay and her colleagues have also been active in using CT-scan data to study asymmetries and have had some success.[16]

### What Do Anatomical Asymmetries Tell Us?

Much of the interest in angiographic and CT-scan techniques to measure asymmetries in the living brain comes from a basic problem in interpreting anatomical asymmetries in general. Are the asymmetries that have been identified related in a meaningful way to functional asymmetries? Are they in fact the physical basis for the functional asymmetries between the hemispheres?

At this point we do not know. Most of the data on anatomical asymmetries have come from post-mortem measurements of brains where nothing is known about the kinds of functional asymmetries that may have existed before death. In many cases even the handedness of the individuals is not known. Clearly, this kind of information is necessary if we are to begin to answer the questions posed in the preceding paragraph.

Procedures that permit measurements in the living brain offer us a way to get that crucial information. Batteries of behavioral and electrophysiological tests designed to study the distribution of functions between the hemispheres can be used together with measurements of brain asymmetry in the same individuals to see whether there is a

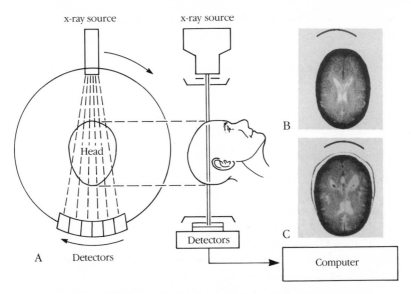

**4.5** A. Computerized tomography (CT scan) uses an x-ray beam and an array of detectors revolved around the subject's head to calculate the densities of tissue in a particular slice of the brain. A computer reconstructs a two-dimensional picture of what the brain looks like in the plane swept by the x rays. The CT pictures shown here are B. normal, with no evidence of any pathologies, and C. abnormal, with enlargement of the ventricles (fluid-filled spaces—the light central areas) especially on the right, moderate atrophy, and right fronto-temporal infarct (stroke).

relationship. Some preliminary data indicate that, overall, left-handers show less anatomical asymmetry than right-handers—an observation that is promising.[17] It is clear, though, that investigators have only barely begun the process of studying how anatomical asymmetries and functional asymmetries are related.

It is also of considerable interest to ask whether there are differences at the cellular level between corresponding regions of the two hemispheres. Microscopic studies were an important complement to classic studies that differentiated various regions of the brain. They may serve the same function in the study of hemispheric asymmetry as well. We also mention in passing the possibility of biochemical differences between corresponding regions of the left brain and right brain. Such a difference has already been reported in a preliminary study of the distribution of norepinephrine, a neurotransmitter found in the human thalamus.[18]

The thalamus is a subcortical structure known to play a role in sensory and speech functions. The posterior regions of the thalamus show a higher concentration of norepinephrine on the left than on the right; the anterior region shows a greater concentration on the right. This work needs extensive replication, and much more needs to be learned about the role of norepinephrine in certain thalamic functions. However, it represents some of the first research to identify a possible neurochemical asymmetry in the nervous system.

## Physiology and Psychology: Building the Link

Anatomical measurements, recordings of electrical activity, blood-flow studies, and the scanning of metabolic processes offer investigators the opportunity to study relationships between mental processes, behavior, and brain activity. These techniques have at least partially validated some of the theoretical insights about brain function and hemispheric asymmetry developed in the brain-damage clinic and from psychological research with normal subjects.

Some researchers have claimed that physiological tools will offer the ultimate resolution of questions that deal with relations between mind and brain; others argue against overreliance on such measures both on philosophical and practical grounds. To conclude this chapter we will review some of the concerns that must be confronted in the attempt to establish relationships between physiological processes and psychological functions. Although these concerns are important for the study of hemispheric asymmetries, their significance extends beyond any specific area of research and has applicability to the study of brain–behavior relationships in general.

One issue is the problem of selecting from among the various physiological measures available those that will prove most informative. Like all other tissues in the human body, the brain is dependent on complex metabolic processes for its functioning. Nutrients like glucose are converted for energy processes; other nutrients are used as cellular constituents; waste products are removed. A great deal of the brain's biochemistry, however, is unique and involves the communication of information between neurons. Biochemical processes operating in each cell generate electrical potentials, and biochemicals operating between cells effectively transmit electrical impulses between groups of neurons.

We do not know what aspects of this activity best reflect the functioning of the brain with which we are concerned. If, for example, we just want to know what areas of the brain are most active during particular human behaviors, we can look at cerebral blood flow, for it responds fairly rapidly to changes in metabolic activity. Yet such measures may not be indicative of the true information-processing strategies or codes of the brain. Such codes could involve chemical pathways extending across many areas of the brain, or perhaps they could be reflected in patterns of electrical-wave activity. Neither would necessarily correlate with regional metabolic activity.

Even after deciding on a measure to study, we may be faced with further choices. The evoked potential, for example, may be broken down into several components and analyzed in different ways. In the absence of a comprehensive theory about the meaning of these components, investigators must decide how best to analyze their data to look for asymmetries or other effects. Anatomists, too, must decide what measurements of what regions of the brain will be most useful for the problem at hand.

Another issue involves the concept of localization of function in general. How much does attributing some psychological activity to a specific area of the brain really contribute to insights about that activity? Certainly findings on localization have been of tremendous clinical value. Furthermore, relationships between location and function may help establish the components of a complex behavior or task in terms of more basic processes. As a hypothetical example, it could possibly be demonstrated that the memory of how to get somewhere involves linguistic processes in the left hemisphere as well as imagery processes in the right hemisphere. It is not clear, however, how far this kind of approach can take us. Ultimately, it is likely that dividing the brain in terms of "where" will not completely answer the question of "how."

. . .

A physiologist discovers that certain cells in the occipital lobe respond when very specific visual patterns, and only those patterns, are shown to subjects. A clinician in a hospital notices that a patient with a combination of lesions in both hemispheres can see clearly but seems to view objects in terms of parts and can't figure out what he is looking at. A psychologist suggests that visual perception involves both a pattern recognition system and some decision system to decide on what is relevant.

Hopefully, an interaction results from all these insights, both modifying what is meant by perception and identifying the processes that are involved. Similar interactions between psychology and physiology are possible in virtually every area of study dealing with brain–behavior relationships. It is our opinion that each component will be essential to achieving an understanding of such relationships.

# 5

# The Puzzle of the Left-Hander

An overwhelming majority of human beings use their right hand almost exclusively for writing and other skilled, unimanual activities. Cross-cultural studies put the incidence of right-handedness at around 90 percent. A variety of indirect evidence suggests that this has been the case as far back as prehistoric times.[1] Drawings of people found on cave walls and inside Egyptian tombs typically show the subjects engaged in activities involving the right hand, and an analysis of paleolithic tools and weapons suggests that they were made with, and for, the right hand.

A study of tracings of the hand believed to have been made by Cro-Magnon people shows over 80 percent to be of the left hand. If we assume the artists traced their own hands, these data also point to a very strong preference for the right hand in skilled activity. Perhaps the most ingenious evidence of all for right-hand preference in early humans comes from an analysis of fossilized baboon skulls with fractures. On the basis of the location of the fractures, the investigator concluded that the injuries were the result of blows inflicted by early humans wielding the fatal clubs with their right hands.

Animals may show preferences for one paw or the other in certain situations, but they divide up fairly evenly in terms of the number preferring the right paw or left paw. Why, then, are most human beings right-handed? Conversely, why does a significant percentage of the population use the left hand, despite subtle and sometimes overt social pressure to conform to the handedness pattern characteristic of the majority?

We have mentioned in earlier chapters that handedness is related in complex ways to the distribution of functions between the left brain and right brain. Any analysis of brain asymmetry must deal with this problem if it is to be complete. What factors determine handedness? In what ways do left-handers and right-handers differ?

In this chapter we consider modern theories proposed to account for variations in handedness and studies designed to examine possible differences between left-handers and right-handers. To provide a historical context for recent work, we turn first to a brief review of some of the older ideas about handedness.

## Historical Notions of Left-Handedness

### Is There Anything Sinister About Being Left-Handed?

*Webster's Third International Dictionary* lists several definitions of the adjective "left-handed" including the following:

> a: marked by clumsiness or ineptitude: awkward; b: exhibiting deviousness or indirection: oblique, unintended; c: obs.: given to malevolent scheming or contriving: sinister, underhand

Left-handers are frequently referred to as "sinistrals," and *Roget's Thesaurus* lists "left-handed" as a synonym for "unskillfulness." In other languages as well, the terms for "left" or "left-handed" have almost always contained at least one derogatory meaning, ranging from clumsy or awkward to evil. The French word for "left," *gauche,* also means clumsy; *mancino* is Italian for "left" as well as for "deceitful." The Spanish word for "left," *zurdo,* appears in the idiom *no ser zurdo* meaning "to be very clever." Its literal translation is "not to be left-handed." Other examples abound.

The Bible, too, reflects a bias against the left hand or side. One example from the New Testament that is especially striking is the Vision of Judgment in Matthew 25:31–34, 41, 46:

> When the Son of man shall come in his glory, and all the holy angels with him, then shall he sit upon the throne of his glory:

> And before him shall be gathered all nations, and he shall separate them one from another, as a shepherd divideth *his* sheep from the goats:

> And he shall set the sheep on his right hand, but the goats on the left.

Then shall the King say unto them on his right hand, Come, ye blessed
of my Father, inherit the kingdom prepared for you from the foundation
of the world. . . .

Then shall he say also unto them on the left hand, Depart from me, ye
cursed, into everlasting fire, prepared for the devil and his angels. . . .

And these shall go away into everlasting punishment: but the righteous
into life eternal.

Michael Barsley, author of *Left Handed People*, has argued that the
Vision of Judgment has been more responsible for "fixing the prejudice
against left handers than any other pronouncement, and that this prejudice has come down through the ages, adopted by Inquisitors, judges,
soldiers, artists, teachers, nurses, and parents as the supreme example
of the association of sinistral people with wickedness and the Devil."[2]
Whether or not Barsley is correct, it is clear that the association between
left and bad is of very long standing.

What is the origin of this bias? We can at this point only speculate.
Carl Sagan of Cornell University has suggested one possibility in *The
Dragons of Eden*, his book on the evolution of intelligence.[3] Sagan
notes that in preindustrial societies, both now and in the past, the hand
has been used for personal hygiene after defecation. This use of one
hand is both unaesthetic and potentially harmful because it can spread
disease, but these drawbacks can be reduced somewhat by using the
other hand to eat and to greet others. Right-handed individuals would
perform activities like eating and throwing weapons with the right hand,
leaving toilet hygiene to the left. Sagan suggests that the left hand
became associated with excretory activities, which have a long history
of negative associations in human cultures. Thus the chain linking "left"
with "bad" was forged.

This explanation assumes that human beings begin with a preference to use the right hand for activities requiring fine control. We
must still explain the basis for that preference. Speculation abounds
on this issue, but we stand a good chance of bringing the tools of
modern science to bear and resolving the question in a satisfactory
way.

### Nineteenth-Century Theories of Handedness

Let's first consider some of the ideas that were proposed in the nineteenth century to account for handedness. One popular theory was
known as visceral distribution. Proponents argued that the asymmetrical
placement of visceral organs such as the liver puts the center of gravity

of the human body slightly to the right of midline, and, as a consequence, human beings are better able to balance on the left foot. This leaves the right hand free, so that over time the muscles on the right side became better developed. This notion, however, does not explain why some people are left-handed, unless we assume a reversal in the orientation of their viscera.

Social evolution explanations of handedness were also popular in the nineteenth century. There are several variations on this general theme, the most common being the sword and shield theory. According to this theory, attributed to English essayist and historian Thomas Carlyle and others, most soldiers hold their shield with their left hand to protect their heart when they are engaged in battle and use their right hand to hold their weapon. As a consequence, during aeons of armed conflict, the right hand gained in manipulative ability and came to be used for other unimanual activities as well. Again there is no attempt to explain left-handedness or the apparently high incidence of right-handedness in early humans before the invention of the shield.

The idea of cerebral dominance emerged in the last quarter of the nineteenth century, and with it came yet another theory of handedness. D. J. Cunningham, a Scottish anatomist, summarized this view in 1902 in a Huxley Memorial Lecture: "Right handedness is due to a transmitted functional preeminence of the left brain. Left brainedness is not the result but, through evolution, it has become the cause of right handedness." As stated, this view would have difficulty accounting for left-handers with left-hemisphere speech, who comprise about 70 percent of all left-handers. In addition, it fails to explain the reasons for the transmitted functional preeminence of the left brain.

## The Difficulty of Determining Handedness

Before we consider more modern theories of handedness, it is important to consider how handedness is actually assessed. We might assume that the best way to find out whether a given individual is a left-hander or a right-hander is simply to ask. Unfortunately, this direct approach does not always work. Few people use one hand exclusively for all unimanual activities, and simple self-classification does not indicate how someone weighed various activities when making his or her determination.

Another approach is to ask people which hand they use for specific activities. The researcher can then compute a handedness preference based on the same weighting scheme for everyone. Questionnaires frequently ask such things as which hand is used to throw a ball, to hold a needle for threading, to hold a tennis racquet, and to hold a pen for writing. Problems arise, however, when answers given on questionnaires are compared to actual behavior. Most investigators now agree that the most accurate way to determine the hand used for various tasks is to observe the individual performing those tasks.

Relatively few studies, though, do this. And even the most careful procedures do not yield a clear left or right preference in all cases. Some subjects show a pattern of mixed handedness. Studies classify such individuals in various ways. Thus it should not be surprising to find that experiments investigating the effects of handedness sometimes yield conflicting results. Differences in the way subjects are classified may account for some or all of the conflict.

Keeping in mind this problem of handedness studies in general, we turn now to consider the major theories of handedness currently receiving attention.

## Is Handedness Hereditary?

Is handedness, like eye color, blood type, and general body build, genetically determined? The probability of two right-handed parents having a left-handed child is 0.02. It rises to 0.17 if one parent is left-handed, and to 0.46 if both are left-handed.[4] These figures are consistent with the hypothesis that genes play a role in determining handedness. The problem with interpreting the data, however, is that environmental factors can account for these differences as well.

Two left-handed parents could provide a child with different experiences relevant to the determination of handedness just as they might provide specific genes. Nature (genes) and nurture (experience) are confounded in these figures, making it impossible to sort out the contribution of each.

One way to approach this problem is to formulate specific models of how handedness might be transmitted from generation to generation through the action of genes. Different models make different predictions of the actual figures. A good fit between the predictions of a specific model and actual data would suggest that genetic factors can account for most of the variations in handedness found among people.

One of the first genetic models of handedness proposed that handedness is a consequence of the action of a single gene that has two different forms, or *alleles*.[5] One allele, *R,* was dominant and coded for right-handedness. A second, *l,* was recessive and coded for left-handedness. An individual inheriting the *R* allele from each parent would be right-handed, as would someone with an *Rl* genotype (*R* from one parent, *l* from the other). Left-handers would be those individuals who inherited the *l* allele from each parent.

This model, however, cannot account for the fact that 54 percent of the offspring of two left-handed parents are right-handed. The model predicts that all offspring of such parents should be left-handed since the *l* allele is the only one that left-handed parents can transmit to their offspring. There have been attempts to rescue this model by introducing the concept of *variable penetrance*. Variable penetrance means that all individuals with the same genotype may not express that genotype in the same way. In this case, it has been suggested that some individuals with the *Rl* genotype will be left-handed. These left-handers could transmit an *R* allele to their offspring, accounting for the nonzero incidence of right-handedness among the children of two left-handed parents. Even with variable penetrance built into the model, however, the model's "goodness of fit" to actual data is less than satisfactory.

A more sophisticated model has been proposed by Jerre Levy and Thomas Nagylaki.[6] They suggest that handedness is a function of two genes. One gene with two alleles determines the hemisphere that will control speech as well as the preferred hand. The allele *L* codes for left-hemisphere speech and is dominant, while the allele *r* codes for right-hemisphere speech and is recessive. The second gene determines whether the speech hemisphere controls the ipsilateral or contralateral hand. Contralateral control is coded for by the dominant *C* allele, while ipsilateral control is coded for by the recessive *c* allele. Someone with an *LrCC* genotype, for example, would have left-hemisphere speech and be right-handed. Another individual with an *Lrcc* genotype would have left-hemisphere speech but would be left-handed.

This model assumes that an individual's handedness is a consequence of the pattern of hemispheric asymmetry as well as the type of motor control present in that individual. It does a better job of accounting for handedness patterns among relatives than do single-gene models, but it too is less than totally satisfactory. There is some question about whether ipsilateral motor control of the sort postulated really exists. Nevertheless, the model is an ingenious attempt to account for variations both in brain organization and in handedness in terms of simple genetic mechanisms.

Marion Annett of the University of Hull has proposed a genetic model of handedness that is very different from those just considered.[7] She hypothesized that most individuals possess a gene that she refers to as the "right shift" factor. This factor, when present, disposes an individual to be right-handed. When the factor is absent, the individual may become either left-handed or right-handed, depending on chance factors.

To test her model, she studied the speed with which the offspring of two left-handed parents could perform a peg-sorting task. About half did better with the left hand and half better with the right, in keeping with her prediction that hand preference in this group would be determined by chance. Left-handed parents who reported birth trauma in their own history, however, had significantly more right-handed children. The history of birth trauma suggests that these parents were not "natural" left-handers; they probably possessed the "right shift" factor but because of early injury they became left-handers. The "right shift" factor would be transmitted to their children, however, and would result in a high incidence of right-handedness in those children. The most general predictions of Annett's model await testing.

## Why Are There So Many Left-Handed Twins?

Assessing the fit of the predictions of specific genetic models to actual data is the approach most frequently taken by researchers testing the hypothesis that handedness is under genetic control. Another approach involves looking at the hand preferences of monozygotic (identical) and dizygotic (fraternal) twins. Monozygotic twins are genetically identical. They began life as a single fertilized egg that divided to form two individuals at some point within the first two weeks after conception. Dizygotic twins, however, are no more similar genetically than ordinary siblings born at different times. They result from the simultaneous fertilization of two separate eggs by two different sperm, and they have on the average 50 percent of their genes in common. Figure 5.1 shows the way in which monozygotic and dizygotic twins are formed.

If a trait is under genetic control to some extent, monozygotic twins should be more similar on that trait than dizygotic twins. A number of studies have looked at handedness in twins. When the results of all these studies are combined, some interesting findings emerge. Concordance for handedness (the percentage of pairs where both twins are left-handed or both are right-handed) is no higher in monozygotic twin pairs than in dizygotic pairs. Moreover, about 25 percent of the total number of pairs of each type are discordant for handedness: in other words, one out of every four pairs of twins contains a left-handed twin and a right-handed twin.

The fact that monozygotic twins are no more similar in hand preference than dizygotic twins has been interpreted as evidence *against* genetic control of handedness. At first glance, the evidence from twins is a major setback for genetic models of any type. Regardless of the specific genetic mechanisms involved, genetic control of a trait means that individuals with all their genes in common should be more similar on that trait than individuals with fewer shared genes. This logic assumes, however, that the nongenetic factors that may affect handedness are the same in terms of their nature and incidence for both types of

Identical Twins                    Fraternal Twins

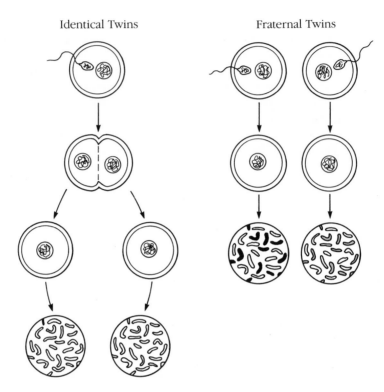

**5.1** The origin of identical and fraternal twins. Identical or monozygotic twins are the product of a single sperm and egg. The resulting embryo divides at an early stage of development to form two individuals. Fraternal or dizygotic twins develop from two different eggs fertilized by two different sperm. On the average they have half of their genes in common.

twins as well as for singletons (nontwins). As we shall see, this assumption is probably incorrect. In addition, we will consider how the factors that determine handedness in twins can help us understand the basis for hand preference in general.

### Brain Damage and Left-Handedness

The incidence of left-handedness in twins is about 20 percent, approximately twice that found in the singleton population. Twins also show a disproportionately high incidence of neurological and other disorders, which are believed to be a consequence of damage resulting from intrauterine crowding during fetal development.[8] It is a simple next step to suggest that the elevated incidence of left-handedness in twins is due at least in part to these factors.

The idea that minor brain damage may underlie much of the left-handedness in twins was first proposed in 1920.[9] Several pieces of evidence support that suggestion. First, the incidence of left-handedness is very high in populations that may have suffered minor brain injury before or during birth. In the mentally retarded, for example, the incidence is 20 percent. Left-handedness is also very common in children with learning disabilities, as well as in epileptics. Perhaps the minor brain damage that is the cause of the problem in many of these cases is also responsible for the shift in hand preference in individuals who otherwise would have been right-handed.

Second, clinical data from sodium amytal work suggest a relationship between handedness and early brain damage. In one study, the majority of left-handed patients with evidence of early damage to the left brain showed right-hemisphere language centers, while left-handers without signs of early damage had left-hemisphere language.[10] This suggests that damage to the left hemisphere early in life may result in a shift in the language hemisphere as well as in hand preference.

Paul Bakan contends that all left-handedness is essentially pathological in origin and that trauma occurring at birth can account for most of it.[11] He collected data showing a high incidence of birth trauma in both left-handers and their families and has suggested that the tendency for left-handedness to run in families is a consequence of a genetically based increase in the risk of birth trauma in such families.

Less extreme views have been taken by others. Paul Satz, for example, believes that pathological factors can account for a good deal of the elevated incidence of left-handedness among certain clinical populations as well as some of the left-handedness in the population at large.[12] The remaining left-handers are, in his view, "natural" left-handers whose left-handedness is genetic in origin.

Most researchers would agree that some left-handedness is pathological in origin, although few would take the extreme view of Bakan that all left-handedness can be explained in this way. Interestingly, the pathological model predicts the existence of pathological right-handedness as well. Some percentage of natural left-handers who sustain brain damage may shift their preference to the right hand. The overall percentage of pathological right-handedness, however, would be quite low because there are relatively few left-handers to begin with.

The popularity of the pathological model of left-handedness has led investigators to compare the cognitive abilities of left-handers and right-handers. The rationale for such studies is simple. If left-handedness is a consequence of brain damage, however mild, then such damage may be reflected in lowered ability in various higher mental functions. We will review studies exploring this possibility in a later section. Before doing so, however, we will return to the issue of the elevated incidence of left-handedness in twins.

## Mirror Imaging in Twins

The evidence linking prenatal brain damage and left-handedness in singletons is sufficiently compelling for such damage to be considered a factor in producing the high rate of left-hand preference in twins, both monozygotic and dizygotic. As a result of their unusual prenatal conditions, twins are particularly susceptible to neurological damage, and left-handedness may be one of the results.

Another factor, operating only in monozygotic twins, may also contribute to the high incidence of left-handedness. About one-fourth of all monozygotic pairs are believed to demonstrate some aspect of a phenomenon known as *mirror imaging*. One twin may be left-handed, the other right-handed. One may have a clockwise hair whorl at the top of the head, the other a counterclockwise whorl. Fingerprints are also reported to show mirror-imaging effects. The print on the left index finger of one twin, for example, is more like the pattern on the same finger of the right hand of the other twin. Mirror imaging is typically limited to bodily tissues that derive from the ectodermal layer during development; it rarely extends to internal organs like the heart and stomach.[13]

The embryological mechanism responsible for mirror imaging is not well understood, but there has been some speculation concerning how it might come about. At some point early in development, chemical gradients that establish an axis of bilateral symmetry are established in the embryo. If the division that forms two individuals occurs after that point (and in the proper plane), one embryo will develop from what was to be the left half of the original embryo, and one will develop from what was to be the right half.

This fortuitous division is believed responsible for the mirror imaging seen in certain monozygotic pairs. Relatively late division (around two weeks after conception) is generally incomplete, and the end result is so-called Siamese twins, joined together at some point along their bodies. Mirror imaging could operate only in monozygotic twins, for dizygotic twins begin life as two separate embryos and division of the sort that occurs in monozygotic pairs does not take place. Thus mirror imaging could help account for left-handedness only in monozygotic pairs.

## Twins and Handedness: Some Further Insights

Two factors—brain damage and mirror imaging—may contribute to handedness discordance in monozygotic pairs. Handedness discordance in dizygotic pairs may be the result of pathological factors and genetic differences since they have, on the average, only one-half of their genes in common.[14] The puzzle that remains is why the factors affecting monozygotic and dizygotic pairs operate in such a way as to produce an incidence of discordance that is almost identical for both types of twin pairs. It may be a coincidence, or perhaps it is indicative of something more significant, possibly another factor associated with twinning in general that we have not accounted for. Nevertheless, this analysis suggests that twins are not a good population with which to test genetic models of handedness. They are subject to the influences of handedness-determining factors that affect singletons to a much lesser extent, if at all.

It is interesting to note that at least one investigator has suggested that all singleton left-handers are the surviving members of monozygotic twin pairs that divided at the time crucial for mirror imaging to occur.[15] We have no evidence either to support or refute this, but it is an intriguing notion. In contrast, we have seen that some investigators are convinced that almost all left-handedness is genetic in origin; others argue that left-handedness is the result of early injury to the left hemisphere. At the present time, none of these extreme views has really convincing evidence to support it, although each may in fact contribute to understanding the incidence of left-handedness overall.

## Handedness and Functional Asymmetry

In what ways does the brain organization of left-handers differ from that of right-handers? Both clinical and behavioral studies have helped answer this question.

The sodium amytal procedure discussed in an earlier chapter temporarily anesthetizes one hemisphere at a time, allowing the neurosurgeon to determine which half of the brain controls speech in a given patient about to undergo brain surgery. A recent summary of sodium amytal testing at the Montreal Neurological Institute reported that over 95 percent of the right-handers had speech localized to the left hemisphere, and 70 percent of the left-handers showed the same pattern. Of the left-handers remaining, half showed right-hemisphere control of speech, and half had speech represented bilaterally.[16]

From these figures, one might conclude that the majority of left-handers are just like right-handers, while many of the others show a simple reversal of the pattern found in right-handers. Other clinical data, however, suggest that the picture is more complex.

Several studies have reported that the prognosis for recovery from aphasia following stroke is much better in left-handers than in right-handers.[17] Many investigators believe that recovery from massive damage to the speech hemisphere is a function of the extent to which the remaining, undamaged hemisphere can take over. If this is so, it suggests that language functions may be bilaterally represented in more than just the 15 percent of the left-handers identified by the sodium amytal data. Left-handers with speech controlled predominantly by one hemisphere may have the other hemisphere available "in reserve" to a much greater extent than right-handers.

Behavioral studies with normal subjects generally confirm this picture of complexity. Dichotic listening and lateralized tachistoscopic studies that compare the performance of left-handers and right-handers show less evidence of asymmetry in left-handers.[18] As a general rule, any asymmetry found with right-handers will be smaller and perhaps in the opposite direction when studied in left-handers.

By themselves, however, these summary statements don't allow us to differentiate between a situation where left-handers truly show no asymmetry in these tasks and a situation where approximately equal numbers show a right or left advantage. When data from individual subjects are examined, we find that left-handed subjects show smaller asymmetries than right-handed subjects, although there are some left-handers with strong left or strong right superiorities. These findings mesh nicely with the clinical evidence pointing to greater bilaterality in left-handers.

### The Role of Familial Sinistrality

The brain organization of left-handers appears to be more complex than the sodium amytal data would lead one to expect. Other clinical work has suggested that some of the variability between left-handers may be accounted for by determining whether a given left-hander has first-degree relatives (parents, siblings, or children) who are themselves left-handed.[19]

Left-handers with a history of *familial sinistrality* (left-handers in the immediate family) showed language disturbances occurring with similar frequency following damage to the left or right side of the brain. In nonfamilial left-handers, language disturbances were almost non-existent after right-hemisphere lesions. This difference suggests that there are at least two kinds of left-handers, and that the patterns of brain organization in the two groups are different.

Studies with normal subjects have looked at the effect of familial sinistrality on performance. In one study using dichotic listening, left-handers without a history of familial sinistrality showed a right-ear superiority, and familial left-handers showed no left–right difference.[20] This difference has been found in several other studies, but some investigators have reported contradictory results.

In some studies, the left-hander with left-handed relatives seemed to show the largest right-sided asymmetry, and the left-hander without left-handed relatives showed signs of bilateral or right-hemisphere speech.[21] Other researchers have reported no difference in asymmetry between familial and nonfamilial left-handers.[22] The bulk of the evidence, however, supports the idea that left-handers with left-handed relatives differ from those without. The conflict exists in showing how they differ.

The evidence pointing to differences in brain organization between persons with and without a family history of left-handedness has been taken by some to be a sign of a genetic component to handedness. The same relationship, however, may also be viewed as support for an environmental determinant of handedness.

### Inverted and Noninverted Writing Postures

The research of Jerre Levy and MaryLou Reid has identified another variable that may help sort left-handers into different groups on the basis of brain organization.[23] Some left-handers write in an inverted or hooked position, holding the pen or pencil above the line of writing. Other left-handers, as well as virtually all right-handers, hold their writing instruments below the line of writing. These hand postures are shown in Figure 5.2.

Levy and Reid have argued that the position of the hand provides useful information about which hemisphere is controlling speech and language in an individual. Their view conflicts with conventional wisdom, which suggests that hand posture is simply a matter of training. According to the conventional view, some left-handers, encouraged to position their writing paper in the same way as right-handers, have adopted the hooked posture out of necessity. Without it, their hand hides most of what they have just written.

In contrast, Levy and Reid argue that the inverted hand posture means that the speech hemisphere is ipsilateral to the preferred hand. Thus the speech of a left-handed inverter would be controlled by the left hemisphere. The speech of a right-handed inverter (their study involved one subject in this category) would be controlled by the right hemisphere. The speech of noninverted writers would be controlled by the hemisphere opposite to the preferred hand.

The basis for Levy and Reid's conclusions is data from two tachistoscopic tests involving lateralized presentation of three-letter syllables or a dot randomly located in 1 of 20 possible locations within the left or right visual field. These tests are shown in Figure 5.3. On verbal trials, subjects were asked to identify the syllable. On dot trials, they

Left-handed Writers

Right-handed Writers

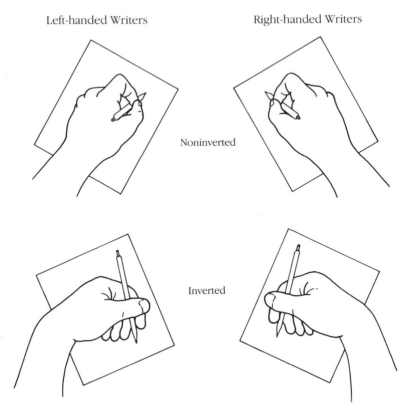

Noninverted

Inverted

**5.2** Noninverted and inverted writing postures of left-handers and right-handers. (From J. Levy and M. Reid, "Variations on Writing Posture and Cerebral Organization," *Science* 194, Fig. 1, p. 337, Oct. 1976, pp. 337–339. Copyright © 1976 by the American Association for the Advancement of Science.)

were to remember the position of a dot and locate it a few seconds later on a matrix of boxes displayed in free vision. Visual-field asymmetries in accuracy (measured as the number correct in the right field minus the number correct in the left field) were computed for each type of stimulus to provide a measure of hemispheric asymmetry for verbal and spatial processing.

The results clearly indicate that right-handers who use the noninverted hand posture show a right visual field superiority for syllables and a left visual field superiority for the spatial task. Left-handers who write with the noninverted posture show the reverse. In contrast, left-handers who write with an inverted posture perform like the right-handers with a noninverted posture. The single right-hander who wrote with an inverted posture generated data comparable to those of left-handers writing in a noninverted fashion.

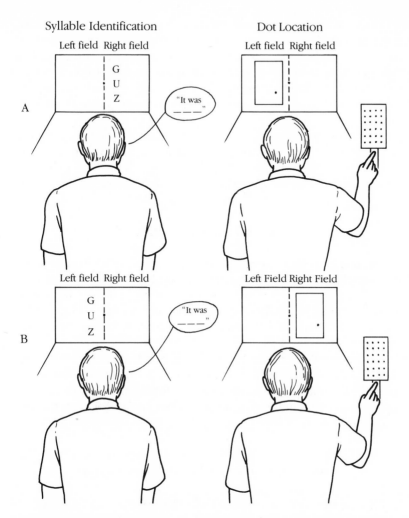

**5.3** Syllable identification ("What did you see?") and dot location tasks ("Point to the dot on the card that is in the same spot as the dot that appeared on the screen."). A. Noninverted right-handers and inverted left-handers were most accurate when the syllable task appeared in the right field and the dot task appeared in the left. B. Noninverted left-handers and inverted right-handers were most accurate when the syllable task appeared in the left field and the dot task appeared in the right.

These results suggest that it is possible to tell a great deal about brain organization from an individual's handedness alone. Like most interesting findings, though, they raise more questions than they answer. What is the evidence for ipsilateral motor control of the sort postulated by Levy and Reid and earlier by Nagylaki and Levy? Assuming it exists, why should it result in an inverted hand posture?

Even more important are the questions raised by other studies using dichotic listening measures to look for differences between inverters and noninverters. These studies have failed to find significant differences between these groups, although attempts to replicate the work with lateralized tachistoscopic presentations have been successful.[24] Why is the difference apparent with visual but not with auditory stimuli?

At this point, the most prudent course of action is to defer judgment on the utility of hand posture as a predictor of brain asymmetry until some of these problems are resolved. It remains, however, a promising variable that may allow researchers to differentiate among individuals.

## Handedness and Higher Mental Functions

Do left-handers differ from right-handers in ways other than brain organization? The search for the relationship between handedness and brain asymmetry has led many investigators to consider the consequences of this relationship for other functions. Recall, for example, the pathological model of left-handedness. According to this view, some (one investigator says all) left-handers have suffered from very early, minimal brain damage that resulted in a shift from what would have been a right-hand preference to a preference for the left hand. The pathological model leads readily to the prediction that minimal brain damage will result in lowered ability on various tests of higher mental functions.

### Evaluating the Case for Deficits in Left-Handers

Studies that compare the performance of left-handers and right-handers on tests of higher mental functions have yielded little in the way of data to support predictions of inferior performance by left-handers. A recent review of the literature cited 14 studies examining reading ability. Only one of them found a difference between left-handers and right-handers, and it reported that left-handers were superior.[25] Using measures of academic achievement, one study found no difference between groups, while another study reported that left-handers did more poorly on a college entrance exam. Three studies reported that left-handers did more poorly in perceptual tasks, although the only one of these studies to be replicated failed to show a difference in subsequent work.

Despite this relatively meager collection of empirical evidence documenting performance differences between left-handers and right handers, the association of left-handedness with deficit persists. This is most likely the result of the high incidence of left-handedness among the mentally retarded and reading-disabled. This association suggests that some of the left-handedness in these groups selected for deficits is pathological in origin. The same damage that produces the impairment may also be responsible for the shift to left-hand usage. It does not follow, however, that a similar relationship holds for unselected groups of subjects obtained outside of clinical settings.

The pathological model of left-handedness, then, has been responsible for much of the interest in the relationship between handedness and cognitive ability. Another theoretical approach to this question has been taken by Levy.[26] She noted that many left-handers show evidence of some language ability in the right hemisphere, in addition to language ability in the left hemisphere. What, she asked, are the consequences of this for the visuo-spatial functions typically controlled by the right hemisphere in the right-hander?

She proposed that language and visuo-spatial functions could compete for available neural tissue within a hemisphere, and that language functions would predominate at the expense of the others. Thus, she predicted that left-handers should do more poorly than right-handers on visuo-spatial tasks but perform similarly on verbal tasks.

To test her hypothesis, she recruited 10 left-handed and 15 right-handed California Institute of Technology graduate students and administered the Wechsler Adult Intelligence Scale (WAIS) to them. The WAIS can be broken down into two parts, a verbal and a performance component. The verbal subtests include general information, vocabulary, and similarities (simple abstraction). The performance subtests include block design (Koh's blocks), object assembly (puzzle assembly), and picture completion (noticing anomalies in drawings).*

Levy's study demonstrated that scores on the verbal component were the same for left-handers and right-handers. Left-handers scored significantly lower than right-handers on the performance score, however. Thus Levy's prediction of a deficit in visuo-spatial tasks was borne out.

It is important to remember, however, that this "deficit" is a relative one only. Levy's subjects, both left-handers and right-handers, showed markedly superior scores on both parts of the WAIS compared to the overall population. The performance scores of the left-handers, though,

---

*The verbal subtests seem most sensitive to damage to the left hemisphere, probably because they are so language dependent. The performance subtests are known to be quite sensitive to damage to either hemisphere, especially in the parietal region. In addition, the performance tests seem to be more sensitive than the verbal tests to brain damage in general, especially diffuse damage. They are first to show decline with increasing age and are the tests most affected by brain trauma and diffuse pathological processes.

were lower than their verbal scores, while there was no difference for the right-handers.

Levy's work has generated considerable interest as well as several attempts at replications.[27] One study using a larger number of subjects from a college population obtained similar results. Three other studies, with large samples from other subject populations, have failed to find any evidence of the differences expected.

Some have argued that Levy's results are an artifact of using a highly select sample of subjects. That objection, however, cannot explain the replication that was successful.

### Leonardo da Vinci Was a Lefty

Some investigators have suggested that the more bilateral distribution of language function that appears to characterize left-handers may result in superior abilities. The argument has been made that creativity might be enhanced in individuals whose brains permit a greater interplay between verbal and nonverbal abilities by virtue of their being housed within the same hemisphere. Occasional studies have reported superior performance by the left-hander, but these studies do not paint any more clear a picture than do those pointing to deficits in left-handers. Proponents, however, are eager to point out that Leonardo da Vinci, Ben Franklin, and Michelangelo were all left-handed.

Despite the suggestion of deficits in left-handers and the amply justified reprisals just mentioned, it is evident that any differences in the cognitive abilities of left- and right-handers in general are very small and of little practical importance. As in many such studies, it is clear that individual variation within a group is much greater than the statistical difference between groups. However, the issue of statistical differences in cognitive functioning and handedness will continue to be pursued because of its significance to theories of brain variability and organization.

# 6

# Sex and Asymmetry

Consider the following simple experiment. In one condition, subjects are asked to run mentally through the alphabet and count the number of letters, including the letter *e,* that when pronounced contain the sound "ee." In a second condition, subjects are asked to count the number of letters that contain curves when they are printed as capitals. In both tasks, the subjects must do everything "in their heads." Writing is not allowed, nor is speaking out loud. Participants are told to do each count as quickly as possible since the results are scored for speed as well as for accuracy.

Which task is harder—counting sounds or counting curves? The outcome of this study depends on whether male or female subjects are being tested. Males are more accurate and slightly faster in the shape task; females do better in the sound task.[1]

This study is one of many pointing to sex differences in certain human abilities—in this case, verbal and spatial skills. Considerable evidence suggests that females are superior to males in a wide range of skills that require the use of language, and extensive evidence shows males to be superior in tasks that are spatial in nature.[2]

Simply identifying sex differences such as these, however, does not reveal anything about the origin of the difference. Biological factors may play an important role, as may sex differences in child-rearing practices. Recent research into the left brain and right brain has suggested that sex differences in verbal and spatial abilities may be related to differences in the way those functions are distributed between the cerebral hemispheres in males and females.

In this chapter we will review the evidence on this question and consider its theoretical and practical significance. The picture we have of sex differences in the brain comes from both clinical and behavioral studies.

## Evidence From the Brain-Damage Clinic

### *Sex Differences in the Effects of Brain Damage*

Herbert Lansdell, working at the National Institutes of Health, was among the first investigators to note that the consequences of damage to one half of the brain appeared to differ for males and females.[3] Lansdell was interested in studying the effects of the removal of part of the temporal lobe on one side of the head in patients operated on to alleviate epileptic seizures. A wealth of earlier research had led him to predict greater deficits in visuo-spatial tasks following operation on the right hemisphere and greater deficits in verbal tasks following left-hemisphere surgery. His predictions were borne out, but only for male patients. These unexpected findings led Lansdell to speculate that some physiological mechanisms underlying visuo-spatial and verbal ability may overlap in the female brain but may be located in opposite hemispheres in the male brain.

Later work has pointed to the same conclusions. For example, psychologist Jeannette McGlone has reported data from 85 right-handed adults with damage to the left or right side of the brain.[4] Most had suffered a stroke, although some were tumor cases. Each patient was given a battery of psychological tests, including the Wechsler Adult Intelligence Scale (WAIS) and an aphasia test, to see whether the pattern of verbal and nonverbal deficits that emerged was a function of both sex and side of damage.

The results for language impairments were striking. Aphasia following damage to the left hemisphere occurred three times more frequently in males than in females. Even when patients showing signs of aphasia were excluded from the analysis, deficits in higher verbal tasks in the remaining patients continued to be more common and more severe in males.

In contrast, performance on the nonverbal subtests of the WAIS did not show any overall significant effects due to sex or side of damage. When performance on the nonverbal tests was compared to performance on the verbal tests, however, differences by sex and side of lesion again appeared. The relevant measure is the difference between the score on the nonverbal IQ items and the verbal IQ score. For men, left-hemisphere damage impaired verbal IQ more than nonverbal IQ, and right-hemisphere damage lowered nonverbal performance relative to verbal. Women showed no effect of side of lesion. Their verbal and nonverbal IQ scores were not significantly different for damage to the left or right side. These data also support Lansdell's speculation that both language abilities and spatial abilities are represented more bilaterally in females than in males.

### Have Sex Differences Always Been Present?

How can these findings be reconciled with almost 100 years of clinical investigations of hemispheric asymmetry that did not report sex differences? One explanation is that many of the older studies were done with patient populations that were predominantly male. Patients in Veterans Administration hospitals have been extensively studied, and they are almost exclusively male. Patients suffering from war-related brain damage have also been the object of much research, and they too are overwhelmingly male. Populations having surgery on the temporal lobe are biased as well. Most surgery of this type is done to alleviate epilepsy, a disease that is much more common among males.

Another important factor in explaining the failure of early work to notice sex differences is simply that no one looked for them. There is tremendous variation from patient to patient (even within one sex) in the effects of unilateral brain damage. Damage to the left hemisphere of some right-handed people can produce a massive disruption of language skills, while comparable damage in other individuals has minimal effect. This variability in the effects of brain damage within groups of males and females makes it difficult to find differences between males and females unless the investigator is working with a large subject population and is specifically looking for differences.

## Evidence From Behavioral Tests

### Auditory and Visual Studies

Many researchers doing behavioral studies of laterality have begun to look for sex differences. Several verbal dichotic listening studies have reported greater right-ear advantages among males than among females. Philip Bryden, a psychologist who has conducted numerous dichotic listening studies to assess brain asymmetry, has combined the data from several of his studies using dichotically presented digit pairs to look for possible sex differences.[5] Of the 98 subjects he tested, 73.6 percent of the males (11 left-handers and 42 right-handers) showed a right-ear advantage, and 62.2 percent of the females (3 left-handers and 42 right-handers) showed right-ear superiority. Sex differences in ear asymmetries have also been found in studies using spoken syllables as dichotic stimuli.

Not all attempts to look for sex differences in verbal dichotic listening performance have found them, however.[6] The failures have led some investigators to question the reality of sex differences in laterality in the first place. Some have argued that this area of research is plagued by the *type I error*.

Type I is the name given to the kind of error made when an investigator concludes that the differences she or he observes in a study are real, when in fact they are due to chance. Investigators are much more willing to report differences between groups (and journal editors are much more eager to accept such studies) than they are to publish negative or "no difference" results. Critics have suggested that journals contain only the tip of the sex-differences-in-laterality-research iceberg, and that the majority of studies with negative results are never published.

Those who believe that sex differences in laterality are real counter this argument with one that challenges the sensitivity of studies that fail to find evidence of sex differences. They note the tremendous variability in lateralization within a given sex and point out that this variability makes it quite difficult to detect real, but small, differences between the sexes. Small studies with 10 or 15 subjects per group (the size of many studies) will especially suffer from this problem.

### Studying Sex Differences in Children

Significant sex differences in the lateralization of spatial functions have been found in children. Standard behavioral techniques for studying the right hemisphere's role in spatial processing proved difficult for young children. Thus Sandra Witelson devised a test of tactual perception that could be used over a wide range of ages.[7]

The test, known as the dichaptic stimulation test, requires that the subject simultaneously feel two different objects held out of view, one in each hand. Figure 6.1 shows the stimuli used. After holding the meaningless shapes for 10 seconds, the subject chooses the two shapes from among a group of six that are displayed visually. The data are then scored for the number of objects correctly selected by each hand.

Witelson tested 200 strongly right-handed children from the ages of 6 to 13. The results showed a significant interaction of hand and sex. The left-hand score of the boys was significantly better than their right-

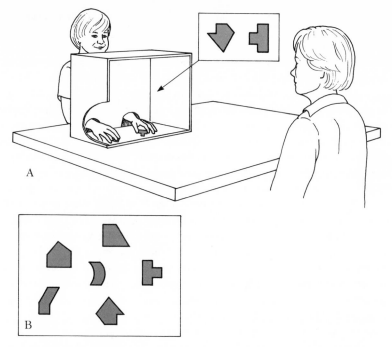

**6.1** Dichaptic stimulation test. A. The subject is given two objects with meaningless shapes such as those shown in the inset. Without being able to see the objects, he simultaneously feels both of them, one with each hand, for 10 seconds. B. The subject is asked to identify the two shapes from among a group of six displayed visually.

hand score, but there was no difference between hands for the girls. A dichotic digits test administered to the same subjects did not show any sex difference in the proportion of children showing a right-ear or a left-ear advantage.

The results of the Witelson study suggest that sex differences in lateralization of spatial abilities may have their origins quite early in life. Later in this chapter we will consider mechanisms that may underlie these differences. In the next section we will summarize some of the remaining bits and pieces of information that provide additional evidence for the existence of sex differences.

## Activity and Anatomy:
## Additional Pieces of the Sex Differences Puzzle

### Differences in Brain Anatomy

In Chapter 4, we reviewed some of the evidence pointing to anatomical differences between the hemispheres. Mounting interest in sex differences in lateralization has encouraged investigators to see whether sex is a factor in these asymmetries, and findings have begun to appear suggesting that it is.

Although data on sex have not been reported in some studies, one large investigation obtained gender information for most of the brains that were examined post-mortem.[8] Results were reported as ratios of the length of the right temporal plane to the length of the left temporal plane for each brain. Overall, this ratio was less than 1, reflecting a longer plane on the left side. Of those individuals showing a reversal of this pattern, however, most were female.

If a reversal is assumed to reflect greater bilaterality of function, these findings are consistent with the other data we have presented so far. Females seem to be less lateralized. We must reemphasize, though, that the link between anatomical asymmetries and functional asymmetries is, at present, an untested assumption. That link must be firmly established before it is wise to use anatomical data to infer function. In addition, relatively few specimens showed a reversal—that is, a right temporal plane longer than the left—so we are talking about an effect that may hold for only a small percentage of females overall.

## Electrical Activity and Sex Differences

Some other evidence pointing to sex differences in lateralization has come from electrophysiological studies. One study correlated the degree of EEG alpha asymmetry (left alpha power minus right alpha power) with the speed of performance on different tasks thought to engage the left and right hemispheres differentially.[9] For males, a significant correlation was found between the magnitude of the asymmetry and performance in the right-hemisphere task. The correlation for the left-hemisphere "vocabulary" condition approached, but did not quite reach, statistical significance; a task believed to involve both hemispheres did not show any correlation with performance. In females, however, none of these correlations was significantly different from zero. These results suggest some differences in laterality as a function of sex, but a direct analysis of alpha power itself did not show any evidence of the sex by type of task by hemisphere interaction that was originally predicted.

Another study looked for sex differences in a situation where subjects were trained to use biofeedback techniques to generate symmetrical or asymmetrical EEG patterns.[10] In a task where the subject can control the onset or offset of a tone by generating a particular EEG pattern (such as greater left-hemisphere alpha, greater right-hemisphere alpha, or low or high alpha in both hemispheres), subjects quickly acquire the ability to produce the required distribution of activity. Results showed that females were better able to maintain asymmetric patterns of alpha activity than males, but there were no sex differences in the ability to maintain *symmetrical* patterns in the two hemispheres.

Although this last study points to a sex difference in brain asymmetry, the difference is the reverse of what would have been predicted on the assumption that females are less lateralized. The investigators proposed that the apparent conflict may be based on the fact that other studies used perceptual tasks to measure asymmetry; they employed a task involving production (the production of the alpha asymmetry). They suggest that sex differences in asymmetry may depend heavily on whether perception or production is studied.

Electrophysiological studies, then, contribute to the idea that the lateralization patterns of males and females differ. This area of research, however, confronts the same difficulties as the electrophysiological work reviewed in Chapter 4. Studies are often difficult to repeat, and even seemingly successful studies are not always clear-cut in their results or their interpretation.

## Are Sex Differences in Laterality Real?

Are there sex differences in the distribution of verbal and spatial functions between the hemispheres? Much of the data reviewed in the preceding sections suggest that there are. A variety of evidence suggests that males tend to be more lateralized for verbal and spatial abilities and women show greater bilateral representation for both types of functions. But what about the type I error? Aren't there studies (some of which we don't know about because they are unpublished) that fail to find these purported sex differences?

Our review of the lateralization literature in general has given us a healthy respect for the type I error and the scientific chaos it can create. The frequency as well as the consistency of reports of sex differences in cerebral organization, however, leads us to accept their reality, at least as a working hypothesis. The strength of the case, in our opinion, rests on the diversity of methodologies (clinical studies, dichotic listening, tachistoscopic presentation, and electrophysiology) that point to the same conclusion: females are less lateralized than males.

A review of the studies that do not support this conclusion shows that most report no differences between the sexes. It is a rare study that reports sex differences in the direction of greater lateralization in females. This consistency suggests that there are true differences that are small in magnitude and easily masked by individual variability or other factors that may not be controlled.

## The Origin of Sex Differences

Assuming for the moment that sex differences are real, how can they be accounted for? Several intriguing proposals have been offered. Deborah Waber has suggested that sex differences of the sort we have reviewed are attributable not to sex per se but rather to differences in the rates at which males and females develop.[11] Waber noted that females generally gain physical maturity at an earlier age than males. She hypothesized that maturational rate might be systematically related to sex differences in verbal and spatial abilities. Specifically, she predicted the following relationships that would be independent of sex. First, early maturers have better verbal than spatial abilities; late maturers perform better on spatial tasks than on verbal ones. Second, early maturers show less speech lateralization than late maturers.

Waber tested her predictions with a sample of 80 children divided into eight groups on the basis of age (10 and 13 for girls, 13 and 16 for boys), sex, and maturational level (early or late based on a medical examination for secondary sexual characteristics). Individuals were classified as early maturers if their chronological age was at least one standard deviation below mean age for their stage of sexual development, as late maturers if their chronological age was one standard deviation above the norms used.

Several standard tests of verbal and spatial ability were administered to each subject, in addition to a consonant–vowel dichotic listening test to assess speech lateralization. In general, the results confirmed Waber's predictions. Within individuals and independent of sex, late maturers scored better on spatial tasks, and early maturers scored better on verbal tasks. Further analysis showed that only the spatial scores were related to maturational rate. The verbal scores did not differ as a function of maturation. Among the older subjects, late maturers also showed larger ear advantages than early maturers. The younger children did not show a difference in ear advantage as a function of maturational rate. Differences due to sex alone were not significant in the study.

Waber's data lead to the proposal that sex differences in verbal and spatial ability and the lateralization of these functions may be due not to sex but to a variable that is *correlated* with sex—maturational rate.

Jerre Levy has suggested an evolutionary basis for sex differences in lateralization.[12] She argues that males have been the hunters and leaders of migrations throughout hominid evolution, and those with good visuo-spatial skills have had a selective advantage. At the same time, females were likely to have had selective pressures exerted on them for skills involved in child rearing, such as the use of language as a tool for communication, the development of social sensitivity, and facility with nonverbal communication. Levy proposes that greater bi-lateralization of function may facilitate the skills needed by females, while stricter separation of function is necessary to ensure a high level of visuo-spatial skills in males.

## The Significance of Sex Differences

From a theoretical standpoint, the significance of sex differences in brain organization is considerable. If sex differences are real, what is (or was) their adaptive advantage? How does brain organization relate to patterns of higher mental function? Do sex differences in child-rearing practices affect brain asymmetries? These are a few of the important questions that are still unanswered.

Particularly interesting is the issue of how ability is related to extent of lateralization. Does greater lateralization for a given function imply superior performance for that function? Is the spatial ability of males better than that of females because males seem to rely more on one hemisphere to process spatial information? There is, of course, no logical reason to expect that greater lateralization necessarily leads to superior ability. In fact, we have to assume the opposite to explain the superior verbal ability of females. According to behavioral tests and clinical data, women appear to be less lateralized for language functions, yet as a group they are superior to men in language skills.

There may be a relationship between lateralization and ability that is different for different tasks. If this is the case, it would be fascinating to know why the brain organizes itself so differently for the optimal functioning of different abilities. At this point we can only speculate about the relationship of lateralization and ability. It is clear, though, that this is an important issue for our ultimate understanding of the sex differences we have considered.

Although most investigators would probably agree that theoretical questions of this sort are significant, there would undoubtedly be less agreement concerning the practical meaning of sex differences in brain organization and their possible correlates in cognitive function. Sex differences in higher mental functions are typically on the order of one-quarter of a standard deviation. This means that there is a great deal of overlap in the distribution of ability across men and women. Some women have better spatial abilities than most men, while some men have better verbal skills than most women. On the average, though, the groups do differ in these abilities to a limited degree.

Awareness of the extent of the overlap in ability tends to temper any suggestion that sex be used as major criterion, by itself, for deter-mining career options and educational opportunities. Witelson has pro-posed that data on sex differences in brain organization be the basis for devising at the elementary-school level educational programs that are best suited to the abilities of each sex. This approach, though, denies the importance of individual differences within groups of males and females. The need for curricula better geared to the abilities of specific groups is clear. It is perhaps wiser, however, to determine the composition of those groups through individual testing rather than to determine it simply on the basis of gender.

# 7

# The Development
# of Asymmetry

At birth, the brain of a human infant is but one-fourth the weight of an adult brain. By the time a child is 2 years of age, however, the brain will have more than tripled its mass and come close to its full size. Accompanying this dramatic change in physical size are equally dramatic changes in the child's capabilities. By the age of 2, the average child has begun to talk and to show the beginnings of many of the higher mental functions that characterize human beings.

In this chapter we ask the question of how and at what point the basic differences between the left brain and right brain found in adults fit into this picture of physical and functional change in childhood. Do these asymmetries emerge over time as the child develops, or are they present at birth or even possibly before? What roles do genetic and environmental factors play in the establishment of asymmetry? Can the pattern of asymmetry be changed, and if so, what are the limiting factors?

These fundamental questions are the focus of considerable research using many different methodologies. The answers have the potential for contributing in important ways to our understanding of language disorders, both in children and in adults. They may also help investigators better understand other problems that have been linked to the division of functions between the hemispheres.

## When Is Lateralization Complete?

### *The Case For Lateralization by Puberty*

The person perhaps most responsible for current interest in the development of lateralization was Eric Lenneberg, a psychologist at Cornell University. In the mid-1960s, Lenneberg reviewed a variety of evidence and concluded that lateralization of function in the brain develops over time but is complete by puberty.[1] His research also indicated that puberty marks a crucial turning point in the ability to learn new languages, without signs of a foreign accent, through mere exposure. Lenneberg believed it was not merely a coincidence that both lateralization and language-learning ability appear fixed at puberty. He saw one as the biological basis of the other.

In drawing his conclusions about the time course of lateralization, Lenneberg relied heavily on clinical data collected by a neurologist named L. S. Basser.[2] Basser reported that about half of a group of 72 children with brain injury occurring before the age of 2 began to speak at the usual time, while the other half showed some delay. The results were the same for children with damage to the left or right hemisphere, suggesting that hemispheric asymmetry for language is not well established by age 2. Results from a group of children with injuries occurring between the onset of speech and age 10, however, showed the emergence of hemispheric differences. In this group, injury to the left side resulted in speech disturbances in 85 percent of the cases, but injury to the right side produced disturbances only 45 percent of the time.

Despite these differential left–right effects, this pattern of impairment is still different from that found in right-handed teenagers and adults who sustain brain injury. Here, aphasia very rarely follows damage to the right hemisphere but occurs even more often after damage to the left half of the brain. On the basis of this evidence, Lenneberg concluded that lateralization begins at the time of language acquisition but is not complete until puberty.

### *Lateralization by Puberty Reconsidered*

Lenneberg's interpretation of these data has not gone unchallenged. A careful reexamination of Basser's findings has shown that each of the cases where damage to the right hemisphere resulted in speech disturbances involved injury occurring before the age of 5. In the one case where right-hemisphere injury occurred after that age, no speech loss was noted. Thus Basser's findings are consistent with the hypothesis that lateralization is complete by age 5, rather than by puberty, and they do not provide an adequate number of patients to test the hypothesis that lateralization is completed later.[3]

Further reevaluation of Basser's work has even led one investigator to argue that the data are consistent with the hypothesis that lateralization is complete at birth, not by age 5 or at puberty. Kinsbourne has reviewed the neurological records in Basser's cases and argues that most of the cases in which right-hemisphere damage in infancy resulted in aphasia were really cases of injury to the left as well as the right hemisphere.[4] If this is so, the early childhood data look no different from adult data in terms of incidence of aphasia following damage to the left or right sides of the brain.

It is clear that new evidence, utilizing sophisticated tools for localizing brain injury, would be helpful in answering the question of whether children and adults differ in the incidence of aphasia following damage to the left or right hemisphere. Regardless of the outcome of such a study, however, we do know that there are dramatic differences in recovery from aphasia in children and in adults. We will consider the theoretical implications of this finding later in the chapter.

## Age and Asymmetry:
## The Search for the Beginnings of Lateralization

Basser's data on the effects of unilateral brain injury have led different investigators to different conclusions about the time course of brain asymmetry. Several other sources of evidence bearing on the issue are also available, and we turn now to consider them.

### Dichotic Listening in the Crib

Many dichotic listening studies have sought to determine the earliest age at which the right-ear advantage may be found. This technique, discussed at length in Chapter 3, involves the presentation of two different speech messages simultaneously, one to each ear. Subjects are typically asked to report what was heard, a procedure that obviously places a lower limit on the age of the children that can be tested. The standard dichotic listening test has been used with children as young as 3, though, and a right-ear superiority is found.[5]

More recently, ingenious methods have been used to take the dichotic technique into the crib to see whether infants show a right-ear advantage. In one study, infants averaging 50 days of age first learned to suck on a nipple in order to receive dichotic presentations of a pair of words. Each time the infants sucked with a previously specified force, the same words were presented to them. This procedure continued until the infant habituated to the dichotic pair as evidenced by a sustained reduction in the sucking rate. At this point, either the left-ear stimulus or the right-ear stimulus was changed, and the investigator monitored the infant for changes in sucking rate. The results of this study showed that the infant noticed a change in either ear (the sucking rate increased), but a change in the right ear produced a larger increase in sucking.[6]

Work by other investigators has shown that infants typically increase their rate of sucking when a novel stimulus is presented. The results with the dichotic speech stimuli, then, suggest that the difference between old and new stimuli is easier to detect in the right ear—a right-ear advantage. A similar study by the same investigator found a greater increase following left-ear change when nonspeech stimuli were used. This is further evidence that the "ear difference" in the dichotic task reflects brain asymmetry.

Although this modification of the dichotic paradigm is ingenious and encouraging to those who believe lateralization of function is present at birth, other investigators have had difficulty replicating the findings. One study repeated the work with speech stimuli modifying the procedures slightly to prevent inadvertent experimenter bias.* That study failed to obtain any evidence of differences in the sucking rate in response to stimuli changed in each ear.[7] Further work is needed to determine whether ear asymmetries may be found in newborns.

Attempts have also been made to see whether the magnitude of the ear advantage in the standard dichotic task changes with age. Perhaps the beginnings of lateralization of function are present at birth, and the degree of asymmetry increases as the child matures. Results on this issue are not clear-cut. Some investigators have reported that the asymmetry does not change from 5 to 12 years of age; others have noted differences over that period.[8]

### Evoked Potentials In Infants

Because electrophysiological recording techniques do not require a deliberate response of any sort from the subject, they are ideally suited

---

*Experimenter bias is a potential problem in all behavioral research that does not strictly control for it. In the study just discussed, the experimenter working with the infant was not "blind" to the order of stimulus conditions (that is, the investigator knew which ear received a change in sound stimuli on a particular trial). Thus the experimenter may have inadvertently influenced the infant to respond in the predicted direction. In the attempted replication of this work, the interaction of experimenter and infant was reduced to a minimum, and the experimenter present in the room with the infant had no knowledge of the particular condition being tested at any given time.

to the study of hemispheric asymmetries in infants. Psychologist Dennis Molfese was one of the first investigators to find evidence of asymmetries in the electrical recordings of the left brain and right brain in neonates. In one study, he and his collaborators presented speech sounds such as "ba" to infants from one week to ten months of age while they recorded evoked potential (EP) activity from both hemispheres.[9] They found responses of greater amplitude, presumably reflecting greater involvement in the processing of the sounds, on the left side in 9 of the 10 infants tested. The effect held for the youngest infants as well as for the older ones. The one infant showing a reversal was eight months of age. When Molfese presented the infants with certain nonspeech sounds such as a noise burst or a piano chord, the opposite results were obtained: all 10 infants showed evoked potentials of greater amplitude in the right hemisphere.

These findings are exciting because they suggest that although the newborn may not "understand" what is being presented, its brain is already equipped with specialized centers that will be responsible for processing these sounds at deeper levels later in life.

Wada and Davis have taken another approach to the study of EP asymmetries in infants. "If fundamental asymmetry of the neurocircuit exists before the development of language and speech function," they note, "then we ought to be able to disclose such a difference without using verbal stimuli."[10] Wada and Davis recorded the EP to clicks and flashes of light and measured the *coherence,* or similarity of the forms, of the EP in the temporal and occipital regions of the brain in infants.

In earlier work with adult patients tested with sodium amytal, they had observed that coherence was largest for clicks in the speech-dominant hemisphere and for flashes in the non-speech-dominant hemisphere. Similar results were found in their study of 50 infants ranging in age from 1 day to 5 weeks. Findings indicated that the forms of the occipital and temporal responses to clicks were more similar within the left half of the brain than in the right half; the similarity shifted toward the right hemisphere when flashes were presented. The investigators have argued that their findings reflect the specialization of the two hemispheres for processing different kinds of information, and that this specialization is present at birth.

### Anatomical Asymmetries In Infants

Other evidence to support the idea that brain asymmetry has its origin early in life comes from anatomical studies in fetuses and infants. In the largest study, 207 brains were measured. Age ranged from 10 to 44 weeks after conception. A longer temporal plane was present in 54 percent of the brains; the relationship was reversed in 18 percent of the cases. In 28 percent, no significant difference in the size of the temporal plane was observed between the two sides.[11]

In another large study of 100 brains, comparable results were found. The mean age in this study was 48 weeks, including the gestational period. The left temporal plane was 77 percent larger, on the average, than the right temporal plane. There were 12 infants with the right side larger than the left side and 32 with approximately equal measurements on left and right.[12]

Once again, we encounter a major difficulty in interpreting such anatomical studies. We do not know the precise nature of the relationship between anatomical asymmetry and functional asymmetry. Is the former the structural basis of the latter? If so, are functional differences between the hemispheres operative whenever we find anatomical differences? Only when we have additional information to help answer these questions will we be able to interpret the asymmetry data with confidence. Until then, the evidence will remain suggestive and intriguing but by no means a complete answer to the issue of whether lateralization of function is present at birth.

### Hemispherectomy: The Removal of Half a Brain

Occasionally, it becomes medically necessary for physicians to remove one cerebral hemisphere. The procedure, known as *hemispherectomy*,* is performed when a cancerous tumor is discovered to have spread throughout one side of the brain. The operation is also done early in infancy when extensive damage to one hemisphere threatens to impair the function of the undamaged side as well.

Reports of several-dozen hemispherectomy cases have appeared in the literature and serve as yet another source of information on the development of hemispheric asymmetry of function. The consequences of the operation are a function of the age of the patient at the time of the surgery and which hemisphere is removed. Adult patients with the right hemisphere removed typically show little or no language impairment, but the removal of the left hemisphere generally results in marked aphasia that improves only slightly with time. Similar lateralized effects occur in children. The severity of impairment is directly related, and the prognosis for recovery of language is inversely related, to the age of the child at the time of surgery.[13]

---

*The term *hemispherectomy* is somewhat of a misnomer, for most operations excise only the cortical regions of one hemisphere, sparing many of the subcortical structures.

Several reports have noted that if surgery is performed early enough in infancy, no signs of lateralized deficits in higher mental functions remain in adulthood. This finding suggests that the remaining hemisphere, whether it is the left or the right, is able to take over for the hemisphere that is removed and to perform those functions that would ordinarily be lateralized to the other half of the brain.

It is possible to draw at least two different theoretical conclusions from these data. One is that no shift of functions has taken place in early hemispherectomy cases because lateralization of function is not present in early infancy. A second interpretation is that hemispheric differences are present early in infancy, but the young brain has tremendous ability to reorganize itself in the face of damage to specific regions.

Some recent, in-depth studies of the abilities of patients with left and right hemispherectomies suggests that of the two possibilities, the latter "plasticity" explanation is more likely to be correct. Maureen Dennis and Harry Whitaker have tested early hemispherectomy patients on various language tests and have found very subtle signs of lateralized effects.[14] Standard measures of verbal intelligence do not seem to differentiate between early left and early right hemispherectomy. This does not mean, though, that other tests might not reveal such a difference.

Dennis and Whitaker studied three 9- to 10-year-olds who had undergone hemispherectomy by the age of 5 months. One was a right-hemispherectomy patient; the other two had had the left hemisphere removed. Results showed that both discrimination and articulation of the sounds of speech were normal in all three children. The three were also equally good at producing and discriminating between words. Important differences between the hemispheres, though, appeared in tests of the patients' ability to deal with syntax—the rules for combining words into grammatically correct sentences. For example, each child was asked to judge the acceptability of the following sentences:

1. I paid the money by the man.
2. I was paid the money to the lady.
3. I was paid the money by the boy.

The right-hemispherectomy patient correctly indicated that sentences 1 and 2 are grammatically incorrect and sentence 3 was acceptable. The two left-hemispherectomy patients did not make these distinctions.

The researchers concluded that the right hemisphere in the left-hemispherectomy cases does not accurately comprehend the meaning of passive sentences. Other tests led them to conclude that the right-hemisphere defect is an organizational, analytical, and syntactic problem rather than one rooted in the conceptual or semantic aspects of language. The results suggest that there are limits to the plasticity of the infant brain and, more importantly for our purposes, that the asymmetries between the hemispheres are present very early in life.

Although plasticity appears to operate within limits, it nonetheless plays an important role in much of the dramatic recovery from aphasia that is found following left-hemisphere damage in children. The ability of a brain to readjust its function relatively quickly makes it hard to distinguish between a system where lateralization does not exist or exists only in rudimentary form, and one where lateralization is extensive but rapid compensation for unilateral damage is possible. Only through the use of very sensitive tests designed to measure subtle differences in performance can we begin to tease apart these alternatives.

## Does Lateralization Change Over Time?

A good deal of the evidence we have just reviewed suggests that hemispheric differences, both functional and anatomical, are present at birth. What changes in this early lateralization take place as the infant matures? How, if at all, does asymmetry change over the life span of a human being?

The brain of most mammals, including humans, is largely underdeveloped at birth and undergoes a major portion of its structural and functional maturation in infancy and early childhood. In addition to its obvious growth, the brain undergoes dramatic changes at the microscopic level. The connections between neurons multiply tremendously in the first few years and are thought to continue changing throughout a person's life time. In addition, insulating fatty layers called myelin are laid down around nerve fibers, making them more efficient conductors of electrical impulses.

The corpus callosum is present at birth but appears disproportionately small in cross section when the brain of a newborn is compared with the brain of an adult. Figure 7.1 shows the growth of the cerebral commissures during three stages of human development. Some investigators feel that the slow maturation of the neocortex and the interhemispheric fibers leads to differential development of the two sides of the brain during the postnatal period.[15]

The fact that the effects of unilateral brain damage occurring early in life contrast with the effects of later damage certainly suggests that important changes in the brain occur with time. Language impairments following damage to the left hemisphere are generally less severe and of shorter duration the younger the individual is at the time of the

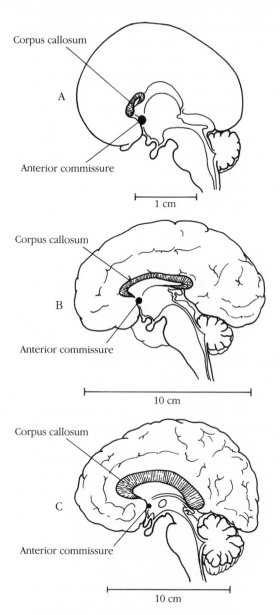

**7.1** The corpus callosum and anterior commissure at three stages of human development. A. Fetal (16 weeks). B. At birth (40 weeks). C. Adult. (From C. Trevarthen, "Cerebral Embryology and the Split Brain," in *Hemisphere Disconnection and Cerebral Function,* Fig. XI-7, pp. 228–229, M. Kinsbourne and L. Smith, eds., 1974. Courtesy of Charles C Thomas, Publisher, Springfield, Illinois.)

injury. Does this imply that lateralization becomes more extensive or complete with age? Not necessarily. Another interpretation of these brain-damage findings is that the plasticity of the brain decreases with age. That is, as the individual grows older, the right hemisphere loses the ability to take over the control of language.

To answer the question of whether lateralization itself changes with age, we must obtain measures of lateralization in subjects of different ages and compare the degree of asymmetry present in each age group. This approach has been used most extensively in investigations of dichotic listening. The pattern of findings, unfortunately, is not consistent. For example, one large study using 30 children at each of five ages (5, 7, 9, 11, and 13) in a dichotic consonant–vowel task found a right-ear advantage across all age groups, with the magnitude of the ear asymmetry consistent at all age levels.[16] In contrast, another study using 24 subjects in each of five age groups (6, 7, 10, 12, and 14) found an increase in the magnitude of the ear asymmetry over this age range. The right-ear advantage was significantly different from zero, in fact, in the 12- and 14-year-old groups only.[17] The stimuli employed were syllables as in the previous experiment. In a review paper dealing with the issue of developmental change, the authors tallied four dichotic listening studies showing an increase in asymmetry over this time period and five showing either a mild decrease or a plateau after 3 to 5 years of age.[18]

Other measures have also been used to address the question of change in lateralization with age. Molfese's study of evoked potentials to speech and nonspeech stimuli mentioned earlier in this chapter also involved children between 4 and 11 years of age and adults from 23 to 29 years old.[19] Analyses showed that the asymmetry in the size of the EP to the nonspeech stimuli was proportionately greater in the infants than in the children and adults. The speech stimuli resulted in a comparable asymmetry in the infants and children, while both groups showed greater asymmetry in response to these stimuli than did the adults. The authors suggest that the EP asymmetry may decline with age because of the maturation of the cerebral commissures that connect the hemispheres. To support their argument they cite anatomical studies showing that the corpus callosum is incompletely developed at birth.

We noted earlier that anatomical asymmetries have been found in infant brains. One study used both infant and adult brains measured in a manner permitting comparison of the degree of asymmetry in the two groups. By expressing the size of the right temporal plane as a percentage of the size of the left temporal plane, a measure independent of absolute size is derived. The investigators could then directly compare the infant and adult series. The average R/L ratio was 67 percent for infants and 55 percent for adults, indicating a greater degree of asymmetry in the adults.[20] These findings suggest that the asymmetry in the size of the temporal plane in the two hemispheres increases with age.

Given the variability in outcome of studies using different methodologies, as well as the variability found in studies using the same measure of lateralization, it is clearly premature to draw conclusions regarding change in asymmetry with age. Further research using more refined measures of lateralization should provide the answers.

## The Role of Nature and Nurture
## in the Establishment of Asymmetries

### *Nature*

Much of the evidence reviewed in this chapter suggests that hemispheric asymmetries in some form are present at or near birth. The earlier the age at which asymmetries are detected, the more confident we may be that they are part of the biological makeup of the organism and independent of experience.*

Several genetic models have been proposed to account for hemispheric asymmetries. We reviewed some of them in Chapter 5 in the context of our discussion of handedness. One model, for example, postulates separate genes coding for both left-hemisphere and right-hemisphere dominance; another holds that only left-hemisphere dominance is controlled genetically.

More recently, some investigators have begun to consider other ways, not genetic in the strict sense, in which patterns of lateralization may be inherited. Research has shown that cytoplasm, the fluid contained in all cells including the maternal egg, can transmit certain traits from parent to offspring in some species. Such "cytoplasmic inheritance" has been proposed as a possible basis for the transmission of asymmetry from parent to offspring in human beings.[21]

Because brain asymmetry is not easily observable, it is difficult to evaluate these various models. Different measures of hemispheric asymmetry are available, yet the measures do not always agree in terms of the direction and degree of asymmetry they reveal in a given subject. Philip Bryden has conducted a family study of dichotic listening performance in which he obtained ear-advantage scores for parents and

---

*Asymmetries occurring later may also be part of an organism's biological makeup. Genetic factors may determine the emergence of asymmetries in later stages of development.

offspring in 49 families. Results showed significant positive correlations between parents and offspring in ear asymmetry but negative correlations between siblings.

Both genetic and cytoplasmic models of inheritance would predict positive correlations between siblings as well as parents and offspring. Bryden notes, however, that the ear-asymmetry score is far from an ideal index of hemispheric differences and that until we have better measures it will be difficult to test models of the inheritance of lateralization of function.[22]

## Nurture

What can be said about the role of experience or environmental factors in determining hemispheric asymmetries? At one extreme, we have seen that early damage to one hemisphere of the brain can result in a dramatic reorganization of lateralized functions. The fact that persons with the left hemisphere removed in infancy develop language skills in the right hemisphere is but one piece of evidence pointing to the tremendous plasticity of the brain. The compensation for early removal of one hemisphere, however, is not total. Sensitive tests reveal language deficits, suggesting that the basic blueprint for asymmetry is present very early in life and that its traces remain despite damage-induced reorganization. In our discussions of left-handedness, we noted that some investigators believe all left-handedness (and presumably all right-hemisphere control of speech) is a result of brain injury, however subtle.

Other evidence has suggested that the quality and quantity of exposure to language itself may affect the development of lateralization. Several studies have looked at the effect of socioeconomic class (SEC) on hemispheric asymmetries as measured by behavioral tests. In one experiment, 104 right-handed children from 4 to 7 years of age from low SEC backgrounds were matched for age and sex with 104 right-handed children from middle SEC homes. All were then given a dichotic digits test. Results revealed a significant right-ear superiority in the 4-, 5-, 6-, and 7-year-old children from the middle SEC group, while only the 7-year-olds from the low SEC group showed a right-ear advantage.[23]

In another study, a right-ear advantage was found in both low SEC and middle SEC children, but the middle SEC children showed right-ear advantages of significantly greater magnitude.[24] SEC differences in the ear asymmetry have not been found in all studies that have looked for them.[25] But if the differences are real, they suggest that environmental factors correlated with SEC affect lateralization of function.

A very different type of finding that also points to early environment as a factor in asymmetry is based on the study of Genie, an adolescent girl who endured eleven and a half years of extreme social and experiental deprivation. Genie was discovered at the age of 13½ after having spent most of her life in almost complete isolation, during which time she was punished for making any noise whatsoever. Two years after she was found, she was reported to have made slow but steady progress in language learning. This fact is of considerable significance for the theoretical issue of whether a first language may be acquired after puberty.

Of particular interest to us here, though, is Genie's performance on dichotic listening tests. Two special tests were prepared for her. One was composed of familiar words, the other familiar environmental sounds. Genie was able to identify correctly each of these stimuli when she was tested one ear at a time. This finding is typical. When the words were presented dichotically, however, her performance departed markedly from what was expected. Instead of the moderate right-ear advantage that is generally found in right-handed subjects, Genie showed an extreme left-ear advantage. Her left ear performed perfectly, while the performance of her right ear was at chance level. For the environmental sounds Genie showed a small left-ear advantage, in keeping with the prediction that such sounds are processed more efficiently in the right hemisphere.[26]

On the basis of dichotic listening performance, then, it appears that the processing of language and nonlanguage stimuli is taking place in Genie's right hemisphere. The investigators working with her have argued that her left hemisphere may have begun language acquisition before her confinement but through disuse was no longer able to fulfill its original function. As Genie began to learn language a second time, the right hemisphere assumed control because its functions had presumably been exercised (by visuo-spatial processes) in spite of her confinement.

The problem with a single-subject study such as this is that we have no way of knowing the pattern of asymmetry that would have developed in Genie's brain had she had a normal childhood. Perhaps she would have shown right-hemisphere specialization for language and nonlanguage stimuli anyway. Nevertheless, the results are intriguing, especially in light of work looking at hemispheric asymmetry in the congenitally deaf.

Walter McKeever and his colleagues at Bowling Green State University have used tachistoscopic presentation to compare the degree of lateral asymmetry in normal subjects and in congenitally deaf persons. They argued that if experience with auditory stimuli plays a major causal role in the lateralization of language, congenitally deaf persons should show smaller visual-field differences for linguistic stimuli than hearing subjects. In several different tasks with words and letters as stimuli, they found that both groups showed a right visual field superiority in identification, but the differences were considerably smaller for the congenitally deaf subjects. They concluded that auditory experience is a major determinant of lateralization of visual language processing in humans.[27]

## In Summary

Although investigators are far from having definitive answers to the questions posed in this chapter, a pattern of findings is emerging.

Of great theoretical significance are the observations suggesting that hemispheric differences are present at birth. In apparent conflict with the lateralization-at-birth view is clinical evidence showing that the effects of very early unilateral brain damage do not vary as a function of the side of injury. The latter data, though, are compatible with the lateralization-at-birth position if we take into account the plasticity that allows the young brain to compensate for the effects of damage. In this context we pointed to the importance of tests that are very sensitive to subtle impairment and could perhaps differentiate between the results of damage-induced reorganization and the absence of lateralization in the first place.

Research investigating the time course of lateralization and the factors that affect it is difficult for several reasons. First, our measures of laterality are far from perfect. Does failing to find differences between the hemispheres mean such differences do not exist? Can we be sure that we have not simply failed to set up conditions that would allow us to detect true differences?

A related issue is that many tests are apparently sensitive to factors other than brain lateralization. In Chapter 3 we discussed how differences in the way a task is approached can dramatically affect the type of asymmetry observed in behavioral tests. Perhaps any differences found in hemispheric asymmetry as a function of age reflect different strategies adopted by the subjects rather than differences in lateralization per se.

A second major problem in studying factors involved in lateralization is related to the difficulty of answering nature–nurture questions with human beings in general. We are severely limited in the kinds of environmental effects that can be studied, and genetic models frequently cannot be adequately tested.

The state of affairs is a challenging one for which there are no simple solutions. As more and more investigators appreciate the significance of the developmental issues and the care with which they have to be investigated, we can expect progress toward some answers.

# 8

# Asymmetries in Animals

Do animals show any evidence of lateral asymmetries similar to those found in humans? Are there differences between the left brain and right brain in creatures other than human beings? Scientists have asked this question for several reasons.

Research demonstrating the existence of hemispheric asymmetries in animals would have important implications for our understanding of the origin and significance of asymmetry in humans. Some people have argued that brain asymmetry is intimately related to higher linguistic abilities. The presence of hemispheric differences in nonlinguistic animals would suggest that this view is not correct. The asymmetries found could then provide clues to the actual evolutionary basis for brain asymmetry. On the other hand, convincing evidence pointing to the absence of asymmetries, even in the closest evolutionary relatives of human beings, would argue that brain asymmetry is unique to *Homo sapiens* and is perhaps fundamentally related to language ability.

On a practical level, research on hemispheric differences in human beings would progress more rapidly if it were possible to study similar asymmetries in animals. Experiments on brain asymmetry involving surgical and environmental manipulations that are not possible with people could be conducted with animals showing hemispheric specialization.

In this chapter we will review the evidence that has emerged from the search for asymmetries in animals. The data, though often conflicting or inconclusive, are also often tantalizing and inspire speculation about the origin of brain asymmetries.

## What Paw Does Your Dog Shake Hands With?

The most obvious sign of lateralization in humans is handedness. Thus investigators have looked for paw or limb preferences in animals as evidence of brain lateralization, and they have found that many species do show such preferences.[1] Cats typically use one paw in tasks that involve reaching for an object. Monkeys too use one limb predominantly in unimanual tasks. Even mice show consistent preferences in a task in which they must use one paw at a time to reach for food.

Although the pattern of limb preference in a given animal bears some resemblance to hand preference shown by human beings, there is an important difference. Approximately 50 percent of the cats, monkeys, and mice show a preference for the right paw, and 50 percent show a preference for the left paw. This is strikingly different from the breakdown found in human beings—90 percent right-hand preference, 10 percent left-hand preference.

The 50–50 split in animals has led some investigators to propose that paw preferences are the result of chance factors. According to this hypothesis, the limb first used by an animal is determined by chance. The additional dexterity gained as a result of the experience increases the probability that the same limb will be used again. This kind of use–dexterity loop rapidly produces preference for that limb in the animal under consideration. Some support for such a mechanism has come from geneticist Robert Collins' work with paw preference in mice.

Collins compared the predictions of the chance, environmental model of paw preference with predictions that follow from the assumption that paw preference has a genetic basis. If a trait is under genetic control, it should be possible to select for it. That is, if individuals with the trait are selectively mated, each successive generation should show a higher incidence of the trait. If the trait is determined by chance, however, no such increase across generations should occur.

Collins began his study by mating mice that shared the same paw preference. In the next generation, he mated those offspring who showed the same paw preference as the parents. After repeating this selective inbreeding three times, Collins looked at the proportion of left-pawed and right-pawed offspring in the last generation. He found a 50–50 split, the same proportion he had started with in generation 1.[2]

Collins interpreted his data as evidence against genetic control of lateral preference in mice and argued that chance is the determining factor in such preferences. His data, of course, speak only to the question of the basis for paw preference in mice. Selective inbreeding studies have not been reported for other animals. However, we can say with some assurance that the favored paw in animals showing a preference is equally likely to be the left or the right. Human beings appear to be the only animals with lateral preferences strongly biased in one direction.

Although the paw preference data are not particularly encouraging for those seeking evidence of fundamental hemispheric asymmetries. in animals, it is important to remember that the relationship between hand preference and hemispheric specialization in human beings is also less than clear-cut. With this in mind, investigators have turned to more direct tests of hemispheric asymmetry of function in animals. They frequently employ the same approaches that have proved useful in studying brain asymmetries in human beings.

## Damage to One Hemisphere:
## Are the Effects Asymmetrical?

Many studies have looked at the kinds of deficits in behavior that follow surgical lesions in specific brain structures. In general, deficits following lesions on one side only (unilateral lesions) are less serious than those that follow bilateral brain damage, regardless of which side the lesion is on. In monkeys, for example, studies have shown that visual discriminations involving color, shape, and orientation are disturbed equally by lesions in a particular region of the left or right hemisphere and the deficits are independent of the monkey's limb preferences.[3] Figure 8.1 shows a typical visual discrimination test. Deficits in the discrimination of complex sequences of auditory stimuli following damage to the auditory region have also been shown to be independent of the side of the lesion.[4]

More recently, however, James Dewson of Stanford University has reported some evidence for hemispheric asymmetry in monkeys in a complex, cross-modal matching task.[5] In this task, monkeys are taught to push a red light after hearing a tone and a green light after hearing a brief noise. The test is conducted with varying delays between the presentation of the noise or tone and the appearance of the lights. The task is a difficult one for monkeys, particularly at delay intervals as long as 15 seconds.

Dewson taught the task to six monkeys and then removed part of the temporal lobe on one side of the brain in each of the six. After

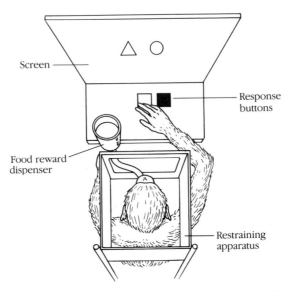

**8.1** Visual discrimination training. A monkey is positioned in front of a screen and a panel containing several buttons. The animal receives a reward such as a raisin if it presses the black button when a pair of similarly shaped figures appear on the screen. It is also rewarded for pressing the white button if the figures are dissimilar.

surgery, the four monkeys with lesions on the left side could no longer do the task when the delays were longer than 2 seconds. The two monkeys with right-side lesions continued to perform normally even at the longest delays.

Dewson's data suggest that animals, or at least monkeys, do show some evidence of hemispheric specialization. Why haven't other lesion studies produced similar results?

Charles Hamilton of the California Institute of Technology has reviewed the evidence on asymmetries in animals and makes two important points.[6] First, the Dewson study and some other studies that have reported asymmetries are based on a very small number of animals. The results are suggestive but cannot be considered definitive until they are replicated on larger numbers of animal subjects. Type I errors are a problem in animal studies as well as in laterality research with humans; the best safeguard against such errors is successful replication.

Hamilton's second point is the importance of the tasks used to study hemispheric asymmetry in animals. He notes that many experiments, particularly those involving visual discriminations of simple patterns and objects, would probably fail to reveal evidence of hemispheric asymmetry in human beings. What is needed are tasks that are sufficiently complex to tap the brain asymmetries that may exist in animals. Dewson's delayed cross-modal matching task certainly meets the criterion of complexity, but it is a difficult one for monkeys to learn.

## Split-Brain Research With Animals

Split-brain studies are also used to test for hemispheric specialization in animals. We have already considered at some length what has been learned about brain asymmetry from split-brain studies with human beings. We noted that findings from animal research played an important role in the decision to try split-brain surgery with epileptic patients. More recently, the dramatic results of human split-brain research have led to a renewed interest in the work of investigators searching for brain asymmetries in other species.

In principle, split-brain research is ideal for this purpose. Cutting the fiber bands that connect the two hemispheres allows the investigator to study separately the abilities of each half of the same brain. Except for possible hemispheric differences, which are the object of the research in the first place, both hemispheres are genetically identical and have been exposed to the same environmental influences.

In contrast to research with human patients, limited by necessity to persons with epilepsy, generally of long standing, animal studies may be done with healthy animals with two intact hemispheres. Interpretation of any differences that might be found is therefore much more clear-cut. In addition, split-brain research avoids the problem of inferring the function of specific regions of the brain from the effects of lesions in those areas. Lastly, investigators must have some idea in advance about which parts of the brain control specific functions in lesion studies. In split-brain work it is not necessary to localize a function to a specific region; the performance of the whole hemisphere is studied.

What are the results of studies with monkeys and cats investigating the relative abilities of the two hemispheres to learn and perform different types of problems? Results from tests of simple pattern discrimination suggest that the two hemispheres possess similar learning capabilities.[7] A few studies have reported quantitative differences between the hemispheres in learning and performance. However, there are no consistent differences favoring one hemisphere in these studies.[8] The absence of consistency within a study suggests that the differences found may be a consequence of asymmetrical damage resulting from the surgical procedure itself.

Like the lesion work, however, most of the tasks used to study asymmetries in split-brain animals are simple and bear little resemblance to the stimuli and tasks that reveal asymmetries in humans. An exception is several studies by Hamilton that have tested the surgically separated hemispheres of rhesus monkeys with stimuli similar to those that show evidence of asymmetry in humans.[9] Hamilton's studies are models of how research in this area should be done, and we will consider them in some detail.

The work used 18 rhesus monkeys, with equal numbers of left-handed and right-handed, male and female individuals trained in each task wherever possible. The surgery for all animals involved midline division of the optic chiasm, corpus callosum, and the anterior and hippocampal commissures. This procedure allows the experimenter to present stimuli to just one hemisphere by presenting it to the ipsilateral eye. For each task, comparisons were made between the left and right hemispheres, and between the hemisphere contralateral and ipsilateral to the preferred hand. The experimental design also eliminated possible biases from asymmetrical surgical procedures or the order in which the two sides of the brain were tested.

Stimuli were projected on a screen located in front of the monkey. The compartment in which the animal sat allowed the experimenter to determine which eye and hand would be used on a particular trial. Hamilton first ran control experiments to determine the ability of each hemisphere to learn simple visual discriminations. Twelve two-choice discriminations were taught to each animal. Animals were taught to press the screen after seeing one member of each pair and to refrain from pressing after seeing the other. The number of trials needed for the animal to reach a criterion of 90 percent was then calculated for each half of the brain.

The results showed no overall difference between hemispheres in the speed of learning these discriminations, nor was there any systematic relationship between sex, hand preference, or hemisphere retracted during surgery. These control tasks demonstrated that Hamilton had been successful in eliminating some of the biasing factors that may have affected other studies, and they provided further evidence that the two hemispheres of the monkey are equally capable of learning a simple pattern discrimination.

The purpose of the experiment, though, was to test tasks that would have a high likelihood of showing hemispheric differences. Two tasks that would be considered right-hemisphere tasks in human terms were used. The first was a facial recognition task in which monkeys were taught to discriminate colored pictures of two monkeys with each hemisphere. Five different pictures of each of the two monkeys were used to reduce the probability that the monkeys would perform the task on the basis of some incidental feature and not the face itself.

The second task was a series of spatial discrimination tests involving (1) two-dimensional drawings of horizontal surfaces that receded toward the horizon from either above or below eye level; (2) lines of different orientation, 0 versus 135 degrees and 45 versus 90 degrees; and (3) a spiral form rotating clockwise or counterclockwise. Again, the monkeys were taught to press the screen in the presence of one member of each pair of stimuli and to refrain from pressing in the presence of the other.

These are difficult tasks for monkeys, but with many weeks of training they can learn to perform them. Results from these tests did not provide any evidence for hemispheric asymmetry of function in rhesus monkeys of the sort that favors the right hemisphere in humans.

Hamilton also employed a more analytic, left-hemisphere task with his animals to see whether asymmetry would be observed. In this task, the monkey was rewarded for a response to two successively presented stimuli that were the same. If the two stimuli were different, the animal was rewarded for withholding a response. The task can be made more difficult by increasing the time between stimuli; the data, however, showed no hemispheric asymmetries even at the longer delays.

Despite the absence of hemispheric asymmetries in these experiments, Hamilton has found evidence for differences in what each hemisphere likes to see. In this study, the monkey holds down a lever for a specified period of time to obtain food. Independent of its relationship to the food, the lever also controls the presentation of a picture projected on a screen in front of the monkey. If the lever is released and then pressed again, the picture changes. Since the lever may be released and pressed again without affecting the food reward, this procedure provides a way to measure a monkey's preference for various pictures.

Hamilton's data using this task suggest that there may be consistent differences between the hemispheres of the same monkey in preferences for pictures. This work is preliminary but promising and suggests that the left hemisphere has a greater preference than the right for viewing colored pictures, especially photos of other monkeys and people, over viewing a plain white screen.

## Anatomical Asymmetries in Animals

Anatomical studies have suggested that in the temporal lobe region of some nonhuman primates there may be structural asymmetries between the hemispheres similar to the asymmetries found in human brains. In one study, comparable measurements were made in the brains of 25 humans, 25 chimpanzees, and 25 rhesus monkeys. Results showed asymmetries favoring the left hemisphere in humans and to a lesser extent in chimps, but no significant differences between sides in the rhesus brain.[10]

Another study examining the brains of a variety of monkeys and apes reached a similar conclusion. Sixteen out of 28 great apes (orangutan, chimp, and gorilla) showed an asymmetry favoring the left hemisphere. One showed the opposite. In contrast, only 3 cases among 41 monkeys and lesser apes (gibbon and siamong) showed a sizable asymmetry.[11] Skull size rather than brain size has been studied by another investigator. In this study examining skull length in three species of gorilla, only the mountain gorilla showed evidence of gross asymmetry. The other species did not.[12]

It is tempting to speculate that these asymmetries are related to the ability of the apes, particularly the chimp, to learn language. Chimpanzees have shown an ability to learn words, some grammar, and even some abstract concepts through the use of sign language or the manipulation of plastic symbols.

Some investigators believe the anatomical asymmetries in the great apes are a reflection of their having reached a "prelinguistic" evolutionary stage where their thought patterns are similar to those of humans but much more primitive. Theorizing about the possible evolutionary significance of these asymmetries should be tempered, however, by our lack of knowledge concerning the relationship between anatomical differences and functional differences.

## Behavioral Tests

We have reviewed lesion, split-brain, and anatomical studies of hemispheric asymmetries in animals. In many respects the search for asymmetries in animals has followed a progression similar to that of laterality research with human beings. A major difference between the human and animal research, however, lies in the role played by behavioral studies. Behavioral work forms a large part of the literature on human laterality; but, with the exception of research on paw preference, there have been very few studies involving behavioral approaches to hemispheric differences in animals.

One recent study, however, fits nicely into this category, and we will present it here because of its relevance to the issue of asymmetry in animals as well as the cleverness of its methodology. The study involved teaching Japanese macaque monkeys to discriminate two different types of vocalizations made by Japanese macaque monkeys. The sounds were prerecorded and presented to the left or right ear in a random sequence. The investigators found that all five of the monkeys tested performed more accurately when the sounds were presented to the right ear. Only one out of five monkeys of other species showed the ear asymmetry when presented with the Japanese macaque vocalizations.[13]

If we assume that sounds presented to the right ear are preferentially delivered to the left hemisphere,* these results suggest a hemispheric asymmetry in Japanese macaques for the processing of vocalizations produced by members of their own species. This, of course, is precisely what we find with human subjects. If these results can be replicated, they open up the exciting possibility that there is at least one hemispheric asymmetry in primates that has striking parallels to hemispheric asymmetry for speech in human beings.

## Avian Asymmetries:
## What the Bird's Brain Can Tell Us

Up to this point we have confined our review of asymmetries in animals to studies working with mammals, in particular the nonhuman primates. There is some evidence to suggest the existence of asymmetries in these species, but the evidence is far from clear-cut. Given this background, it is especially interesting to note that researchers working at Rockefeller University have discovered a striking asymmetry between the halves of the brain in an unexpected source—song birds. To appreciate their findings, we must make a brief digression to consider how bird song is produced.

The vocal system of birds consists essentially of a set of bellows that act on an air-driven structure called the syrinx. The position and tension of tissue folds and membranes in the syrinx determine the frequency and amplitude of the sounds produced. The syrinx is divided into a left half and a right half, which are controlled independently by the left and right hypoglossus nerves, respectively.† Song birds typically develop song during the first year of life. They require auditory feedback to both acquire and maintain normal song.

Fernando Nottebohm and his colleagues demonstrated that sectioning the left hypoglossus in adult chaffinches and canaries results in

---

*It is normally assumed that dichotic presentation involving simultaneous presentation of material to the two ears is necessary to lateralize auditory inputs. A few studies, however, have reported monaural ear differences in human subjects.

†Notice that control of the syrinx is same-sided or ipsilateral, in contrast to the crossed or contralateral control we have come to expect.

a dramatic change in song. Most of the song components disappear and are replaced either by silence or by poorly modulated sounds. The sectioning of the right hypoglossus, in contrast, has minimal effects on song; for the most part, song remains intact.[14]

Further work has shown that the right hypoglossus may come to control song to varying degrees, depending on the age at which the left hypoglossus is cut. Canaries with the left hypoglossus cut within two weeks after hatching develop song of normal complexity that is completely controlled by the right hypoglossus. Birds operated on as adults also show some plasticity in that they can learn new song under control of the right hypoglossus. The end result, though, is less accomplished than that produced by intact canaries and canaries with damage occurring earlier in life.

These asymmetries in control of bird song appear to extend to the highest vocal control stations in the brain itself. Results show that lesions of the left hemisphere produce a song almost completely lacking in structure, without any of the components that were present preoperatively. In contrast, the song in right-lesioned birds retains its structure, although some components are lost. With time, canaries with damaged left hemispheres recover their ability to sing; the right hypoglossus assumes control as it did when the left hypoglossus was cut. Here too, though, the resulting song is less accomplished than that found in normal birds.

### In Summary

Comparative research with nonhuman species may help to answer two fundamental questions about brain lateralization. One is why there are asymmetries in the first place. The other is why such asymmetries are generally consistent in their direction: why is speech usually represented in the left and not in the right hemisphere?

Research with song birds and other animals suggests possible answers to each of these questions. The general similarity of Nottebohm's findings with song birds and the situation with human-brain damage and speech is quite startling. Both, perhaps, may be the by-products of selective evolutionary processes operating to ensure optimal control of the vocal apparatus needed for song and speech.*

With regard to the issue of the direction of asymmetries, embryologists have noted that in many species the left side normally develops slightly faster than the right side.[15] This difference may be the basis for

---

*It is also possible that the asymmetries in birds and humans are unrelated, having evolved independently and serving different adaptive functions.

consistency in the direction of asymmetries when they are found. The hemisphere developing fastest may assume control of functions that are represented in a lateralized fashion.

Although these ideas are speculative, they are representative of the problems that neuroscientists wishing to understand lateralization are starting to confront. By extending the search for asymmetries beyond human beings, researchers have begun the process of discovering the answers.

# 9

# Pathology and the Hemispheres

Research in the area of hemispheric differences has had an impact on many fields involved in the investigation of human function and dysfunction. In Chapter 1 we discussed some of the clinical symptoms of damage to the right and left hemispheres. In this chapter, we will consider some other disabilities and abnormalities in human behavior that have been related to the division of function between the hemispheres.

Is stuttering the result of competition for control of speech by the two hemispheres in a less than normally lateralized individual? Does incomplete lateralization predispose a child to reading problems, despite otherwise normal intelligence? Why does psychiatric depression seem to respond better to right-hemisphere than to left-hemisphere shock treatment? These are a few of the questions investigators have pursued in an attempt to determine the role of the left brain and right brain in pathological processes.

Some of the evidence we will discuss, such as the connection between schizophrenia and dysfunction of the speech-dominant (usually left) hemisphere, is very indirect and inconclusive. Other relationships, such as the link between a syndrome in which a patient neglects stimuli presented in the left side of space and damage to the nonspeech (usually right) hemisphere, are more widely accepted.

There are at least two ways in which pathological processes can be related to hemispheric asymmetry of function. The pathology can be directly related to dysfunction in one of the hemispheres—that is, to dysfunction of one or more of the hemisphere's specialized abilities. Alternatively, the pathology can be associated with *patterns* of hemispheric asymmetry that differ from normal. Both kinds of dysfunction have been claimed to play a role in pathology.

## Reading Disability:
## A Failure of Dominance?

One of the first investigators to propose a link between lateralization and reading disability was Samuel T. Orton. Orton was a physician who had worked during the early decades of this century with children suffering from reading and writing problems. In the course of his work he noticed that these children sometimes wrote in mirror form, reversing the orientation of individual letters as well as their sequence within a word. For example, the word "cat" might be written "ƚɒɔ," such as it would appear if one viewed "cat" in a mirror. Similarly, these children often reversed letter sequences in reading, so that "saw" was read as "was."

Orton observed that children who made mirror-image reversals in reading and writing also tended to have unstable preferences for one hand. He interpreted this finding as a sign of incomplete cerebral dominance. This association of reading disability and incomplete cerebral dominance led him to propose that the two are related:

> Since the normal pattern in the adult is a concentration of control of the functions under discussion in the hemisphere opposite to the master hand, and since our clinical observations show so wide a variation both in time and degree in the development of a selective preference for either side in many children, it is suggested that these disorders may derive from a comparable variation affecting the essential language areas of the brain and thus rest on a basis largely physiological in nature.[1]

Because the two sides of the brain are symmetrical about the midline, he suggested, information about the visual world is represented in mirror-image form on each side: "The exact symmetrical relationship of the two hemispheres would lead us to believe that the group of cells irradiated by any visual stimulus in the right hemisphere are the exact mirror counterpart of those in the left." Figure 9.1 shows the end result.

Orton argued that information represented in the dominant hemisphere was oriented correctly, while information in the nondominant hemisphere was in mirror-image form. In the absence of sufficiently developed cerebral dominance, the two representations, one normally

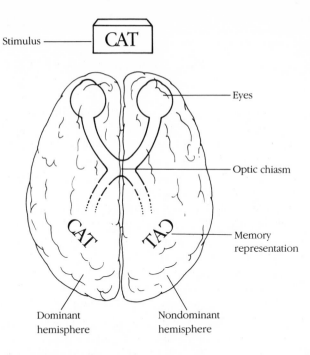

**9.1** Schematic representation of Orton's theory. Orton assumed that a visual stimulus is represented in opposite orientations in the two hemispheres. (From M. C. Corballis, "The Left-Right Problem in Psychology," *Canadian Psychologist* 15, 1974.)

oriented and one reversed, would cause confusion in reading and writing. Orton used the term "strephosymbolia" to describe the condition that would result.

Orton's term for this type of reading and writing difficulty is no longer used, and his ideas of how mirror-image representations are laid down in each hemisphere have been shown to be incorrect. Nevertheless, the basic notion that reading disability may be linked to hemispheric asymmetry is still under active investigation. With the development of behavioral tools to study hemispheric asymmetry, it has become possible to test more directly the idea that reading disability is linked to atypical brain asymmetry. It turns out that Orton may have been right, but for the wrong reasons.

### Behavioral Studies With Normal And Impaired Readers

Dichotic listening tasks have been popular in studies investigating the relationship between lateralization and reading. One of the first studies to use this approach compared the dichotic listening performance of

14 normal fourth-graders with that of 14 boys who had been classified as dyslexic.[2] *Dyslexia* is the term applied in cases where reading disability is present but is not associated with other problems such as sensory impairment, retardation, or emotional difficulties.

The dichotic digits tasks showed a significant right-ear advantage for the normal children and a weak, nonsignificant left-ear advantage for the dyslexics. Consistent with this finding are other studies showing a higher incidence or magnitude of right-ear advantage among good readers than among poor readers.[3]

Lateralized tachistoscopic presentation has also been used to investigate hemispheric asymmetry in dyslexic children. Using letters and words as stimuli, several studies have pointed to greater right visual field superiorities in normal readers than in dyslexic readers.[4]

In contrast to these findings suggesting that dyslexia may be related to the direction and degree of hemispheric asymmetry are a number of studies reporting no differences between normals and dyslexics on behavioral tests. Both dichotic listening and tachistoscopic studies have reported comparable asymmetries for both groups using verbal stimuli.[5] One study even reported a right visual field effect larger for dyslexic subjects than for normal ones.[6] The authors proposed that too much lateralization can adversely affect reading ability. This, of course, is the opposite of Orton's view that too little lateralization poses a problem for reading.

What can we make of this diversity of findings? A review of the literature leads to the conclusion that much of the conflict between studies is traceable to the way in which the investigators defined their subject populations. Dyslexia is not a unitary disorder; it may take different forms, each probably having different causes. The dyslexic children most likely to show reduced asymmetry in behavioral tests appear to be those with deficits that extend beyond reading difficulties to include auditory-linguistic deficits—problems with the sounds of language and language more generally.

Up to this point we have concentrated on the hemispheric organization of linguistic functions. Are there differences between normal and dyslexic children in hemispheric specialization for spatial functions? One large-scale study by Witelson using dichaptic stimulation, discussed in Chapter 6, suggests that there are.[7]

When given two novel forms to feel simultaneously, one in each hand, normal children were better able to make a visual match to the form held in the left hand. Dyslexic children, however, showed no differences. The same study failed to find any differences between the groups on a verbal dichotic listening task. Witelson concluded that developmental dyslexia may be associated with bilateral representation of spatial functions and left-hemispheric representation of language functions. She argued that the existence of spatial functions in both hemispheres may disrupt left-hemisphere language functions during the reading process.

Still other work suggests that when the recognition of faces is studied with lateralized tachistoscopic presentation, the performance of dyslexic children is similar to that of normal readers.[8] Thus, dyslexics may show bilateral representation of certain aspects of presumed right-hemisphere function (visual–tactile matching of forms), but other aspects (face recognition) are lateralized to the same degree as in normals. These findings emphasize the importance of the specific task in the outcome of lateralization studies. Certain tasks may lead to one set of conclusions; others can lead to very different conclusions.

### Anatomical Asymmetries in Dyslexics

Some anatomical evidence pointing to a relationship between brain asymmetry and dyslexia have been reported recently.[9] Computerized brain scans were obtained for 24 patients classified as developmentally dyslexic and ranging in age from 14 to 47. Six were left-handed.

Measurements of the width of the brain in the region where the parietal and occipital lobes meet were made on each side and then compared. Results showed that 42 percent of the patients had brains with parieto-occipital regions wider on the right side than on the left, and 33 percent had brains wider on the left. Twenty-five percent showed virtually no asymmetry.

When data from dyslexic patients was subdivided by handedness, 50 percent of the left-handers and 39 percent of the right-handers showed a reversal of the asymmetries found in normal subjects. Only 9 percent of the normal left-handers examined showed wider parieto-occipital regions on the right. It is also interesting to note that the patients with reversals of brain asymmetry had lower scores on tests of verbal intelligence than did the patients with normal patterns of asymmetry, although there were no differences between the two groups in performance or nonverbal IQ.

The authors emphasize that a reversal of brain asymmetry alone is not sufficient to produce dyslexia. The incidence of dyslexia in the population is from 1 to 3 percent; brain-asymmetry reversal is considerably more frequent. They suggest that reversal interacts with other factors to produce dyslexia. From their data, though, they estimate that individuals with reversals in brain asymmetry are at five times greater risk for dyslexia than are other individuals.

*Evaluating the Evidence*

The data just presented are highly suggestive of a relationship between brain lateralization and reading disability, although differences among subjects and tasks clearly play an important role in the outcome of such studies. Even if this relationship were to be reliably established, however, we could not be sure that the extent or type of brain lateralization *determined* reading abilities.

Orton assumed that weak cerebral dominance caused reading disability. One could just as easily argue from the data we have reviewed that some third factor is responsible for the relationship we observed and that there is no direct causal link between lateralization and reading skill. It is even possible to argue that reading ability itself may affect lateralization. Good readers may spend more time reading than poor readers, and this could conceivably affect brain lateralization.

Each of these alternatives must be considered speculative at best, and much additional work will be necessary before these possibilities will be disentangled. For now, it is important to keep two points in mind when considering the relationship between lateralization and reading ability. First, most people who show little evidence of asymmetry (or even reversed asymmetry) on dichotic listening tests and other measures of lateralization do not show any evidence of reading problems. Second, many people with such problems have normal lateralization as measured by these tests. Thus, reduced lateralization is neither a necessary nor a sufficient condition for reading problems. Reading difficulties are a complex class of problems to which many different factors may contribute. Similarly, brain lateralization is but one aspect of a complex of brain functions that provide the neurological substrate for reading.

## Stuttering: The Case for Competition for Control of Speech

Most people have probably heard the claim that it is unwise for parents to try to force a child showing a natural preference for the left hand to use the right hand. It has been argued that such attempts have potentially serious consequences for the child's overall adjustment, including increasing the chances that the child will stutter.

Samuel Orton played an important role in establishing this idea. Orton believed that stuttering in some cases is the result of competition between the hemispheres for the control of speech. In individuals with cerebral dominance well established, the left hemisphere assumed control, whereas those with poorly established dominance were at risk for stuttering. Forcing a child to switch hands against his or her natural preference could disrupt the establishment of dominance and result in a stuttering problem. In his own practice with stutterers, Orton had observed that children allowed to use their naturally preferred hand after having been forced to use the right hand would stop stuttering.

What evidence links hemispheric organization to stuttering? One piece of evidence sometimes mentioned is the purported higher incidence of left-handedness and ambilaterality among stutterers than in the general population. Since left-handers and ambidextrous people tend to be less lateralized for language functions than right-handers, the increased incidence of left-handedness and ambilaterality among stutterers is certainly consistent with Orton's ideas. Recent studies, however, have challenged the figures showing a higher incidence of left-handedness among stutterers.[10]

The general consensus now appears to be that the frequency of left-handedness is not significantly higher among stutterers than among nonstutterers. In any case, the status of the relationship between hemispheric organization and stuttering should not rest solely on handedness data. Before a convincing case can be made that stuttering is a disorder of cerebral organization, what is needed is direct evidence bearing on the hemispheric asymmetry of stutterers themselves.

Some evidence addressing this question has come from behavioral studies of brain asymmetry. Again, dichotic listening has been a popular technique. One of the first studies showed that 55 percent of adult stutterers had a left-ear advantage in a dichotic task, while only 25 percent of normal subjects showed a left-ear advantage.[11] Later studies, however, have been unable to replicate these findings with either adults or children. No differences were found between normal subjects and stutterers in the size of the ear-asymmetry effect.[12]

Another interesting approach has involved stutterers tested with sodium amytal. One study looked at four stutterers who underwent sodium amytal testing for an unrelated neurological problem.[13] All four of the patients, three left-handers and one right-hander, showed evidence of bilateral control of speech. Sodium amytal was injected on each side on successive days. Speech impairment followed injection on either side.

This is in contrast to the typical sodium amytal finding, in which transient aphasia follows injection on one side (usually the left) but not on the other. Moreover, in each case stuttering was reported to have stopped after the surgical removal, for medical reasons, of one of the presumed speech centers. This finding is perhaps the strongest evidence linking stuttering to the bilateral distribution of speech.

An attempt to replicate the sodium amytal work, however, failed to obtain very similar results.[14] The subjects in this study were four right-handers, only one of whom showed any evidence of bilateral representation of speech. The fact that even one of the right-handers showed bilateral speech is important, however, for it is extremely rare in normal right-handers. The sodium amytal data can thus be viewed as a partial, but certainly not a total, confirmation of the idea that stutterers have speech bilaterally represented in the brain.

The case for the role of brain asymmetry in stuttering is not as strong as that for its role in reading disability. First, far fewer studies have looked for such a relationship in stutterers. Second, stuttering is now viewed as a disorder with many possible causes, only one of which may be related to brain organization. Differences in subject populations could be a major factor in failures to replicate results, and until we are able to identify specific subgroups the replication problem will persist.

What of the claim that forcing a child to switch hands increases the likelihood the child will stutter? At this point we do not know for sure that brain lateralization and stuttering are related, let alone if switching hand usage at an early age has important consequences for the distribution of language functions between the hemispheres. One older study reported that the incidence of stuttering in college students with an early, forced hand switch was no higher than that found in control populations.[15] However, observations such as Orton's persist.

There may well be a link between stuttering and forced switching that is independent of brain lateralization. A general increase in stress may be caused by insisting the child use a hand she or he is not comfortable with. This stress, in turn, may be the factor that is causally related to the stuttering. Relevant to this point is the observation that the incidence of stuttering is not reported to be particularly high in mainland China, a society that has exerted considerable pressure toward the use of the right hand. This would argue against the neurological basis for the link between hand switching and stuttering and would suggest that any association is the result of processes of a different sort.

## Hemispheric Asymmetry and Psychiatric Illness

Within the last decade, investigators have begun to explore the possibility that certain psychiatric disorders, particularly schizophrenia and depression, may involve the hemispheres asymmetrically. The first evidence suggesting such a link came from the clinical study of patients with brain lesions. It was noted that schizophrenic-like symptoms were more likely to occur after lesions on the left side, and symptoms of affective disorders (depression) were more likely to arise after lesions on the right side. Other clinical evidence also pointed to an asymmetric role of the hemispheres in mental illness.

Although the evidence from clinical work was not particularly strong, it meshed well with general notions about the functions of the left and right hemispheres. The thinking disorders and verbal hallucinations that are frequently symptoms of schizophrenia fit with the view of the left hemisphere as the analytic, language half of the brain. The mood disorders characteristic of affective illness are consistent with the conceptualization of the right hemisphere as the half controlling nonverbal functions.

## Observations From the Clinic

Pierre Flor-Henry has presented data bearing on the relationship of hemispheric asymmetry to mental illness from patients with temporal lobe epilepsy.[16] Epilepsy patients are often found to have an abnormality in the part of the brain where the epileptic activity originates. Flor-Henry compared 50 cases of temporal lobe epilepsy that also showed psychotic symptoms with 50 cases without psychotic symptoms. When both groups were subdivided on the basis of left hemisphere, right hemisphere, or bilateral location of the epileptic focus, he found significant differences between the groups. The psychotic group had a greater incidence of left-hemisphere focus than the nonpsychotic group. A further breakdown of the psychotic group into four subgroups based on the nature of their illness suggested that a left-hemisphere focus was more common in schizophrenia and the right-hemisphere focus was more common in affective psychoses.

This work has been criticized on the grounds that the results are weak statistically; other studies, however, have produced results pointing in the same general direction. One large study looked at the effect of head injury sustained during World War II.[17] The Minnesota Multiphasic Personality Inventory (MMPI) was administered to all participants, who were classified into one of two groups on the basis of whether they showed any language deficits as a result of their injury. The investigators found an increased frequency of high scores on the schizophrenic scale of the MMPI in the group with language disturbances. By dividing subjects on the basis of language impairment rather than side of injury, this study more directly addresses the question of the link between impaired language centers and schizophrenia.

Additional clinical evidence pointing to right-hemisphere involvement in affective illness comes from findings on unilateral electroconvulsive shock (ECS), in which current is delivered through electrodes placed on the scalp. Electroconvulsive shock is occasionally used in the treatment of depression and is quite effective in many cases. Although the conventional treatment has generally been bilateral, numerous reports have suggested that posttreatment confusion and memory loss frequently accompanying ECS can be reduced by using electrodes placed on only one side of the head. Furthermore, when unilateral shock is used, it is more effective when applied to the right hemisphere.

These claims have important implications for lateralization of function in affective illness. If the effectiveness of ECS as a treatment for depression varies as a function of the side of the brain to which it is administered, the result is strong evidence for the lateralized nature of the disorder.

Of three well-done studies comparing the therapeutic effect of left, right, or bilateral ECS, two found the left-hemisphere-only condition to be less effective in relieving depression than the right-hemisphere-only treatment. One study found no difference.[18] The studies assessed the effectiveness of ECS at least one month after the last treatment by means of a blind evaluation of each patient.

Results in this area are not totally consistent, but the general picture that emerges is one in which depression responds more effectively to right-hemisphere ECS than to left-hemisphere ECS. Thus we have another piece of evidence pointing to the lateralized nature of certain forms of mental illness.

### Behavioral and Electrophysiological Studies

A variety of behavioral and electrophysiological techniques have been used to explore the role of brain organization in mental illness. Some support for the lateralized dysfunction model of mental illness has come from studies of the orienting response measured by skin conductance. When a subject is alert and presented with a novel stimulus, the resistance of the skin on the arm to mild electric current decreases. This is one of several peripheral physiological changes that take place when a person is alerted to something new or different. With repeated presentation, this response diminishes and is said to have habituated.

John Gruzelier and his colleagues studied the skin conductance of both schizophrenic and depressed patients to repeated auditory stimuli.[19] Among the schizophrenics there was a trend in the direction of no response in the left hand. In contrast, the response amplitudes of depressed patients were smaller for the right hand than for the left. Gruzelier notes that these orienting responses are believed to be controlled by the *ipsilateral* hemisphere, so that a left-hemisphere disorder and a right-hemisphere disorder are implicated by his findings in schizophrenia and depression, respectively.

Some evidence consistent with a relationship between brain organization and psychiatric illness has come from work on lateral eye movements. In Chapter 3 we reviewed evidence suggesting that the direction of lateral eye movements (LEMs) after the presentation of a question reflects differential hemispheric activation. Several studies have reported a greater frequency of left LEMs following spatial questions.

In a study of 29 schizophrenic and 31 control subjects, all right-handed, a series of verbal nonemotional, spatial nonemotional, verbal emotional, and spatial emotional questions were presented and lateral eye movements were recorded. Results showed that schizophrenics produced more right LEMs than controls to all but the spatial emotional questions.[20] If one interprets lateral eye movements as a measure of cerebral activation, these findings suggest that schizophrenic patients utilize the left hemisphere to a greater extent than the right, both for questions for which left-hemisphere processing is presumed more appropriate and for questions for which it is not.

A somewhat different approach to the relationship between brain organization and mental illness has been taken by Stuart Dimond and Graham Beaumont.[21] Evidence from post-mortem examinations shows a significant increase in the size of the corpus callosum in chronic schizophrenics. Dimond and Beaumont speculated that the increase reflects compensation for defective interhemispheric communication. To test this hypothesis they used tachistoscopically presented material lateralized to one hemisphere at a time, and they asked subjects to identify the stimuli, which were letters, digits, and abstract shapes. In this condition the schizophrenic subjects performed as well as non-schizophrenic patients and nonpsychiatric medical patients.

When two stimuli were presented simultaneously, however, and the task was modified to require judgments of same or different, differences between the schizophrenic and control patients appeared. The largest differences were found when each of the two stimuli in a pair was presented to separate hemispheres. Smaller differences between schizophrenic and normal subjects were observed when the two stimuli on each trial were presented to the same hemisphere. Figure 9.2 shows the test procedures. Dimond and Beaumont argue that the difficulty had by the schizophrenic patients in the task involving both hemispheres is the result of a defect in communication between the two sides, which is greater than what can be accounted for on the basis of deficits within each hemisphere.

Electroencephalographic measures have been used by Flor-Henry in a study with 28 schizophrenic, 18 manic depressive, and 19 control subjects performing verbal and visuo-spatial tasks.[22] Schizophrenic subjects had significantly more EEG power in the left temporal region than

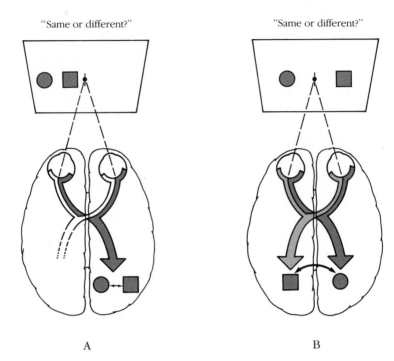

"Same or different?"                              "Same or different?"

A                                                              B

9.2   Intrahemispheric versus interhemispheric same–different judgments. A. When both stimuli are presented in one half of the visual field, they project directly to one hemisphere. B. When the stimuli to be compared are presented to each side of the fixation point, they are initially processed by separate hemispheres. Comparing them involves some information transfer across the corpus callosum.

normal subjects; power in the right temporal region was comparable to that in normals. Manic depressives, however, had more power on both sides of the head in parts of the EEG than did normals, with the right side showing greater power than the left.

### Hemispheric Differences in Emotion

With the exception of the work on the effects of electroconvulsive shock, most of the research we have reviewed makes a stronger case for a link between schizophrenia and the left hemisphere than it does for a link between depression and the right hemisphere. A variety of indirect evidence dealing with right-hemisphere involvement in the control of emotion, however, is available and plays an important role in current thinking about depression and hemispheric differences. We first intro-duced the possibility that the right hemisphere is specialized for the

  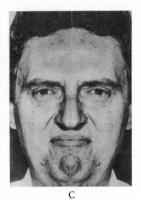

| A | B | C |

9.3 Comparison of the intensity of emotional expression in composite faces. A. Left-side composite. B. Original face. C. Right-side composite. (From H. Sackheim, "Emotions Are Expressed More Intensely on the Left Side of the Face," *Science* 202, Oct. 1978, Fig. 1, p. 434. Copyright © 1978 by the American Association for the Advancement of Science.)

processing of emotional stimuli when we discussed lateral eye movements in Chapter 3. We noted there that the preponderance of left LEMs to emotionally laden questions had been interpreted as a reflection of right-hemisphere involvement in the processing of those questions.

Some clinical evidence has also suggested a role for the right hemisphere in the processing of emotional information. Kenneth Heilman and his colleagues, for example, report that patients with damage in the right hemisphere have greater difficulty picking up on the emotional messages conveyed by speech intonations than do patients with damage in the left hemisphere.[23]

Evidence has also begun to appear pointing to hemispheric differences in the control of emotional expression. In one study, full-face photographs and their mirror-reversals were split down the midline. Composites were put together from two "left sides" or two "right sides."[24] Subjects were asked to rate the intensity of emotional expression evident in a series of such pictures depicting different emotions. Figure 9.3 shows one such face and the composites formed from it.

Left-side composites were judged to express emotion more intensely than right-side composites. The researchers noted the preponderance of contralateral projections controlling facial muscles and argue that these results point to greater involvement by the right hemisphere in the production of emotional expression.

There thus appears to be a good case for believing that the right hemisphere is involved both in the processing of emotional information and in the production of emotional expressions to a greater degree than is the left. Since affective illness is characterized by mood changes, the findings on hemispheric differences in emotion are at least consistent with the idea that affective disorders involve the right hemisphere in some way.

### Some Theoretical Considerations

In our brief review of evidence suggesting a relationship between brain lateralization and psychiatric disorder, we have looked at a number of different ways the question has been studied experimentally as well as clinically. Investigators have proposed three different models of the nature of that relationship. Each of the studies we have reviewed can be interpreted in terms of one or more of these models.

1. The *lateralized deficit model* holds that deficits in one hemisphere are associated with particular forms of mental illness. These deficits are believed to be quite subtle, requiring highly sensitive measures of lateralization to detect them.

2. The *cognitive-style model* views certain forms of mental illness as characterized by atypical modes of information processing that result from nonoptimal utilization of hemispherically linked functions. There are no hemispheric deficits per se; rather, the illness is the result of inappropriate patterns of hemispheric involvement.

3. The *interaction model* ties psychopathology to a problem between the hemispheres, rather than to a deficit in either hemisphere alone. Here, the difficulty is seen to lie in the faulty exchange of information between the halves of the brain.

It is clearly premature to argue strongly for one model over the other. In fact, although all the evidence we have reviewed points to some involvement of brain lateralization in psychopathology, each piece by itself is not particularly compelling. Like reading disability and stuttering, mental disorders probably have a number of different causes, many of which produce the same overall symptomatology. Perhaps brain asymmetry is involved in some forms of schizophrenia and affective illness, but not in all. We need better ways to subdivide patients into appropriate groups. It is even possible that the measures of lateralization themselves may be useful in this task.

## The Neglect Syndrome

A patient in a rehabilitation hospital wakes up in the morning and proceeds to shave his face. When he puts the shaver down to go eat breakfast, one notices that he shaved only the right side. While eating breakfast, the patient starts to look feverishly for his coffee cup until someone points out that it is just slightly over to the left of his dish. At lunch or dinner he may leave the food on the left half of his plate untouched while asking for more, only to be reminded that there is still food on the plate. If asked to draw a clock, the patient will draw a circle correctly but then crowd all the numbers into the right half. If asked to draw a person, he will draw only the right side of the body, leaving out the left arm and leg. If questioned about the drawings, the patient states that they look all right to him.

This phenomenon, known as the *neglect syndrome,* is observed in stroke or accident victims who have fairly extensive damage to the posterior (parietal or parieto-occipital) regions of the right hemisphere.[25] It sometimes occurs after similar damage to the left hemisphere, but much less frequently and in milder form. The impression one gets in observing such a patient is that he or she behaves as if the whole left side of space, and sometimes even the left side of his or her own body, does not exist. Figure 9.4 shows drawings made by a patient with neglect.

Several questions have long been asked about the syndrome. Why is there such blatant inattention to one half of space? To what extent is it related to damage in the visual system? Why are patients with damage to the right hemisphere much more likely to show long-lasting neglect symptoms than patients with equivalent damage to the left hemisphere? The answers are still not clear, but the phenomenon of neglect provides some valuable clues about the working relationship between the left brain and right brain.

Although they may be initially unaware of it, many neglect patients are actually blind in their left visual field. Because information from the left half of visual space is initially processed in the visual area of the right hemisphere, damage there can produce a hemianopic (literally, "half-blind") observer who can't see any object to the left of the point of fixation. This half-blindness, though, does not by itself explain the inattention in neglect patients.

Many examples can be found of patients who are blind to half of the visual field but do not show neglect of that side of space. Patients in whom damage is restricted to the optic-nerve pathways or to the primary visual areas of either hemisphere typically compensate for their half-field blindness through eye and head movements. Patients with damage to the left hemisphere who are blind in the right visual field rarely display the kind of persistent functional neglect to one half of space shown by right-hemisphere patients.

Moreover, some neglect patients are not hemianopic at all. In testing situations, they can accurately report simple visual stimuli flashed alone in the left visual field. However, when stimuli are presented simultaneously in both visual fields, experimentally or in everyday situations, they will report only the items in the right half of visual

Model                    Patient's Copy

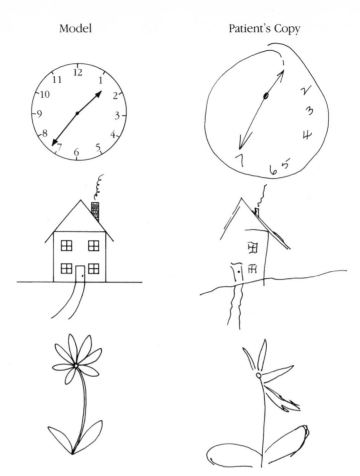

9.4   Drawings by a neglect patient. A patient with a stroke in the
posterior regions of the right hemisphere was asked to copy the model
pictures. Notice the profound neglect of the left side in each of his
drawings. This patient's pictures are quite representative of those of
many such patients.

space. Input from the right field reaching the undamaged left hemisphere appears to interfere with the brain's ability to process input
from the left field coming into the damaged right hemisphere. The left
half of the stimulus is "extinguished" by the right, but the patients see
the left half of the pattern clearly if it is presented alone. Figure 9.5
shows typical stimulus presentations.

The extinction effects seen in these patients explain at least part
of the neglect patient's inattention to the left half of the world. Events
in the right visual field may continuously extinguish information in the
affected left field and consequently lead to orientation only to the right.
This class of nonhemianopic neglect patients is particularly interesting
to investigators of visual perception.

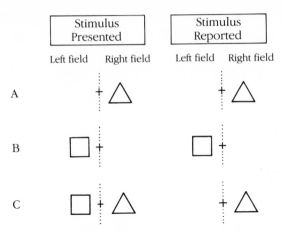

**9.5** Visual extinction. The left column shows three stimulus patterns as they were presented for 100 milliseconds each. The right column shows what the patient reported seeing. In stimulus conditions A. and B. the patient reports stimuli in either half of the visual field. In condition C., however, the patient does not see the item in the left field when another item is present in the right.

What happens to extinguished left-field information? Is it truly lost? Or is it present in the nervous system but unavailable to conscious experience? Several lines of research have studied this question. Some investigators have found that under certain circumstances the patients are able to report what appeared in the left field even when there was stimulation in the right. If forced to guess from among several choices, they perform much better than chance, although they may never acknowledge having actually seen the pattern in the left visual field.[26]

In a somewhat different line of research, patients who normally extinguished the left-field stimulus when two discrete patterns were presented did not do so when a single large pattern crossing the midline between the left and right fields was used. They were consistently able to identify meaningful drawings like a key or safety pin presented on midline, even though relying only on the information in the right half of the drawing would not have provided them with enough information to recognize it.[27] Figure 9.6 illustrates stimuli of this type.

These findings can be interpreted in terms of a speculative but intriguing theory of why the neglect syndrome seems to arise from damage to the right hemisphere. The left hemisphere normally possesses most of the speech and language skills of the brain. Furthermore, work with split-brain patients has shown that their left hemisphere often confabulates incorrect verbal responses based on that part of the

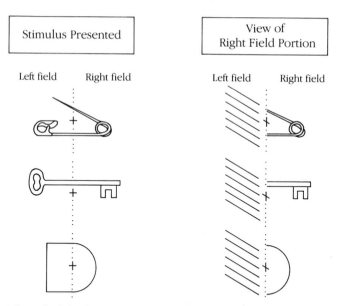

9.6  In the left column are examples of continuous figures used to test bilateral processing in neglect patients. Neglect patients with true left-field cuts (partial blindness) were not able to report what these figures depicted following a 100-millisecond presentation. The right column shows how the stimuli would appear to a patient with a left-field cut. Neglect patients who normally exhibited the extinction phenomenon reported these figures accurately, thus showing bilateral processing ability under certain conditions.

visual information available to it. Perhaps after damage to the right hemisphere, the dominant left hemisphere of the neglect patient acts in an egotistical fashion and assumes that what it sees encompasses everything there is. In other words, the left hemisphere, because it appears to be more self-sufficient than the right on account of its verbal capabilities, is more likely to act as if nothing is wrong in the presence of right-hemisphere damage than would the right hemisphere in the presence of left-hemisphere damage.

In the extinction patients just discussed, the left hemisphere seems very willing to report only information in its visual field as long as it can interpret that information in some comprehensible manner. If it cannot make sense out of what is presented to it, or if there is nothing at all in its field, only then does the left hemisphere make use of some of the information projected to the damaged right half of the brain.

Other explanations as well have been proposed for the asymmetrical nature of the neglect syndrome. One possibility is that mechanisms controlling selective attention or even arousal are lateralized to the right hemisphere. Another possibility is that the right hemisphere is more spatially adept in general and thus, in its absence, the left does a poor job of comprehending space.

These last two theories share the idea that neglect involves damage to centers responsible for proper orientation to the world, centers located in or at least controlled by the right cerebral hemisphere. This is in contrast to the notion of the egocentricity of the left hemisphere, an idea postulating that neglect is a result of the left hemisphere's inappropriate rationalizations in the face of impaired or inefficient input from the right.

We have stressed the visual problems and anomalies usually accompanying the neglect syndrome. Yet many investigators believe that thinking about neglect in purely perceptual terms doesn't capture all its manifestations. A subtle aspect of the syndrome may be independent of any sensory processing problems. An anecdote about a neglect patient serves to illustrate this point.

An Italian neglect patient was asked to *imagine* entering a well-known plaza in Rome from the north end and to describe what he saw. The patient had been very familiar with the plaza prior to his stroke. He proceeded to describe all the buildings to the west—that is, to the right—of where he would have entered, but he failed to mention any of the buildings to the east. He was then asked to imagine entering the plaza from the south and to describe what he saw. The patient proceeded to describe all the buildings in the eastern half of the plaza.

This story suggests that neglect can be independent of visual processing since it even affects the recall of images from memory. If neglect truly is a visual deficit, it must be a high-level one involving complex aspects of perception. The fact that some neglect patients even deny their illness further attests to this point. An understanding of this unusual, lateralized deficit may add in important ways to our knowledge of how the left brain and the right brain contribute to awareness and perception.

## The Role of the Left Brain and the Right Brain in Pathology

The pathologies considered in this chapter are diverse, ranging from stuttering to schizophrenia to neglect of one half of space. Of all the examples, the neglect syndrome is the only one that has been directly tied to lateralized damage. In the other cases a lateralized abnormality of some sort is believed to exist but has not been unequivocally demonstrated. Before attempts are made to apply research findings to the treatment of persons with the sorts of problems just considered, we must be sure that the findings are firmly established.

We repeatedly noted the importance of recognizing that many dysfunctions probably have more than one cause. To assume that similar symptoms always result from the same cause is to oversimplify grossly the intricacies of human brain–behavior relationships. Lateralized dysfunction may be involved in some, but not all, forms of a disorder. It is also important to remember that lateralized dysfunction may not be sufficient by itself to result in a particular problem; other factors may have to operate at the same time before a deficit will occur. We have noted that a full range of patterns of lateralization are observed in normal persons, suggesting that particular patterns of lateralization per se are not sufficient causes for certain deficits.

# 10

# Beyond the Data: Speculative Issues

A great deal more has been said about the left brain and right brain than we have reported in the preceding chapters. Speculation concerning the implications of hemispheric asymmetry has followed closely behind discoveries with split-brain patients and other investigations into the functioning of the halves of the brain. This is not surprising, for great indeed is the temptation to account for observations about our own minds and the varieties of human experience in light of discoveries about the brain.

Much speculation has touched on the nature of consciousness and the existence of different styles of thinking. What does laterality research have to offer the age-old question about the relationship of mind and body (or mind and brain)? Does it provide any experimental evidence for Freud's concept of the "unconscious"? Does each hemisphere in a split-brain patient possess a consciousness of its own?

Does the specialization seen in the hemispheres of normal individuals correspond to distinct modes of thought? Do some people rely more on the left side of the brain, others more on the right? Are there cultural differences in hemisphericity? Do the educational systems of western civilization emphasize so-called left-brain thinking and perhaps neglect the potential of the right brain?

These are some of the popular issues raised by the discoveries discussed in this book. In addition, researchers have posed and attempted to answer on a provisional basis a great many theoretical questions concerning the "how" and "why" of hemispheric special-ization. Why is language localized in the left brain? What is the evolu-tionary reason for lateralization? Just how much of one hemisphere is different from the other? To what extent are the many observed asym-metries a consequence of hemispheric differences in language capacity rather than a sign of some other processing differences? Does the verbal left hemisphere truly dominate behavior? Is it instrumental in creating a feeling of mental unity?

The issues are diverse, and discourse about even one topic may operate at several levels. For example, consciousness is an especially confusing topic because it means different things to different investi-gators. One calls consciousness a style of thinking or a way of viewing the world. Another may use the term to mean "self-awareness." Yet another may mean all the information of which one is aware at a given moment. Despite these and other problems, in this chapter we will survey some of the often complex and frequently controversial ideas that have emerged as investigators have attempted to extend the im-plications of the left brain and right brain beyond the data.

## Two Brains, Two Minds?

Over four centuries ago, the great French philosopher René Descartes concluded that the pineal gland at the base of the brain is the seat of consciousness. He reached his conclusion on the basis of his belief in the unity of consciousness and the fact that the pineal gland was the only brain part he could find that was not double in structure.

Assigning consciousness to part of the body seems an inconsistent twist in Descartes' thinking if one examines his writings on the rela-tionship of body and mind. Although Descartes enjoyed mechanically analyzing some of the functions of living things and had great interest in human anatomy (see Figure 10.1), he felt there was something about human beings that could not be explained in these terms. He saw the human body as similar to the bodies of animals, but he questioned whether the human mind could be part of the same physical world. An analysis of one's own thought, he felt, cannot prove the existence of anything outside personal experience. Descartes concluded that an ab-solute distinction must be made between the mental and the physical.

The assertion that the mind is independent of the body came to be known as Cartesian dualism. Some modern skeptics have referred to it as the "ghost in the machine" idea. The philosophical issues re-volving around the relationship between body and mind in general are referred to as the *mind–body problem.*

Within the past two decades, work with split-brain patients has raised questions about the implications of split-brain surgery for the

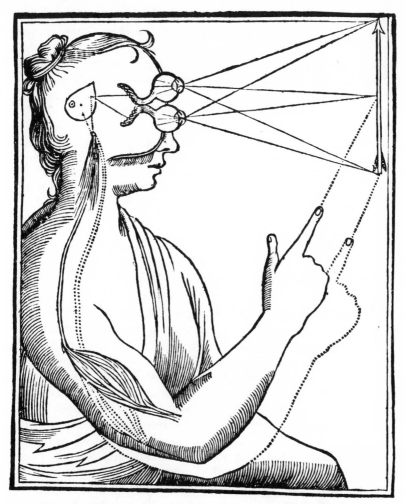

**10.1** Descartes' diagram illustrating the interaction of mechanistic and mental processes in the pineal body. Light reflected from an object (an arrow) is imaged on the retinas of the eyes and conducted by the optic nerves to the brain. There it is apprehended by the soul at the pear-shaped pineal body, which also initiates responsive movements. (Reprinted by permission of Sandford Publications, Oxford, England.)

mind–body problem. If the surgeon's knife accomplishes a separation of consciousness, then splitting the brain *is* splitting the mind. One is then forced, the argument goes, to accept the fact that mind is brain, or at least that mind arises from the workings of the brain.

Although one can argue with the premise that split consciousness implies mind is brain, most of the controversy in this area focuses on whether such patients can actually be shown to possess two realms of consciousness, at least some of the time. In Chapter 2 we noted that this question was discussed on a theoretical level by Gustav Fechner and William McDougall. Fechner argued that the split-brain operation would result in a doubling of consciousness. McDougall argued that consciousness would remain unaffected by such a procedure.

Roger Sperry has argued that the results of split-brain research point to a doubling of consciousness in these patients:

> Everything we have seen so far indicates that the surgery has left these people with two separate minds, that is, two separate spheres of consciousness. What is experienced in the right hemisphere seems to lie entirely outside the realm of experience of the left hemisphere. This mental dimension has been demonstrated in regard to perception, cognition, volition, learning, and memory.[1]

For Sperry, the impression of mental unity in split-brain patients is an illusion, a consequence of the fact that the two sides of the brain share the same position in space, the same sensory organs, and the same experiences in everyday situations outside the lab.

In contrast, Sir John Eccles, winner of the Nobel Prize for his work in physiology, does not believe that there are two separate minds in a split-brain patient or that consciousness is in any way split by commissurotomy.[2] He claims that the right hemisphere cannot truly think. He makes a distinction between "mere consciousness," which humans share with animals, and the world of language, thought, and culture, which is uniquely human and essential to any idea of a mind.

In Eccles' opinion, everything that is truly human derives from the left hemisphere, where the speech center resides and where interactions between brain and mind occur. The split-brain patient who blushes or smiles when a pinup is flashed to her right hemisphere not only can't report why she did so but truly doesn't know why she blushed. The right hemisphere can't know because only the left hemisphere can have thoughts or knowledge.

Although such controversies are highly confounded by subjective definitions of *consciousness,* some attempts have been made to be more precise in using this term. One approach is to form an operational definition. An operational definition of a concept is a definition in terms of the procedures that may be used to measure the concept. Along these lines, Donald McKay, who theorizes about artificial intelligence, has noted that the split brain cannot be viewed as a split mind until it can be shown that each separated half has its own independent system for assigning values to events, setting goals, and establishing response priorities.

Recently, a fascinating experiment to address this point was conducted by Joseph LeDoux and Michael Gazzaniga with their unique commissurotomy patient P. S. The study took advantage of the considerably greater than usual linguistic capabilities in P.S.'s right hemisphere, which we discussed in Chapter 2. P.S.'s right hemisphere was able to express itself by arranging Scrabble letters with the left hand in response to questions. LeDoux and Gazzaniga's intention was to ask subjective questions of each hemisphere separately and to compare the results.

On each trial, P.S. was asked a question orally. The key word or words were replaced by the word "blank." The missing word or words were then visually presented in either the left visual field (to the right hemisphere) or the right visual field (to the left hemisphere). The questions included "who *(are you)?*" "Would you spell the name of your favorite *(hobby)?*" "What is *(tomorrow)?*" The italicized items were the key words actually flashed in the respective visual field. When they were presented to the right hemisphere, P.S. was asked to spell out his answers using the Scrabble letters.

P.S. was also asked to rate how he felt about a particular word by pointing to a number from 1 ("like very much") to 5 ("dislike very much"). Some of the words were chosen because of their personal significance to the patient. They included "Paul" (his name) and "Liz" (his girl friend's name). He would be asked, "How much do you like blank?" and then the appropriate word would appear in either the left or the right visual field.

The results showed both that P.S.'s right hemisphere could answer the questions asked of it and that its answers and evaluations sometimes differed from those of the left hemisphere. For example, ratings by the right hemisphere were consistently closer to the "dislike" end of the scale in the word-rating test than were ratings by the left hemisphere. When asked the job he would pick, the right hemisphere spelled out "automobile race," in contrast to P.S.'s normal left-hemisphere verbal assertion that he wanted to be a draftsman.

LeDoux and Gazzaniga further noted that the answers to a few questions varied in several different testing sessions. Sometimes the answers given by the left and right were similar; sometimes they were discordant. P.S. appeared to be in a better mood on the days when the opinions and values of the left brain and right brain overlapped.

Regarding the issue of double consciousness, the investigators stated:

> Each hemisphere in P.S. has a sense of self and each possesses its own system for subjectively evaluating current events, planning for further events, setting response priorities, and generating personal responses. Consequently, it becomes useful now to consider the practical and theoretical implications of the fact that double consciousness mechanisms can exist.[3]

Although P.S. is a special case because of the extent of verbal capabilities in both of his hemispheres, the theoretical implications of creating double consciousness mechanisms in the same person extend beyond this one case. In addition to illustrating the older claim that splitting the brain can split the mind, LeDoux and Gazzaniga feel that their observations suggest "the nature and origin of those mental qualities unique to man." These, they feel, are dependent on an active language system:

> When this system is absent, as in the right hemisphere of most split brain patients, . . . the organism functions mainly at the perceptual motor level. Though certain cognitive skills can be demonstrated in such instances, the richness and characteristic flexibility of human behavior seems to be lacking in the absence of linguistic sophistication. . . . Add a rich linguistic system to an isolated mass of non-verbal tissue as in the right hemisphere of P.S., and a human being with the capacity to value, aspire, and reflect on life experience emerges.[4]

The idea that consciousness is dependent on language or linguistic processes is not entirely new. Several philosophers and linguists have subscribed to so-called verbal access theories of consciousness. What these theories have in common is the concept that the brain events we experience as conscious are the events processed by the language system of the brain. We shall return to this idea later in the chapter.

## Two Brains, Two Cognitive Styles?

We have seen evidence that, after the surgical division of the two hemispheres, learning and memory can continue separately in the left brain and right brain. Each half of the brain of a split-brain patient is able to sense, perceive, and perhaps even conceptualize independently of the other. Furthermore, in virtually every approach to the study of hemispheric processes, including approaches using normal individuals, findings support the existence of hemispheric differences. In earlier chapters we have dealt with investigators' difficulty in characterizing the differences. Some talk of a verbal–nonverbal distinction. Others argue that the halves of the brain differ in terms of how they deal with information in general.

Since the first split-brain operations, a progression of labels has been used to describe the processes of the left brain and right brain. The most widely cited characteristics may be divided into five main groups, which form a kind of hierarchy. Each designation usually includes and goes beyond the characteristics above it:

| Left Hemisphere | Right Hemisphere |
|---|---|
| Verbal | Nonverbal, visuo-spatial |
| Sequential, temporal, digital | Simultaneous, spatial, analogic |
| Logical, analytic | Gestalt, synthetic |
| Rational | Intuitive |
| Western thought | Eastern thought |

The descriptions near the top of the list seem to be based on experimental evidence; the other designations appear more speculative. The verbal–nonverbal distinction, for example, was the earliest to emerge from split-brain research and behavioral research with normal subjects. The sequential–simultaneous distinction reflects a current, though not universally accepted, theoretical model holding that the left hemisphere tends to deal with rapid changes in time and to analyze stimuli in terms of details and features, while the right hemisphere deals with simultaneous relationships and with the more global properties of patterns. In this model, the left hemisphere is something like a digital computer, the right like an analog computer.

Many investigators speculating on these issues have attempted to go beyond these distinctions. A popularly accepted view of the differences between the hemispheres is that the left brain operates in a logical, analytic manner and the right brain works in a Gestalt, synthetic fashion.

Once one starts using such labels to describe the operation of the hemispheres, several questions come to mind. Are they just convenient descriptions of how the hemispheres deal with information? Or do they imply that the hemispheres differ in their styles of thinking? Is it possible to view the specialized functions of the left brain and right brain as distinct modes of thought?

Historically, philosophers and students of the mind have shown a tendency to divide intellectual faculties into two types. For example, consider the following quotation from a yogic philosopher who wrote in 1910:

The intellect is an organ composed of several groups of functions, divisible into two important classes, the functions and faculties of the right hand, the functions and faculties of the left. The faculties of the right hand are comprehensive, creative, and synthetic; the faculties of the left hand critical and analytic. . . . The left limits itself to ascertained truth, the right grasps that which is still elusive or unascertained. Both are essential to the completeness of the human reason. These important functions of the machine have all to be raised to their highest and finest working-power, if the education of the child is not to be imperfect and one-sided.[5]

Many Western thinkers have also talked of mental organization as if it were divided into two parts. Rational versus intuitive, explicit versus implicit, analytic versus synthetic, are some examples of these dichotomies. More are listed in Table 10.1. Although these terms are quite varied, they do seem to have something in common. Perhaps, as some have suggested, they correspond to the separate processes of the two cerebral hemispheres.

*Table 10.1*
*Dichotomies*

| | |
|---|---|
| *Intellect* | *Intuition* |
| *Convergent* | *Divergent* |
| *Intellectual* | *Sensuous* |
| *Deductive* | *Imaginative* |
| *Rational* | *Metaphoric* |
| *Vertical* | *Horizontal* |
| *Discrete* | *Continuous* |
| *Abstract* | *Concrete* |
| *Realistic* | *Impulsive* |
| *Directed* | *Free* |
| *Differential* | *Existential* |
| *Sequential* | *Multiple* |
| *Historical* | *Timeless* |
| *Analytic* | *Holistic* |
| *Explicit* | *Tacit* |
| *Objective* | *Subjective* |
| *Successive* | *Simultaneous* |

Why so many two-part divisions? Do they label truly distinct and separate qualities, or do they just describe the extremes of a set of continuous behaviors? In other words, are we dealing with all-or-none differences, or are there gradations in between? Some have insisted on the former view because, they claim, it conforms best to a neuroanatomical reality—the existence of the left brain and right brain capable of operating independently. Another view is that the formulation of dichotomies or opposites is just a convenient way of viewing complex situations.

The idea that different modes of knowing are reflected in hemispheric functions has become associated in recent years with psychologist Robert Ornstein. In addition to his electroencephalographic (EEG) studies of hemispheric asymmetry, Ornstein has been interested in the nature of consciousness and its relationship to hemispheric function.

In 1970, Ornstein published a book entitled *The Psychology of Consciousness*. In it he set forth the message that Western men and women have been using only half of their brain and hence half of their mental capacity.[6] He noted that the emphasis on language and logical thinking in Western societies has ensured that the left hemisphere is well exercised. He then went on to argue that the functions of the right hemisphere are a neglected part of human abilities and intellect in the West and that such functions are more developed in the cultures, mysticism, and religions of the East. In short, Ornstein identified the left hemisphere with the thought of the technological, rational West and the right hemisphere with the thought of the intuitive, mystical East.

Many outlandish claims and misinterpretations have followed in the wake of Ornstein's book. For example, some have equated the left hemisphere with the evils of modern society. Ornstein, however, has stressed that the cerebral hemispheres are specialized for different types of *thought*. He also insists that schools spend most of their time training students in what seem to be left-hemisphere skills.

Ornstein has become an advocate of the idea that there are alternate ways of knowing and alternate forms of consciousness. He feels that our intellectual training unduly emphasizes the analytic,

> ... with the result that we have learned to look at unconnected fragments instead of at an entire solution. ... As a result of this preoccupation with isolated facts, it is not surprising that we face so many simultaneous problems whose solutions depend upon our ability to grasp the relationship of parts to wholes. ... Split- and whole-brain studies have led to a new conception of human knowledge, consciousness, and intelligence. All knowledge cannot be expressed in words, yet our education is based almost exclusively on its written or spoken forms. ... But the artist, dancer, and mystic have learned to develop the nonverbal portion of intelligence.[7]

As we have seen, ideas about the nature of hemispheric differences are diverse. They have evolved from verbal–nonverbal distinctions to ever more abstract notions of the relationship between mental function and the hemispheres. In this process, ideas concerning hemispheric differences have moved further and further away from basic research findings. Some have found this progression disconcerting because the distinction between fact and speculation is often blurred. The term "dichotomania" has been coined to refer to the avalanche of popular literature fostered by the most speculative notions. One investigator has noted:

> It is becoming a familiar sight. Staring directly at the reader—frequently from a magazine cover—is an artist's rendition of the two halves of the brain. Surprinted athwart the left cerebral hemisphere (probably in stark blacks and grays) are such words as "logical," "analytical," and "Western

rationality." More luridly etched across the right hemisphere (in rich orange or royal purple) are "intuitive," "artistic," or "Eastern conscious-ness." Regrettably, the picture says more about a current popular science vogue than it does about the brain.[8]

## Cultural Differences in Hemisphericity?

Some attempts by anthropologists to characterize the cognitive process-es of different cultures and subcultures seem similar to many notions about the left brain and right brain. One school of thought suggests that there are qualitatively distinct intersocietal, interclass, and interindi-vidual ways of thinking. Most anthropologists, however, insist that "av-erage" human minds function in the same way regardless of cultural differences. Some have suggested that there is an inconsistency in si-multaneously asserting that the human mind functions the same every-where and that fundamental ways of thinking differ radically with cul-tural background.[9]

One way out of the dilemma is to say that every human brain is capable of more than one kind of logical process, but cultures differ with respect to the processes used to deal with various situations. The idea that within the brain are two different structures capable of qual-itatively distinct logical processes appealed to investigators interested in resolving the "culture–cognition" paradox.

Can differences in cognitive style between cultures be accounted for on the basis of differences in left- versus right-hemisphere usage? One study compared the performance of 1220 persons of varied back-ground, including Hopi Indians, urban blacks, and rural and urban whites, on two tests considered reasonably selective in the hemispheric performance they tap. One test, the Street Gestalt Completion Test, is believed to involve primarily processing in the right hemisphere (see Figure 10.2). The other test, the Similarities Subtest of the Wechsler Adult Intelligence Scale, is thought to involve processing primarily in the left hemisphere. In the latter test, the questions are similar in form to "How are a screwdriver and hammer alike?"

The investigators estimated the relative "right versus left hemi-sphere mode of thought" in each subject group by constructing a ratio of the average Street Gestalt/Similarities scores for each group. High ratios (larger numerator) were interpreted as signifying more right-hemisphere thought; lower ratios (larger denominator) were believed to signify greater left-hemisphere thinking. The results showed rural Hopi Indians to have the highest ratio, followed by urban black women, urban black men, rural whites, and urban whites. The investigators concluded that Hopis and blacks rely relatively more on their right hemispheres in thinking than do the other groups.[10]

10.2 Examples from the Street Gestalt Completion Test. What do these figures depict?

A critique published soon after this research appeared argued convincingly that the reported cultural differences were simply a re-statement of cultural differences on verbal IQ tests rather than evidence for greater right-hemisphere thinking among oppressed groups. The authors stated that there are no appreciable differences between the groups on the Street Gestalt ("right hemisphere") Test and that the groups differ only on the verbal Similarities Subtest. If one is to interpret the findings in hemispheric terms, they conclude, the only thing that can be said is that "the right hemisphere appears to develop similar levels of ability in radically different cultural groups while develop-ment of the left hemisphere is depressed by lack of educational oppor-tunity."[11]

Another problem with this and many studies that claim to show patterns in the use of the two sides of the brain is the questionable nature of the measures employed. Although tests such as the Similarities test certainly seem verbal rather than spatial, it is by no means certain that they are just testing the abilities of the left hemisphere. The situation is even more questionable with many of the standardized nonverbal tests. Many so-called tests of spatial ability have been shown to involve a large and sometimes essential verbal component. At the present time there are no confirmed right-hemisphere-only or left-hemisphere-only tests.

Of course, these criticisms do not rule out the possibility that in certain situations there are cultural differences in hemispheric involve-ment. In Chapter 3 we considered the importance of the subject's strategy in determining the outcome of laterality studies. If specific groups consistently use different strategies in a wide variety of tasks, we would expect to find some evidence of those differences in laterality studies. Studies looking specifically for these effects, however, will re-quire the use of tests that are sensitive to small differences in hemi-spheric utilization.

## Occupational Differences in Hemisphericity?

Do artists make greater use of the right hemisphere than lawyers? The evidence for this and related questions is controversial. Robert Ornstein and David Galin recorded and compared EEG activity over the right and left hemispheres of lawyers and clay modelers (ceramists) while they performed several tasks. The tasks included assembling blocks into specified patterns and tracing a complex pattern viewed through a mirror, both supposedly involving the right hemisphere more than the left. The subjects were also asked to write a description of a passage of prose from memory and to copy a similar passage, tasks thought to involve primarily the left hemisphere.

The investigators expected the lawyers to show more left-hemisphere activity than the ceramists in all these situations. They found that the lawyers showed a greater change in left-hemisphere activity as the task changed. The relationship between differential EEG activity, occupational group, and task, however, was complex and difficult to interpret with any simple generalization.[12]

Some studies to see whether there is differential utilization of the hemispheres in college students pursuing different majors were done at Simon Fraser University by Paul Bakan.[13] Bakan monitored lateral eye movements (LEMs). Among the undergraduates he tested, those who had the most left LEMs were most likely to be majoring in literature or the humanities. Science or engineering majors tended to be right-lookers. If we assume that left LEMs reflect greater right-hemisphere involvement and vice versa, these findings point to differences in occupational hemisphericity—that is, differences in the degree to which individuals in different occupations utilize each cerebral hemisphere.

It is important to keep in mind that effects suggesting differential hemispheric involvement as a function of occupation are generally weak and have failed to replicate in some studies. Differences in the sensitivity of the tests used, as well as variability in the subject populations tested no doubt contribute to these problems. Further work is clearly needed before a strong statement for or against the notion of occupational hemisphericity can be justified.

## Education and the Right Brain

Does an elementary-school program restricted to reading, writing, and arithmetic educate mainly one hemisphere and leave half of an individual's potential unschooled? Is the entire educational system biased against developing right-hemisphere talents?

Joseph Bogen, one of the pioneers of the commissurotomy procedure, has been an especially avid proponent of developing what he calls "appositional thinking" in school.[14] The word "propositional" was adopted by neurologist John Hughlings Jackson in the nineteenth century to describe the left hemisphere's dominance for speaking, writing, calculation, and related tasks. In contrast, Bogen coined "appositional" to refer to the information processing of the right hemisphere in well-lateralized right-handers.

In Bogen's view, society has overestimated propositionality at the expense of appositionality. IQ tests, for example, are aimed at propositional left-hemisphere abilities. Their use is justified by the claim that they predict success in a society that most often measures success monetarily and in terms of productivity. Bogen argues that such measures are very narrow and do not take into account artistic creativity and other not easily quantifiable right-hemisphere skills.

The idea that half of our mental capability is neglected, more precisely the right half, has been appearing with increasing frequency in educational journals, self-help manuals, and a variety of other publications. Articles usually include a background summary of some of the data on laterality along with the author's personal interpretation of what the data mean. Some end with advice about "boosting right-hemisphere thinking" or "training the right hemisphere."

The major business of the left hemisphere, these articles often claim, is the logical representation of reality and communication with the external world. Thinking, reading, writing, counting, and worrying about time are also usually attributed to the left hemisphere. The business of the right hemisphere, in contrast, is said to be understanding patterns and complex relationships that cannot be precisely defined and may not be logical. The qualities of the right hemisphere, an author will state, are essential for creative insight but tend to be inadequately developed.

One writer's statement is representative of a common interpretation of why the right side of the brain is neglected:

> Because we operate in such a sequential-seeming world and because the logical thought of the left hemisphere is so honored in our culture, we gradually damp out, devalue, and disregard the input of our right hemispheres. It's not that we stop using it altogether; it just becomes less and less available to us because of established patterns.[15]

Later in the same article, this author proposes "Ten Ways to Develop Your Right Brain." Here are four examples:

> When presenting information, have a musical background that occasionally drowns out the presentation.
> Give a 30 second explanation of something, and ask people to guess what you're getting at.

One day a week, make it a rule that no one in the office or plant can use the word no. (The right hemisphere has no equivalent of no.) If something is not acceptable, the person must deal with it by saying, "yes, if . . ."

Before a meeting when new speculative thinking is needed, have a ritual idea "dance" and light some punk so you can each read an idea in the smoke.[16]

Our educational systems may be deficient and may limit a broad spectrum of human capabilities. We question, however, the division of styles of thinking along hemispheric lines. It may very well be that in certain stages the formation of new ideas involves intuitive processes independent of analytic reasoning or verbal argument. Preliminary schemes ordering new data or reordering preexisting knowledge could possibly arise from even aimless wanderings of the mind during which a connection is seen between a present and past event or a remote analogy is established. But are these right-hemisphere functions? We don't think it is as simple as that, and there is certainly no conclusive evidence to that effect. Our educational system may miss training or developing half of the brain, but it probably does so by missing out on the talents of both hemispheres.

### Science, Culture, and the Corpus Callosum

After accepting the distinction that the left hemisphere is analytic and the right is intuitive, astronomer–biologist Carl Sagan has gone on to speculate about how the two modes have interacted to generate the accomplishments of our civilization. In his book *The Dragons of Eden,* Sagan describes the right hemisphere as a pattern recognizer that finds patterns, sometimes real and sometimes imagined, in the behavior of people as well as in natural events. The right hemisphere has a suspicious emotional tone, for it sees conspiracies where they don't exist as well as where they do. It needs the left hemisphere to analyze critically the patterns it generates in order to test their reality:

There is no way to tell whether the patterns extracted by the right hemisphere are real or imagined without subjecting them to left hemisphere scrutiny. On the other hand, mere critical thinking, without creative and intuitive insights, without the search for new patterns, is sterile and doomed. To solve complex problems in changing circumstances requires the activity of both cerebral hemispheres: the path to the future lies through the corpus callosum.[17]

Sagan goes on to suggest that intuitive thinking does well in situations where we have had previous personal or evolutionary experience. "But in new areas—such as the nature of celestial objects close up—intuitive reasoning must be diffident in its claims and willing to accommodate to the insights that rational thinking wrests from Nature."[18] Sagan describes science as paranoid thinking applied to nature, a search for natural conspiracies, for connections in data:

> Our objective is to abstract patterns from Nature (right hemisphere thinking), but many proposed patterns do not in fact correspond to the data. Thus all proposed patterns must be subjected to the sieve of critical analysis (left hemisphere thinking). The search for patterns without critical analysis, and rigid skepticism without a search for patterns, are the antipodes of incomplete science. The effective pursuit of knowledge requires both functions.[19]

He concludes that the most significant creative activities of a culture—legal and ethical systems, art and music, science and technology—are the result of collaborative work by the left and right hemispheres. We completely agree. Sagan also suggests, "We might say that human culture is the function of the corpus callosum."[20] This may be true, but not so much because the corpus callosum interconnects "analytic" with "intuitive" thinking but because every structure in the brain plays a role in human behavior, and human culture is a function of human behavior.

## More About Consciousness

### The Origins of Consciousness: Verbal Access Theories

Until as recently as 3000 years ago, members of the group *Homo sapiens* were virtually automatons, lacking both a concept of self-fulfillment and a sense of the brevity of life. They heard voices inside their heads and called them gods. These gods told them what to do and how to act. Their minds were divided into two parts—an executive part called "god" and a follower part called "man." When writing and more complex human activity started weakening the authority of the auditory hallucinations, this "bicameral mind" slowly broke down. The voices of the gods fell silent, and what we call consciousness was born.

This is the radical theory of Princeton psychologist Julian Jaynes. Jaynes proposes that the speech of the gods occurred in the right hemisphere and was heard by the auditory and speech centers of the left hemisphere by means of the cerebral commissures. Perhaps, he suggests, the pattern recognition and spatial processing mechanisms of the right hemisphere were communicating with the left hemisphere through primitive language.

Jaynes supports many of his contentions by reference to ancient literature and to history. He feels that the *Iliad,* for example, describes a people who are not conscious. They don't decide to fight, and they don't plan strategy or do anything else without the intervention of a god or some hallucination:

> These auditory and visual hallucinations, occurring whenever a novel situation arose, show us the structure of the bicameral mind. Achilles, like all bicameral people, had a split mind. One part, the executive god part, stored up all admonitory experience and fitted things into a pattern and told the follower or person part what to do through an auditory hallucination.[21]

To Jaynes, consciousness depends on linguistic processes and the creation of an internal, metaphorical "I." Consciousness is a smaller part of our mental life than we have assumed. A great deal of our mental activity is not conscious but automatic: we don't think about it. This is one reason why it should not be so difficult to imagine ancient humans going through life without the "self-consciousness" we have developed. They may not have been able to view themselves at a distance or to imagine themselves doing something in the future:

> Consciousness is learned on the basis of language and taught to others. It is a cultural invention rather than a biological necessity. . . . We know now that the brain is more plastic, more capable of being organized by the environment than we previously supposed. . . . We can assume that the neurology of consciousness is plastic enough to allow the change from the bicameral mind to consciousness to be made largely on the basis of learning and culture.[22]

Although there is considerable controversy concerning Jaynes' theory, the idea of connecting the voices of gods in ancient times to a stage in the cultural development of language is fascinating. In addition to his view, there are other ways in which the development of language may have been responsible for some of the earlier beliefs of human beings. Instead of equating the voices of the gods with the right hemisphere's attempt to speak to the left, perhaps we should view ancient men and women as having misinterpreted internalized speech developing in the left hemisphere. It is possible that in the early phases of the evolution of language, humans were caught off guard by the fact that they could speak to themselves.

Jaynes' theory is a rather bold example of theories dealing with the topic of consciousness in terms of linguistic mechanisms. Since verbal skills are the most clearly lateralized functions of the brain, such verbal access theories of consciousness lead to questions about the relationship of hemispheric function to consciousness.

### The Right Hemisphere and the Unconscious

Arthur Koestler, a well-known writer, argued that the "creative act" usually occurs through other than conscious analytic intention. In his book *The Act of Creation,* Koestler mentions the idea of incubation periods, putting a problem aside for a time in the hope of coming up with an insight later. He also suggests that the unconscious does a great deal of matchmaking or forming of analogies.

Several famous scientists have told how they found a solution to a problem during a dream. Otto Loewi, who won the Nobel Prize for showing that nerve impulses are transmitted by means of chemical agents, described how the critical experiment came to him in a near-sleep state. He had come up with the idea of chemical transmission 17 years earlier but had put it "aside" for lack of a way to test it. Fifteen years later he performed experiments (unrelated to his old idea) for which he had designed a technique to detect fluids secreted by a frog's heart. One night, two years later:

> I awoke, turned on the light, jotted down a few notes on a tiny slip of thin paper. Then I fell asleep again. It occurred to me at six o'clock in the morning that during the night I had written down something most important, but I was unable to decipher the scrawl. The next night, at three o'clock, the idea returned. It was the design of an experiment to determine whether or not the hypothesis of chemical transmission that I had uttered seventeen years ago was correct. I got up immediately, went to the laboratory, and performed a simple experiment on a frog heart according to the nocturnal design.[23]

Loewi isolated two frog hearts, the first with its nerves intact, the second without. He stimulated the vagus nerve of the first heart. The vagus nerve has an inhibitory effect on the heart, so its beats slowed down. He immediately removed some of the salt solution in which the heart was kept bathed and applied it to the second heart. It slowed down. By going a few steps further, Loewi unequivocally proved that nerves influence the heart (and most other tissue) by releasing specific chemical substances from their terminals.

A careful review of the chain of events leading to Loewi's experiment dispels any notion that it was an accidental or purely intuitive discovery. The background for it had been set by years of rigorous work. However, the act of connecting two critical ideas apparently came while he was in an unconscious or semiconscious state.

Koestler attributes a role to the unconscious in discovery, calling it the "type of thinking prevalent in childhood and in primitive societies, which has been superseded in the normal adult by techniques of thought which are more rational and realistic."[24] As for the incubation period (such as the 17-year period in Loewi's case), Koestler calls it "thinking aside" or a rebellion against constraints that is "a temporary liberation from the tyranny of overprecise verbal concepts, of the axioms and prejudices ingrained in the very texture of specialized ways of thought."[25]

The temptation to reinterpret such ideas in terms of the laterality data is obviously great. Several investigators have suggested that dreaming is part of the realm of the right hemisphere. Some believe that the right hemisphere does all the dreaming; others feel that the dream state allows the right hemisphere to express itself more freely than usual because the left hemisphere doesn't dominate or interfere. Sigmund Freud, the father of psychoanalysis, believed that the qualities of the unconscious mind are revealed through the logic of dreams.

Do the discoveries with split-brain patients have any consequences for Freud's theories? David Galin thinks they do. He believes they provide a neurological validation for Freud's notion of an unconscious mind. Galin points out that the right hemisphere's mode of thought is similar to Freud's description of the "unconscious," and he notes a parallel between the functioning of the isolated right hemisphere and mental processes that are repressed, unconscious, and unable to control behavior directly: "Certain aspects of right hemisphere functioning are congruent with the mode of cognition psychoanalysts have termed primary process, the form of thought that Freud originally assigned to the system Ucs (unconscious)."[26] These include the extensive use of images, lesser involvement in the perception of time and sequence, and a limited language of the sort that appears in dreams and slips of the tongue.

Galin believes that normally the two hemispheres operate in an integrated fashion, but at certain times they may be blocked from communicating with each other. As a result, a situation similar to what is found in split-brain patients may occur in a normal individual. Galin describes several ways in which the two hemispheres of an ordinary person could function as if they had been surgically disconnected. In one interesting example, he talks of the inhibition of information transfer because of conflict: "Imagine the effect on a child when his mother presents one message verbally, but quite another with her facial expression and body language; 'I am doing it because I love you, dear,' say the words, but 'I hate you and will destroy you' says the face."[27]

Galin believes that although each hemisphere is exposed to the same sensory input, it effectively receives a different input because each emphasizes only one of the messages. The left will attend to the verbal cues, and the right will attend to the nonverbal cues. He continues with the following conjecture:

In this situation, the two hemispheres might decide on opposite courses of action; the left to approach and the right to flee. . . . The left hemisphere seems to win control of the output channels most of the time, but if the left is not able to "turn off" the right completely, it may settle for disconnecting the transfer of the conflicting information from the other side. . . . Each hemisphere treats the weak contralateral input in the same way in which people in general treat the odd discrepant observation that does not fit with the mass of their beliefs; we first ignore it, and then if it is insistent, we actively avoid it.[28]

Galin believes that during such moments of disconnection, the left hemisphere alone governs consciousness. Mental events in the right hemisphere, however, continue a life of their own and act as a "Freudian" unconscious, as an "independent reservoir of inaccessible cognition," which may create uneasy emotional states in a person.

It is interesting to note that LeDoux and Gazzaniga make some observations about their patient P.S. that, at least anecdotally, seem psychodynamic in nature. They refer to the experiments where they addressed subjective questions to P.S.'s left and right hemispheres separately:

The day that case P.S.'s left and right hemispheres equally valued himself, his friends, and other matters, he was a calm, tractable, and appealing adolescent. On the days that the right and left sides disagreed on these evaluations, case P.S. became difficult to manage behaviorally. Clearly, it is as if each mental system can read the emotional differences harbored by the other at any given time. When they are discordant, a feeling of anxiety, which is ultimately read out by hyperactivity and general overall aggression, is engendered. The crisp surgical instance of this dynamism raises the question of whether or not such processes are active in the normal brain, where different mental systems, using different neural codes, coexist within and between the cerebral hemispheres.[29]

### *The Role of Verbal Mechanisms in Mental Unity, or the Chicken and Snow Shovel Experiment*

Gazzaniga and LeDoux recently conducted on P.S. another series of experiments, which they claim provides a clue to a major mechanism of personal thought—the process by which we construct a reality based on actual behavior.

P.S. was tested with pairs of visual stimuli presented simultaneously to each side of a fixation point located on a projection screen. The picture falling into each visual field was thus processed by the hemisphere normally receiving input from that side of the fixation point.

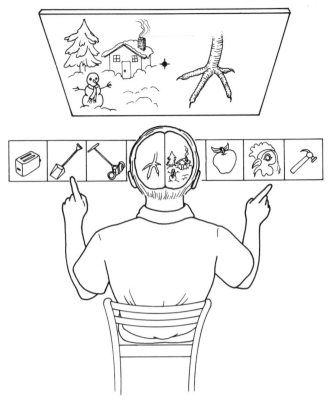

**10.3** Simultaneous presentation of two different tasks, one to each hemisphere of patient P.S. P.S.'s left hemisphere saw the chicken claw while the right hemisphere was presented with a snow scene. Each hemisphere responded by choosing, with the contralateral hand it controlled, a picture related to what it had seen. The patient was then asked to "explain" his choices. (From M. S. Gazzaniga and J. E. Le Doux, *The Integrated Mind,* Fig. 42, p. 149. New york: Plenum Press, 1978.)

P.S. was asked to use his hands to point to pictures that were related to what he had seen flashed on the screen from among several placed in front of him. Figure 10.3 shows the procedure.

He did this quite well. His right hand pointed to a picture related to one that had been flashed in his right visual field (to the left hemisphere), and his left hand pointed to a picture related to one that had been flashed in his left visual field (to the right hemisphere). Of particular interest was the way in which P.S. verbally interpreted these double responses:

> When a snow scene was presented to the right hemisphere and a chicken claw was presented to the left, P.S. quickly and dutifully responded correctly by choosing a picture of a chicken from a series of four cards with

his right hand and a picture of a shovel from a series of four cards with his left hand. The subject was then asked, "What did you see?" "I saw a claw and I picked the chicken, and you have to clean out the chicken shed with a shovel."

In trial after trial, we saw this kind of response. The left hemisphere could easily and accurately identify why it had picked the answer, and then subsequently, and without batting an eye, it would incorporate the right hemisphere's response into the framework. While we knew exactly why the right hemisphere had made its choice, the left hemisphere could merely guess. Yet, the left did not offer its suggestion in a guessing vein but rather a statement of fact as to why that card had been picked.[30]

Gazzaniga and LeDoux see in these results the suggestion that the major task of our "verbal self" is to construct a reality based on our actual behavior. They feel that our verbal mechanisms are not always privy to the origin of our actions and can attribute cause to actions not actually accessible to them: "It is as if the verbal self looks out and sees what the person is doing, and from that knowledge it interprets a reality." They raise the question of whether we indeed know whence our many separate behaviors arise.

They also offer the hypothesis that a developing organism contains a constellation of mental systems—emotional, motivational, and perceptual—each with its own values and response probabilities:

Then, as maturation continues, the behaviors that these separate systems emit are monitored by the one system we come to use more and more, namely, the verbal, natural language system. Gradually, a concept of self-control develops so that the verbal self comes to know the impulses for action that arise from the other selves, and it either tries to inhibit these impulses or free them, as the case may be.[31]

They conclude that the left hemisphere, in most of us, contains that which makes us feel like single, purposeful beings—that is, our language system.

### The "Why" and "How" of Hemispheric Specialization: An Evolutionary Perspective

Although much has been said about what each hemisphere can and cannot do, there is still little understanding of the reasons for hemispheric specialization in the first place. There is also little knowledge about the physiological mechanisms that may underlie these fundamental differences. Dealing with these "why" and "how" issues should help us answer the "what" of specialization, a question that has preoccupied us in so much of this book. It is not clear which question is more important or should be answered first. Insight into any one helps reformulate ideas about the other two. An ultimate understanding of hemispheric specialization will undoubtedly arise from the interaction of successively better answers to all three questions.

In earlier chapters we mentioned different investigators' speculations concerning the evolution and the mechanisms of hemispheric asymmetry. As we close this chapter as well as the book, it is appropriate to bring these speculations together and consider them in more detail.

Why is the hemisphere that controls speech also the one that usually controls a person's dominant hand? Is it a coincidence, or is there a profound relationship that should tell us something about what is involved in both speech and manipulative skills?

Doreen Kimura and her colleagues have obtained evidence that the left hemisphere may be essential for certain types of hand movement.[32] Patients with damage to the left hemisphere, but without paralysis of the right side, may have difficulty copying a sequence of hand movements and complex finger positions with either the left hand or the right hand. Kimura suggests that this finding bears a relationship to reports in the clinical literature of deaf mutes who sustained left-hemisphere damage in addition to their earlier speech and hearing disabilities. These individuals had used hand movements for communication, but after damage to the left hemisphere they displayed disturbances of these movements similar to the disruption of speech suffered by normal speakers who sustain such damage.

Kimura has also studied the gestural hand movements of a group of normal subjects, including individuals with right-hemisphere speech dominance as determined by dichotic listening tests. If speech is controlled by the left hemisphere, as it is in most people, the right hand makes more of the free hand movements; whereas if speech is controlled by the right hemisphere, the left hand makes more of those movements.

Kimura and others have proposed that left-hemisphere specialization for speech is a consequence not so much of an asymmetric evolution of symbolic functions as it is a consequence of the evolution of certain motor skills "that happen to lend themselves readily to communication."[33] In other words, the left hemisphere evolved language not because it gradually became more symbolic or analytic per se, but because it became well adapted for some categories of motor activity.

It is possible that the evolutionary advantages offered by the development of a hand skilled at manipulation also happened to be a most useful foundation on which to build a communication system, one that was gestural and utilized the right hand first, but later came to utilize the vocal musculature. As a result the left hemisphere came to possess a virtual monopoly on control of the motor systems involved in linguistic expression, whether by speech or writing.

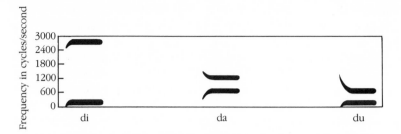

10.4   Idealized spectrogram of sound frequencies produced in voicing "di,"
"da," and "du." Each sound consists of air vibration concentrated mainly within
two frequency ranges, called the first and second formants. Recognizing these
sounds involves perceiving the rapid change at the beginning of the formants.
Even this early part of the formant changes as the vowel sound changes, despite
the fact that all sounds start with *d.*

Although the differences are considerably less striking than in the
case of expression, the left hemisphere also appears to be somewhat
superior to the right in its comprehension ability. Researchers at the
Haskins Laboratories have shown that the left hemisphere is better at
decoding the extremely rapid transitions in frequency that are part of
certain speech sounds. Using the dichotic listening technique, they
found that right-handed subjects show a right-ear advantage for consonant–vowel syllables such as "ba," "da," and "ga." These differ only
in terms of the rapid frequency changes taking place in the first 50
milliseconds or so of the syllable, so the left hemisphere appears to
have an advantage in processing this quickly changing information.[34]

But is the left-hemisphere advantage simply one of being able to
track rapid frequency changes in speech? There is reason to believe
that more is involved. Investigators at Haskins have discovered that the
rapid frequency changes that signal *b* in the syllable "ba" are different
from those that signal *b* in "be" or "bo." Similarly, the acoustic config-
uration of other consonants also changes as a function of the vowel in
the syllable.[35] Figure 10.4 shows the nature of these changes for *d.*

What then do all the different *b*'s or *d*'s have in common that allow
our perceptual systems to hear them as identical sounds? Haskins researchers have noted that they are similar in terms of the way they are
*produced.* The similarity in production, they argue, is responsible for
the similarity in perception.

This idea, the motor theory of speech perception, holds that to
perceive speech sounds the human brain actually figures out what it
would have had to do to produce them. Speech researchers have
worked hard to explain what allows speech pronounced in so many
different ways to be understood so readily. One quality that seems

invariant across any particular sound is the way the throat, mouth, lips, and tongue are controlled in its production. The Haskins workers have proposed that in perceiving speech, a listener is in some manner figuring out how he or she would produce the same sounds. Although this theory is not universally accepted, it is of interest to our discussion, for it suggests that finely controlled motor sequences may be an inseparable part of our language communication system, in terms of both production and perception.

What about the right hemisphere? Has it changed during the period in which the left hemisphere acquired its motor and communication skills? Abilities unique to the right hemisphere remain elusive and difficult to define, although spatial ability is strongly implicated. Just as the left hemisphere evolved language, a symbolic system surpassing any single sensory modality, perhaps areas in the right hemisphere evolved ways of representing abstractly the two- and three-dimensional relationships of the external world grasped through vision, touch, and movement. In addition to the spatial tasks considered in earlier chapters, the ability to visualize a complex route or to find a path through a maze seems to depend on the right hemisphere. Although it is usually characterized as more spatial than the left, it is probably more accurately described as more manipulo-spatial—that is, possessing the ability to manipulate spatial patterns and relationships.

We have just considered how verbal skills may have grown out of the fine movement skills of the left hemisphere. Perhaps the spatial skills of the right hemisphere are due to another kind of motor skill— the ability to manipulate spatial relationships. Our ability to generate mental maps, rotate images, and conceptualize mechanical contraptions could very well be an abstract, internalized right-brain counterpart to the motor skills of the left brain.

Are these right-hemisphere skills a result of evolutionary specialization that developed in a complementary fashion to those occurring in the left brain? Or are they more ancient abilities that were at one time bilaterally represented but were essentially displaced in the left by the emergence of language? As we mentioned in Chapter 2, different investigators hold different views on this issue. Jerre Levy, for example, has argued that the cognitive processes used for language and for spatial-perceptual functions are incompatible and therefore had to develop in separate areas. By analyzing the tasks and questions most difficult for each hemisphere of split-brain patients, she inferred that the left and right modes of processing would mutually interfere if they existed within the same hemisphere.

These kinds of data yield insights into why lateralization took place, but they do not necessarily invalidate the idea that it was mainly the left hemisphere that changed. The issue is not readily decided. Its resolution will depend on much more complete knowledge of what is both common and different about the two hemispheres as well as the neural mechanisms behind the similarities and differences. Even when we achieve this knowledge, however, it is likely that several equally compatible evolutionary schemes for hemispheric specialization will remain.

Our brief review of some of the theories concerning the "why" of lateralization helps place the very large quantity of "what" data we have reviewed in some perspective. In the process of reviewing the literature for this book and reflecting on our own direct involvement in the area of hemispheric specialization for several years, we have become increasingly aware of the "dichotomania" problem. One symptom of the problem is to exaggerate hemispheric differences and to ignore other forms of brain organization such as the orderly differences within a hemisphere.

At the same time, we have become even more impressed with the reality of hemispheric differences and with their potential for helping us understand the brain mechanisms underlying higher mental functions. It is possible that some of the most profound human mental abilities are a result of nature's forfeiting, to an extent, a very old, stable, and successful method of changing the brain—bilaterally symmetric evolution. Why so much of nature involves mirror symmetric structure, and why the brain has for the most part evolved in a mirror symmetric fashion, is a theoretical issue that largely remains a subject of conjecture.

One suggestion is that a doubled structure is less subject to damage. Mechanisms in one side can easily take over functions lost in the other because they are basically doing the same thing. Once asymmetries developed, this advantage was lost. Substituting for this loss of redundancy, however, was the added survival value of language, sophisticated mental mapping capabilities, and whatever other talents the integrated action of the asymmetric components of the two hemispheres can generate.

In studying these asymmetries, researchers are going beyond what is different about the halves of the brain. They are uncovering ways in which the brain deals with different kinds of information in the environment and ways in which it generates some of our behavior. The discovery of different processes and mechanisms in the brain encourages the idea that mental abilities may be explained in these ways. Investigators have touched on issues of consciousness, emotion, and the unity of experience. Some of these may be premature attempts using insufficient data and inappropriate definitions, but they are steps, first steps, in the long endeavor ahead to understand the brain and perhaps ourselves.

# Appendix

## Functional Neuroanatomy
## and Clinical Disorders:
## A Brief Review

Modern functional mapping of the human brain has been attempted through the study of the effects of brain damage, electrical stimulation, neurosurgical procedures, and neuroanatomical studies coupled with animal research. The history of thought on the relationship between neuroanatomy and behavior has revolved around two opposing views. At one time, fanciful maps of the brain were drawn allotting specific regions to "thrift," "love of family," "greed," "memory," and so on. At the other extreme was the view that the brain operates as a unit and within the brain there are no relationships between particular regions and specific mental functions.

Brain researchers today have moved away from these extremes. The brain is now thought to be organized in both a focal and a diffuse manner, depending on what functions are being studied. Basic sensory and motor functions are controlled by very specific regions, while higher mental functions involve a constellation of regions across the brain.

In the Appendix, we will review some basic neuroanatomy, concentrating on the cortical regions of the cerebral hemispheres—the regions of the human brain involved in most of the debate about asymmetry of function. We will also review some of the classic dysfunctions resulting from selective brain damage. Some of these dysfunctions were responsible for current structure–function views of the brain. Others have led investigators away from overly simple views relating brain areas to higher mental function.

In writing this Appendix, we have tried to present views that represent a consensus among brain researchers, although there is still considerable controversy in many instances. Because of these uncertainties, it is necessary to treat the newest "maps" of the brain as a rough guide rather than as a definitive road atlas.

## Neuroanatomy

The central nervous system consists of the spinal cord and the brain. The brain is conventionally divided into three major regions: the hindbrain, the midbrain, and the forebrain. These areas and some of the structures within them are demarcated in Figure A.1.* The major divisions are made on an embryological basis. Each develops from a different embryonic layer and is roughly related to different evolutionary stages in the development of the vertebrate nervous system.

Hindbrain and midbrain structures have traditionally been thought to control the more automatic, unconscious aspects of behavior. These include basic functions essential to life such as breathing, the sleep–wake cycle, and levels of arousal or degrees of responsiveness to external events. It is becoming more apparent that these deeper structures of the brain also contribute to the processing of information necessary for higher mental functions.

The forebrain is the largest and most highly developed section of the brain in humans and higher animals. It consists of a complex of anatomically distinct groups of nerve-cell bodies called nuclei, which are surrounded by nerve fibers sheathed in myelin and covered by the cerebral cortex.† The cortex forms the familiar convoluted surface of the brain and consists of multiple layers of complexly interconnected neurons. It is the "newest" structure in evolutionary terms and is well developed only in mammals. It is most expansive and convoluted in humans. The neocortex, as most of the human cortex is called, contains approximately 9 billion of the 12 billion neurons of the central nervous system. It is generally considered to be responsible for the highest functions of the human brain, such as abstract thought and language.

---

*Reference is often made to the brain stem and to the cerebrum. The brain stem includes the hindbrain and midbrain structures, excluding the cerebellum. Some anatomists also include the very central nuclei of the forebrain (the thalamus), located immediately above the midbrain. The cerebrum refers to the forebrain.

†The nerve fibers sheathed in myelin are known as "white matter" because of their white appearance in fresh brain tissue. The cortex, which has a gray appearance, is known as "gray matter."

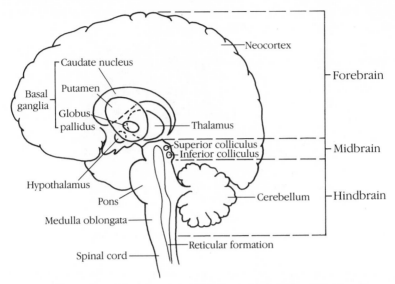

**A.1** Schematic view of the brain showing the basic relationships of deep nuclear groups and brain-stem structures. (From M. S. Gazzaniga, D. Steen, and B. Volpe, *Functional Neuroscience,* Fig. 3.13, p. 61. Copyright © 1979 by Harper & Row Publishers, Inc.)

The entire central nervous system is essentially bisymmetric. A sagittal plane (front to back) through the middle of the human body will divide the nervous system into two mirror-image sections. The left and right halves of the brain stem do not physically separate until the thalamus of the forebrain. The forebrain looks like separate mirror-image halves connected by fiber bundles. These halves are the cerebral hemispheres.

### Functional Areas of the Cortex

Almost the entire surface of each cerebral hemisphere consists of neocortex. Each hemisphere can be divided into four lobes, using the major folds of the cortex, called gyri (ridges) and sulci (valleys), as landmarks. Figure A.2 shows the divisions along the surface of one hemisphere. The central sulcus separates the frontal lobe from the parietal lobe. It also serves as the landmark for separating the anterior or front half of each hemisphere from the posterior areas.

The other major fissure, called the lateral sulcus (sylvian fissure), separates the temporal lobe from the frontal and parietal lobes. The most posterior portion of the cortex is called the occipital lobe.

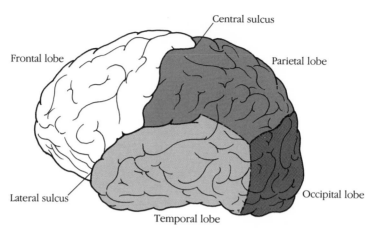

**A.2** Division of the cerebral hemisphere into lobes.

Each lobe is known to serve a different sensory or motor function. The occipital lobe is a visual center. Parts of the temporal lobe are involved with hearing. The anterior part of the parietal lobe is concerned with somatosensory function. The posterior part of the frontal lobe mediates motor function. Figure A.3 shows the areas involved.

The areas of the cortex receiving input from the sense organs or controlling the movements of particular body parts are called primary zones or primary projection areas. The primary motor areas of the frontal lobe control specific parts of the body (see Figure A.4). The

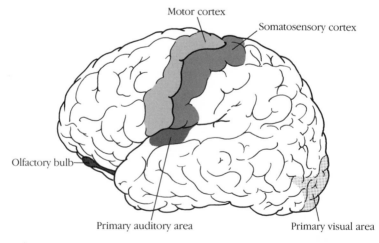

**A.3** Primary sensory and motor areas of the brain. The remaining areas are often termed "uncommitted" or "association" cortex.

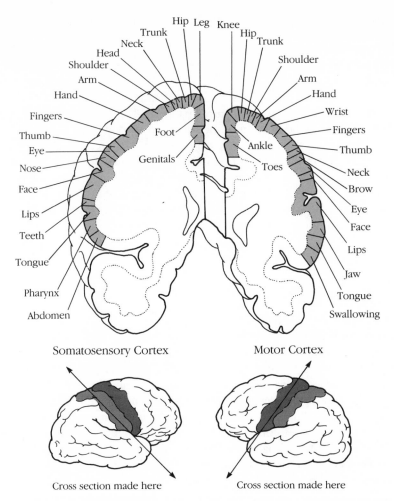

Somatosensory Cortex     Motor Cortex

Cross section made here     Cross section made here

**A.4** The motor and somatosensory areas of the cortex are projections of areas of the body. Some areas, such as those representing the face, the tongue, and the fingers, are disproportionately large because the amount of cortical surface devoted to a given part of the body reflects the requirements of that body part. The lips take up more space in the motor cortex than they do in the somatosensory cortex. Lips do more muscle-controlled moving than they do sensing. (From N. A. Lassen, D. H. Ingvar, and E. Skinhoj, "Brain Function and Blood Flow," Copyright © 1978 by Scientific American, Inc. All rights reserved).

primary sensory areas in the parietal, temporal, and occipital lobes are said to possess high modal specificity: each is active only when there is stimulation in its particular modality. In addition, within each primary sensory area, smaller areas respond only to highly specific properties or parts of its "sensory window."

All primary areas are topologically arranged so that there is a systematic, orderly representation in the cortex of different parts of the body, different auditory qualities, and specific parts of the visual field. Lesions in these areas lead to highly specific deficits, such as blindness in one part of the visual field, a selective hearing loss, a loss of sensation in one part of the body, or a partial paralysis. The extent of the damage will determine the amount of the "sensory window" that is lost.

Figure A.5 shows the primary projection areas in the brains of four animals and in the human brain. In lower animals most of the brain is devoted to sensory and motor functions; there is little else. In higher animals, and especially human beings, a great deal of the cortex does not seem to be committed to the specific senses. These areas are known as "uncommitted" cortex or "association" areas.

### The Association Areas
### of the Parietal, Occipital, and Temporal Lobes

Some investigators make a distinction between secondary and tertiary association cortex. Secondary zones are the areas adjacent to the primary projection areas and are still considered to have some modal specificity—that is, they are higher level processing centers for the specific sensory information coming into the primary area. Modality-specific information becomes integrated into meaningful wholes in secondary zones. Single sensory stimuli are combined and elaborated into progressively more complicated patterns. Damage to secondary zones gives rise to perceptual disorders restricted to a specific modality. In visual agnosia, for example, a patient can see but does not recognize or comprehend what he or she is looking at. There are also auditory and tactile agnosias.

Tertiary zones* lie at the borders of the parietal, temporal, and occipital secondary zones. In these association areas or "zones of over-lapping," modal specificity disappears. Neural activity does not seem to depend on stimulation of any single sensory modality. Various sensory fields overlap, and combinations of sensations become perceptions of a progressively higher order. Tactile and kinesthetic impulses are built up into perceptions of form and size and are associated with visual information from the same objects. It is thought that objects come to be represented ultimately by a constellation of memories compounded from several sensory channels. Damage to areas such as the parietal-occipital junction and parietal-temporal junction result in disorders transcending any single modality.

---

*The definition of tertiary zones is from A. R. Luria, *Higher Cortical Functions in Man* (New York: Basic Books, 1966).

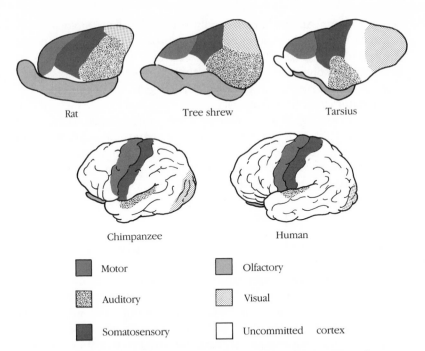

Rat         Tree shrew         Tarsius

Chimpanzee         Human

- Motor
- Auditory
- Somatosensory
- Olfactory
- Visual
- Uncommitted cortex

**A.5** The brains of five mammals showing the increase in the proportion of "uncommitted" cortex to areas devoted primarily to sensory and motor functions. (From W. Penfield in J. C. Eccles, ed., *Brain and Conscious Experience.* New York: Springer-Verlag, Inc., 1966. Copyright © 1966 Pontifica Academia Scientiarum).

It is at this level that hemispheric asymmetries appear. Damage to the right hemisphere within these zones may produce disorders of manipulo-spatial abilities or the neglect syndrome in which a patient ignores the left half of space. Damage within these zones in the left hemisphere may interfere with language comprehension or the ability to name objects. Thus the association areas of the posterior of the brain seem to be concerned with high-level perceptual processes and more abstract "manipulation" of these processes. The left and right hemispheres seem to differ in what processes they handle best.

### The Association Areas of the Frontal Lobes

The rear of the frontal lobes is the primary motor area. The secondary motor area, analogous to the secondary sensory zones of the posterior of the brain, lies immediately in front of the motor strip and is called the premotor area. This area is involved in higher level motor organization. Damage to this region leads to disturbances in the organization of movements (damage to the motor strip itself leads to paralysis). In the left hemisphere, damage to specific parts of the premotor area (Broca's area) leads to disorganization of speech—the expressive dysfunction known as Broca's aphasia.

The functions of the remaining areas of the frontal lobes seem more elusive. The areas in the anterior part of the frontal lobes (called prefrontal) are no longer directly tied in to motor control and are believed to serve higher integrative functions. This prefrontal area is often referred to as frontal granular cortex because of the characteristic "granular" neurons of which it is mostly composed. As shown in Figure A.6, these areas are particularly enlarged in the human brain. They account for humans' distinctively high forehead when the shape of their skulls is compared with the skulls of other primates.

Damage to these prefrontal areas can result in both intellectual and personality changes. Although patients still seem capable of performing many different types of tasks, deficits in executing sequences of operations or solving complex problems become evident. A patient may have trouble shifting "set" and become stuck on a task. There is an inability to inhibit the first tendency aroused by a problem. Having done one step properly, the patient may continue to use the same strategy in totally inappropriate contexts. This is often referred to as perseveration. These syndromes suggest that the frontal lobes are involved in the planning and organization of actions.

The inflexibility seen in certain frontal syndromes has often been called a deficit in abstract thinking, but this label is controversial. Some investigators claim a "dissociation between thought and action." The patient can verbalize what he or she should be doing, yet is unable to carry it through.

The personality and emotional changes associated with damage to the frontal lobes are even more elusive than the intellectual deficits. Earlier in this century, the frontal regions were the object of many experimental surgical procedures that attempted to control several forms of mental illness. Despite a great deal of literature on the subject, the question of how the frontal lobes function and the actual effects of the operations remain controversial.

In general, it appears that the frontal association areas not only play a major role in planning and controlling action, but may also control or inhibit emotional tendencies. Luria has suggested that the frontal areas serve as a tertiary integrative zone for the motor system as well as for the limbic system, an older region deeper in the forebrain believed to play a major role in emotion.

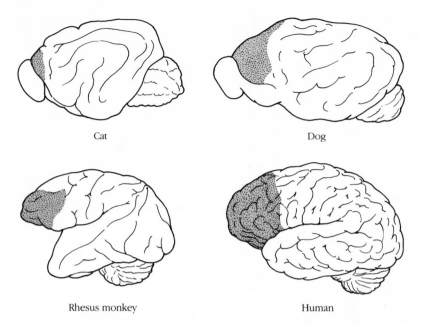

Cat

Dog

Rhesus monkey

Human

**A.6** The frontal granular cortex in the brains of three animals and in the human brain (not drawn to scale). (From K. W. Walsh, *Neuropsychology—A Clinical Approach,* Fig. 4.1, p. 110. Edinburgh: Churchill Livingstone Ltd., 1977.)

## Classic Dysfunctions Arising From Brain Injury

A good deal of the theoretical view of cortical function presented in the preceding section is based on clinical observation of the deficits and abilities of patients with damage to specific regions of the brain. In this section we will discuss some of the traditionally labeled dysfunctions associated with selective brain damage. Some of them have directly contributed to the concepts of the previous section. Others provide additional insight into the interaction of various brain areas in complex behaviors. Several forms of apraxia, for example, show that more is involved in voluntary movement than the motor region of the frontal lobes.

It must be kept in mind that rarely do any of these disorders occur in isolation from other problems or from each other. Of the various consequences of brain injury, these dysfunctions are only the most obvious and most amenable to labeling.

### Agnosia

*Agnosia* means "failure to recognize." Various agnosias have been defined according to the sensory modality that is affected and sometimes according to the class of objects or sounds that cannot be recognized.

*Visual agnosia* is a failure to recognize objects that cannot be attributed to a defect of visual acuity or to intellectual impairments.* Many forms of visual agnosia have been described, including an agnosia for faces, *prosopagnosia*. Prosopagnosia arises from damage involving the posterior regions of the right (nondominant) hemisphere, although the most severe cases usually have bilateral damage. Most severe agnosias for objects occur with bilateral damage to parietal-occipital regions of the brain, or with damage involving these areas in the left (dominant) hemisphere coupled with damage to interhemispheric pathways. The latter situation is thought to mimic bilateral damage effectively by disconnecting any remaining intact visual processing areas from the language centers of the left hemisphere. A patient with visual agnosia may still be able to recognize objects tactually, although extensive parietal damage often leads to problems in both modalities.

*Auditory agnosia* is a condition in which a patient with unimpaired hearing fails to recognize or distinguish what she or he hears. These sounds may include musical tones or familiar noises such as a telephone ring or running water. They may also be only speech sounds, but such an auditory agnosia, known as word deafness, is usually considered a type of aphasia. Auditory agnosia is associated with damage to regions of the temporal lobe in the left (dominant) hemisphere, although these disturbances are more severe when the injury is bilateral.

*Astereognosis* is an inability to recognize familiar objects through touch or palpation even though sensation in the hands appears to be normal. This condition usually results from damage to regions in the parietal lobe adjacent to the somatosensory projection areas. It is thought that such damage interferes with tactile-kinesthetic memories that have been acquired and stored over the years and built up into perceptions of form, size, and texture.

### Aphasia

*Aphasia* is a disturbance in the ability to speak or understand language resulting from brain damage. In the great majority of humans this usually arises from damage to any of several regions of the left (dominant) hemisphere. The speech organs and musculature (larynx, tongue, lips, etc.) are intact, and there is no disruption of the neural wiring to these organs.

---

*Not all clinicians insist that good visual acuity has to be demonstrated. Some term cases of mixed sensory and perceptual loss as agnosias. The decision as to whether a visual deficit is "purely" sensory or a higher level perceptual problem is often very difficult to make. Most cases fall somewhere in between.

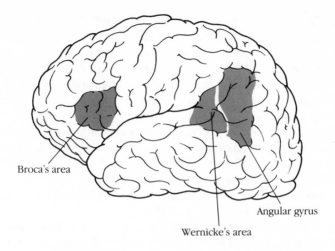

Broca's area

Angular gyrus

Wernicke's area

**A.7** The areas of the left hemisphere in humans associated with speech and language.

There are many different types of aphasia, depending on the location and extent of damage. The two main categories are expressive ("motor") aphasia and receptive ("sensory") aphasia.

*Expressive (or Broca's) aphasia* is a deficit involving primarily the patient's own speech; the patient's comprehension of the speech of others remains relatively intact. This type of aphasia is associated with damage to frontal regions of the left hemisphere controlling speech output, especially Broca's area (see Figure A.7). A patient with Broca's aphasia speaks very little. When the patient attempts to speak, he or she is halting and has difficulty getting the words out. There is an absence of small grammatical parts of speech and proper inflection. Writing is comparably disordered. Most of these patients seem to understand spoken and written language, so the problem is considered to be at the motor output stage of language rather than in comprehension. Broca's aphasics seem aware of most of their errors.

*Receptive (or Wernicke's) aphasia* is a disturbance in which the patient has great difficulty comprehending speech in general. It is associated with damage to the posterior region of the first temporal gyrus (Wernicke's area; see Figure A.7). The speech of a patient with receptive aphasia is much more fluent than that of an expressive aphasic but, depending on the extent of damage, may vary from being slightly odd to completely meaningless. Patients often use inappropriate words (paraphasias) or nonexistent words (neologisms). In some cases the patient's output sounds like complete jargon or "word salad," although the rhythm and flow of speech seem preserved. In severe cases, the speech may not even have wordlike structures. It may consist mostly of phonemic jargon, yet sound fluent. Such patients often seem unaware that their speech is defective or meaningless and continue to talk as if nothing is wrong. Reading and writing are comparably impaired.

Though relatively pure receptive or expressive forms of aphasia do occur, the division of aphasias into these two types implies a more clear-cut distinction than is generally the case. Expressive aphasics, for example, also suffer from subtle comprehension problems, probably having to do with the information conveyed by the grammatical structure of more complex sentences.

A few other types of aphasia have been labeled and interpreted in terms of different patterns of brain damage.

*Conduction aphasia* is thought to result from a disconnection of the fiber tracts connecting Wernicke's area to Broca's area. A patient sounds like a Wernicke's aphasic (speech is fluent but somewhat meaningless) but shows evidence of comprehension and some reading ability. The patient may understand what is said but not be able to repeat it correctly.

*Word deafness* results from a lesion disconnecting Wernicke's area from auditory inputs. Comprehension is impaired for *spoken* language only. Comprehension of writing is normal, as is verbal and written expression. This disorder is essentially an auditory agnosia.

*Anomic aphasia* involves difficulty in naming objects. Although this condition is present in most aphasics, a "purer" or isolated form results from damage limited to cortical areas at the junction of the temporal, parietal, and occipital lobes—an area called the angular gyrus (see Figure A.7). A purely anomic patient will have normal comprehension and be able to speak almost normally in spontaneous casual conversation. When confronted with objects, however, or when trying to think of a word or name for something or somebody, the patient will falter badly. The difficulty is often very severe and disheartening. It has been suggested that this impairment is a result of disruption of the multisensory associations involved in the naming act. The fact that it is associated with damage to the multimodal association areas of the posterior of the brain supports this contention.

*Global aphasia* refers to the severe impairment of all language-related functions. Comprehension and production of speech are defective or absent. Communication may be attempted with a symbol system, but even this is difficult and sometimes unsuccessful. Global aphasia results from widespread damage to the left hemisphere involving most of the areas thought to play a role in language.

### Apraxia

*Apraxia* is the inability to perform certain learned movements despite the absence of paralysis or sensory loss.* Patterns of complex learned movements are organized in space and time and follow intricate sequences established through experience. Reaching out and properly grasping an object consists of a largely unconscious series of movements that depend on a built-up memory of acts similarly performed. Apraxia may be regarded as a breakdown in the program or "memory" of the motor sequences necessary to perform some basic act.

*Kinetic apraxia* ("limb-kinetic apraxia") is most frequently associated with lesions of the premotor region of the frontal lobes. It is a disturbance that can be confined to one limb, depending on which hemisphere is damaged. The dysfunction is an inability to execute fine acquired motor movements, such as properly holding a pen.

*Ideomotor apraxia* is usually due to damage in the parietal lobe of the left (dominant) hemisphere, but it seems to have bilateral effects behaviorally. A patient is unable to perform many complex acts on command, although he or she may perform them spontaneously in appropriate situations. The difficulty is especially noticeable when the patient is asked to use pantomime—for example, "Pretend you are brushing your teeth." "How do you strike a match?" "How do you wave good-by?" The patient seems to know what he or she has been told to do but is unable to do it. Given the actual objects and appropriate context, the patient will usually perform much better. Ideomotor apraxia is considered by many to be a result of the interruption of pathways between the center for verbal formulation of a motor act and the motor areas (of the frontal lobe) necessary for its execution.

*Ideational apraxia* involves an inability to formulate an appropriate sequence of acts or use objects properly. A patient seems to know how to perform isolated movements, such as how to strike against a match cover, but will do them inappropriately. For instance, given a candle and a pack of matches, she or he will strike the candle tip against the match cover. A patient may pick up a perfume bottle and bring it up to her mouth instead of her nose. Sometimes complex sequences are done out of order, such as when a patient starts the hand motions involved in writing before picking up a pen.

The patient's appreciation of what she or he is doing often seems to be defective, so it has been suggested that such apraxia is a form of agnosia. The locus of damage in such disorders has been controversial.

---

*There are some exceptions. Luria, in *Higher Cortical Functions in Man,* describes *kinesthetic apraxia* as apraxia resulting from the loss of feedback from the limbs concerning their position in space.

A classic view was that ideational apraxia arose from lesions in the parietal lobe of the left (dominant) hemisphere or in the corpus callosum. It is most frequently found, however, in cases of diffuse bilateral damage, such as that following anoxia.

*Constructional apraxia* involves a loss in the ability to reproduce figures by drawing or assembling. There seems to be a loss of visual guidance or an impairment in visualizing a manipulative output, although basic visual and motor functions appear intact. It is not considered a purely motor disorder. It is seen in certain cases of damage to the occipital and parietal cortex, perhaps to pathways between them. Many studies have reported that constructional apraxia is more severe in patients with right-hemisphere lesions. Other investigators claim there is a qualitative difference in the types of errors made in visuo-constructive tasks, depending on which hemisphere is damaged. Part of the difficulty in reconciling opinion on constructional apraxia, as well as other disorders, is that it is not clearly a separate entity. The relationship between visuo-perceptive deficits (hemispatial neglect, spatial agnosia, etc.) and visuo-constructive deficits is complex, and their symptoms are not easy to dissociate.

### Amnesia and Localization

Concepts of localization in the brain have long included the idea that specific storage sites exist for human memories. The search for the "engram" or storage unit of memory has continued for decades. Localization of memory was supported clinically by cases of *amnesia,* severe memory loss, following relatively focal damage to certain areas of the brain, notably the temporal lobes and hippocampus (an older part of the cortex deep within the temporal lobes). Figure A.8 shows some regions that have been implicated in memory disorders. In addition, hemispheric differences were reported in the kind of memories most affected by damage to the temporal lobes. Damage to the left-hemisphere temporal lobe appeared to impair verbal memory more than visual memory. Damage to the right-hemisphere temporal lobe tended to do the opposite.

Most amnestic syndromes do not convincingly show a true obliteration of long-term memories. Memory disorders typically affect recent events and new learning. When older memories are affected, there is evidence that the defect is in access; time or cuing can usually bring them back.

Some evidence for the localization of long-term memories was said to come from the stimulation studies of Canadian neurosurgeon Wilder Penfield and his associates. As part of the procedure to remove

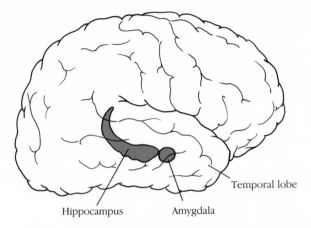

**A.8** The areas of the human brain involved in memory disorders. Certain memory processes appear to be associated with structures on the inner surface of the temporal lobes, such as the hippocampus and amygdala. Unilateral lesions of these structures have been reported to impair memory selectively, depending on which hemisphere is involved. Bilateral lesions have been known to cause severe memory disorders.

diseased brain tissue in certain patients, Penfield electrically stimulated the brain at various points in the vicinity of the diseased region. He reported interesting responses from stimulation of points in the temporal lobes, the hippocampus, and the amygdala (another structure deep in the temporal lobes). Patients at times reported experiencing visual or auditory memories and claimed that these experiences were very vivid, as though they were being lived over again. However, excision of the whole area did not seem to erase any memories. It is likely that most memory impairment consequent to focal brain damage is not so much a removal of localizable "engrams" as an interference with *part* of the mechanisms or steps involved in forming or retrieving memories.

# Notes

Chapter 1    A Historical Overview of Clinical Evidence for
Brain Asymmetries

[1]R. W. Sperry, "Brain Bisection and Consciousness," in *Brain and Conscious Experience,* ed. J. Eccles (New York: Springer-Verlag, 1966).

[2]R. Ornstein, *The Psychology of Consciousness,* 2nd ed. (New York: Harcourt Brace Jovanovich, 1977).

[3]R. Ornstein, "The Split and Whole Brain," *Human Nature* 1 (1978): 76–83.

[4]P. Bakan, "The Eyes Have It," *Psychology Today* 4 (1971): 64–69.

[5]J. E. Bogen, "The Other Side of the Brain. VII: Some Educational Aspects of Hemispheric Specialization," *UCLA Educator* 17 (1975): 24–32.

[6]W. Gibson, "Pioneers in Localization of Brain Function," *Journal of American Medical Association* 180 (1962): 944–951.

[7]P. Broca (1863), cited in R. J. Joynt, "Paul Pierre Broca: His Contribution to the Knowledge of Aphasia," *Cortex* 1 (1964): 206–213.

[8]P. Broca (1864), cited in M. Critchley, *Aphasiology and Other Aspects of Language* (London: Edward Arnold, 1970).

[9]P. Broca (1865), cited in S. Dimond, *The Double Brain* (London: Churchill-Livingstone, 1972).

[10]J. H. Jackson, *Selected Writings of John Hughlings Jackson,* ed. J. Taylor (New York: Basic Books, 1958).

[11]Ibid.

[12]Ibid.

[13]Ibid.

221

[14]T. Weisenberg and K. E. McBride, *Aphasia: A Clinical and Psychological Study* (New York: Commonwealth Fund, 1935).

[15]H. Hecaen and M. Albert, *Human Neuropsychology* (New York: Wiley, 1978).

[16]O. Dalin (1745), cited in A. L. Benton and R. J. Joynt, "Early Descriptions of Aphasia," *Archives of Neurology* 3 (1960): 205–222.

[17]A. Gates and J. Bradshaw, "The Role of the Cerebral Hemispheres in Music," *Brain and Language* 4 (1977): 403–431.

[18]J. Semmes, "Hemispheric Specialization, a Possible Clue to Mechanism," *Neuropsychologia* 6 (1968): 11–26.

[19]B. Bramwell, "On Crossed Aphasia," *Lancet* 8 (1899): 1473–1479.

[20]W. Penfield and L. Roberts, *Speech and Brain Mechanisms* (Princeton, N.J.: Princeton University Press, 1959).

[21]J. A. Wada and T. Rasmussen, "Intracarotid Injection of Sodium Amytal for the Lateralization of Cerebral Speech Dominance: Experimental and Clinical Observations," *Journal of Neurosurgery* 17 (1960):266–282.

[22]T. Rasmussen and B. Milner, "The Role of Early Left-Brain Injury in Determining Lateralization of Cerebral Speech Functions," in *Evolution and Lateralization of the Brain,* ed. S. Dimond and D. Blizzard (New York: New York Academy of Sciences, 1977).

## Chapter 2    Split-Brain Research

[1]T. C. Erickson, "Spread of Epileptic Discharge," *Archives of Neurology and Psychiatry* 43 (1940): 429–452.

[2]W. Van Wagenen and R. Herren, "Surgical Division of Commissural Pathways in the Corpus Callosum," *Archives of Neurology and Psychiatry* 44 (1940) 740–759.

[3]G. Fechner (1860), cited in O. Zangwill, "Consciousness and the Cerebral Hemispheres," in *Hemispheric Function in the Human Brain,* ed. S. Dimond and G. Beaumont (New York: Halsted Press, 1974).

[4]A. J. Akelaitis, "Studies on the Corpus Callosum. II: The Higher Visual Functions in Each Homonymous Field Following Complete Section of the Corpus Callosum," *Archives of Neurology and Psychiatry* 45 (1941): 799–796.

A. J. Akelaitis, "The Study of Gnosis, Praxis and Language Following Section of the Corpus Callosum and Anterior Commissure," *Journal of Neurosurgery* 1 (1944): 94–102.

[5]R. E. Myers, "Function of Corpus Callosum in Interocular Transfer," *Brain* 79 (1956): 358–363.

R. E. Myers and R. W. Sperry, "Interhemispheric Communication Through the Corpus Callosum. Mnemonic Carry-Over Between the Hemispheres," *Archives of Neurology and Psychiatry* 80 (1958): 298–303.

[6]R. W. Sperry, "Hemisphere Deconnection and Unity in Conscious Awareness," *American Psychologist* 23 (1968): 723–733.

[7]M. S. Gazzaniga and S. A. Hillyard, "Language and Speech Capacity of the Right Hemisphere," *Neuropsychologia* 9 (1971): 273–280.

[8]M. S. Gazzaniga, *The Bisected Brain* (New York: Appleton-Century-Crofts, 1970).

[9]J. Levy, C. Trevarthen, and R. W. Sperry, "Perception of Bilateral Chimeric Figures Following Hemispheric Disconnection," *Brain* 95 (1972): 61–78.

[10]L. Franco and R. W. Sperry, "Hemisphere Lateralization for Cognitive Processing of Geometry," *Neuropsychologia* 15 (1977): 107–114.

[11]P. Greenwood, D. H. Wilson, and M. S. Gazzaniga, "Dream Report Following Commissurotomy," *Cortex* 13 (1977): 311–316.

[12]E. Zaidel and R. W. Sperry, "Memory Impairment Following Commissurotomy in Man," *Brain* 97 (1974): 263–272.

[13]J. E. LeDoux, G. Risse, S. P. Springer, D. H. Wilson, and M. S. Gazzaniga, "Cognition and Commissurotomy," *Brain* 100 (1977): 87–104.

[14]Gazzaniga, *The Bisected Brain.*

[15]E. Zaidel, "A Technique for Presenting Lateralized Visual Input With Prolonged Exposure," *Vision Research* 15 (1975): 283–289.

[16]E. Zaidel, "Auditory Language Comprehension in the Right Hemisphere Following Cerebral Commissurotomy and Hemispherectomy: A Comparison With Child Language and Aphasia," in *Language Acquisition and Language Breakdown,* ed. A. Caramazza and E. Zurif (Baltimore: Johns Hopkins University Press, 1978).

[17]M. S. Gazzaniga and J. E. LeDoux, *The Integrated Mind* (New York: Plenum Press, 1978).

[18]M. S. Gazzaniga, B. Volpe, C. Smylie, D. H. Wilson, and J. E. LeDoux, "Plasticity in Speech Organization Following Commissurotomy," *Brain* 102 (1979): 805–816.

[19]R. Nebes, "Dominance of the Minor Hemisphere in Commissurotomized Man in a Test of Figural Unification," *Brain* 95 (1972): 633–638.

[20]J. Levy-Agresti and R. W. Sperry, "Differential Perceptual Capacities in Major and Minor Hemispheres," *Proceedings of the National Academy of Science, U.S.A.* 61 (1968): 1151.

[21]J. E. LeDoux, D. H. Wilson, and M. S. Gazzaniga, "Manipulo-Spatial Aspects of Cerebral Lateralization: Clues to the Origin of Lateralization," *Neuropsychologia* 15 (1977): 743–750.

[22]Levy-Agresti and Sperry, "Differential Perceptual Capacities in Major and Minor Hemispheres."

[23]J. Levy, "Psychobiological Implications of Bilateral Asymmetry," in *Hemispheric Function in the Human Brain.*

[24]C. Trevarthen, and M. Kinsbourne, cited in J. Levy, "Cerebral Asymmetries as Manifested in Split Brain Man," in *Hemispheric Disconnection and Cerebral Function,* ed. M. Kinsbourne and W. L. Smith (Springfield, Ill.: Charles C. Thomas, 1974).

[25]Levy, Trevarthen, and Sperry, "Perception of Bilateral Chimeric Figures Following Hemispheric Disconnection."

[26]Levy, "Psychobiological Implications of Bilateral Symmetry."

[27]J. Levy and C. Trevarthen, "Perceptual, Semantic Language Processes in Split-Brain Patients," *Brain* 100 (1977): 105–118.

[28]J. Levy and C. Trevarthen, "Metacontrol of Hemispheric Function in Human Split Brain Patients, *Journal of Experimental Psychology: Human Perception and Performance* 2 (1976): 299–312.

[29]Ibid.

[30]R. W. Sperry, "Lateral Specialization in the Surgically Separated Hemispheres, in *The Neurosciences Third Study Program,* ed. F. O. Schmitt and F. G. Worden (Cambridge, Mass.: MIT Press, 1974).

[31]G. L. Risse, J. E. LeDoux, S. P. Springer, D. H. Wilson, and M. S. Gazzaniga, "The Anterior Commissure in Man: Functional Variation in a Multi-Sensory System," *Neuropsychologia* 16 (1977): 23–31.

[32]M. P. Bryden, and E. B. Zurif, "Dichotic Listening Performance in a Case of Agenesis of the Corpus Callosum," *Neuropsychologia* 8 (1970): 371–377.

R. E. Saul and R. W. Sperry, "Absence of Commissurotomy Symptoms With Agenesis of the Corpus Callosum," *Neurology* 18 (1968): 307.

[33]Gazzaniga and LeDoux, *The Integrated Mind.*

## Chapter 3    Studying Asymmetries in the Normal Brain

[1]M. Mishkin and D. G. Forgays, "Word Recognition as a Function of Retinal Locus," *Journal of Experimental Psychology* 43 (1952): 43–48.

[2]M. I. Barton, H. Goodglass, and A. Shai, "Differential Recognition of Tachistoscopically Presented English and Hebrew Words in Right and Left Visual Fields," *Perceptual and Motor Skills* 21 (1965): 431–437.

[3]G. Geffen, J. L. Bradshaw, and G. Wallace, "Interhemispheric Effects on Reaction Time to Verbal and Nonverbal Visual Stimuli," *Journal of Experimental Psychology* 87 (1971): 415–422.

G. Rizzolatti, C. Umilta, and G. Berlucchi, "Opposite Superiorities of the Right and Left Cerebral Hemispheres in Discriminative Reaction Time to Physiognomical and Alphabetic Material," *Brain* 94 (1971): 431–442.

[4]D. Kimura, "Spatial Localization in Left and Right Visual Fields," *Canadian Journal of Psychology* 23 (1969): 445–458.

[5]M. P. Bryden and C. Rainey, "Left-Right Differences in Tachistoscopic Recognition," *Journal of Experimental Psychology* 66 (1963): 568–571.

H. L. Dee and D. Fontenot, "Cerebral Dominance and Lateral Differences in Perception and Memory," *Neuropsychologia* (1973): 167–173.

D. Kimura, "Dual Functional Asymmetry of the Brain in Visual Perception," *Neuropsychologia* 4 (1966): 275–285.

[6]D. Kimura, "Some Effects of Temporal Lobe Damage on Auditory Perception," *Canadian Journal of Psychology* 15 (1961): 156–165.

[7]M. R. Rosenzweig, "Representation of the Two Ears at the Auditory Cortex," *American Journal of Physiology* 167 (1951): 147–158.

[8]D. Dirks, "Perception of Dichotic and Monaural Verbal Material and Cerebral Dominance in Speech," *Acta Otolaryngologica* 58 (1964): 73–80.

[9]B. Milner, L. Taylor, and R. W. Sperry, "Lateralized Suppression of Dichotically Presented Digits After Commissural Section in Man," *Science* 161 (1968): 184–185.

S. P. Springer and M. S. Gazzaniga, "Dichotic Listening in Partial and Complete Split Brain Patients," *Neuropsychologia* 13 (1975): 341–346.

[10]D. Kimura, "Cerebral Dominance and the Perception of Verbal Stimuli," *Canadian Journal of Psychology* 15 (1961): 166–171.

[11]M. P. Bryden, "Tachistoscopic Recognition, Handedness, and Cerebral Dominance," *Neuropsychologia* 3 (1965): 1–8.

[12]D. Kimura, "Functional Asymmetry of the Brain in Dichotic Listening," *Cortex* 3 (1967): 163–178.

[13]D. Kimura and S. Folb, "Neural Processing of Backwards Speech Sounds," *Science* 161 (1968): 395–396.

M. Studdert-Kennedy and D. Shankweiler, "Hemispheric Specialization for Speech Perception," *Journal of the Acoustical Society of America* 48 (1970): 579–594.

[14]D. Kimura, "Left-Right Differences in the Perception of Melodies," *Quarterly Journal of Experimental Psychology* 16 (1964): 355–358.

[15]F. W. K. Curry, "A Comparison of Left-Handed and Right-Handed Subjects on Verbal and Nonverbal Dichotic Listening Tasks," *Cortex* 3 (1967): 343–352.

[16]R. Klatzky and R. Atkinson, "Specialization of the Cerebral Hemispheres in Scanning for Information in Short-Term Memory," *Perception and Psychophysics* 10 (1971): 335–338.

[17]J. G. Seamon and M. S. Gazzaniga, "Coding Strategies and Cerebral Laterality Effects," *Cognitive Psychology* 5 (1973): 249–256.

[18]M. P. Bryden, "Strategy Effects in the Assessment of Hemispheric Asymmetry," in *Strategies of Information Processing,* ed. G. Underwood (London: Academic Press, 1978).

[19]D. Hines and P. Satz, "Cross-Modal Asymmetries in Perception Related to Asymmetry in Cerebral Function," *Neuropsychologia* 12 (1974): 239–247.

E. B. Zurif and M. P. Bryden, "Familial Handedness and Left-Right Difference in Auditory and Visual Perception," *Neuropsychologia* 7 (1969): 179–187.

[20]S. Blumstein, H. Goodglass, and V. Tartter, "The Reliability of Ear Advantage in Dichotic Listening," *Brain and Language* 2 (1975): 226–236.

Hines and Satz, "Cross-Modal Asymmetries in Perception Related to Asymmetry in Cerebral Function."

[21]M. Kinsbourne, "The Mechanisms of Hemisphere Asymmetry in Man, *Hemispheric Disconnection and Cerebral Function,* ed. M. Kinsbourne and W. L. Smith (Springfield, Ill.: Charles C. Thomas, 1974).

[22]M. Kinsbourne, "The Control of Attention by Interaction Between the Cerebral Hemispheres," in *Attention and Performance IV,* ed. S. Kornblum (New York: Academic Press, 1973).

[23]J. Morais and M. Landercy, "Listening to Speech While Retaining Music: What Happens to the Right Ear Advantage?" *Brain and Language* 4 (1977): 295–308.

[24]M. Moscovitch, "Information Processing," in *Handbook of Neurobiology-Neuropsychology,* ed. M. S. Gazzaniga (New York: Plenum Press, 1979).

[25]M. E. Day, "An Eye Movement Phenomenon Relating to Attention, Thought, and Anxiety," *Perceptual and Motor Skills* 19 (1964): 443–446.

[26]P. Bakan, "Hypnotizability, Laterality of Eye Movement, and Functional Brain Asymmetry," *Perceptual and Motor Skills* 28 (1969): 927–932.

[27]M. Kinsbourne, "Eye and Head Turning Indicates Cerebral Lateralization," *Science* 176 (1972): 539–541.

[28]D. Galin and R. Ornstein, "Individual Differences in Cognitive Style. I: Reflexive Eye Movements," *Neuropsychologia* 12 (1974): 367–376.

K. Kocel, D. Galin, R. Ornstein, and E. Merrin, "Lateral Eye Movement and Cognitive Mode," *Psychonomic Science* 27 (1972): 223–224.

[29]G. E. Schwartz, R. J. Davidson, and F. Maer, "Right Hemisphere Lateralization for Emotion in the Human Brain: Interactions With Cognition, *Science* 190 (1975): 286–288.

[30]R. E. Gur, R. C. Gur, and L. J. Harris, "Cerebral Activation, as Measured by Subjects' Lateral Eye Movements, Is Influenced by Experimenter Location," *Neuropsychologia* 13 (1975): 35–44.

[31]H. Ehrlichman and A. Weinberger, "Lateral Eye Movements and Hemispheric Asymmetry: A Critical Review," *Psychological Bulletin* 85 (1979): 1080–1101.

[32]M. Kinsbourne and R. E. Hicks, "Mapping Cerebral Functional Space: Competition and Collaboration in Human Performance," in *Asymmetrical Function of the Brain,* ed. M. Kinsbourne (Cambridge, England: Cambridge University Press, 1978).

[33]M. Kinsbourne and J. Cook, "Generalized and Lateralized Effects of Concurrent Verbalization on a Unimanual Skill," *Quarterly Journal of Experimental Psychology* 23 (1971): 341–345.

[34]R. E. Hicks, "Intrahemispheric Response Competition Between Vocal and Unimanual Performance in Normal Adult Human Male," *Journal of Comparative and Physiological Psychology* 89 (1975): 50–60.

[35]M. Kinsbourne and J. McMurray, "The Effect of Cerebral Dominance on Time Sharing Between Speaking and Tapping by Preschool Children," *Child Development* 46 (1975): 240–242.

C. Krueter, M. Kinsbourne, and C. Trevarthen, "Are Deconnected Hemispheres Independent Channels? A Preliminary Study of the Effect of Unilateral Loading on Bilateral Finger Tapping," *Neuropsychologia* 10 (1972): 453–461.

## Chapter 4  Activity and Anatomy: Physiological Correlates of Function

[1]D. Galin and R. Ornstein, "Lateral Specialization of Cognitive Mode: An EEG Study," *Psychophysiology* 9 (1972): 412–418.

[2]R. Cohn, "Differential Cerebral Processing of Noise and Verbal Stimuli," *Science* 172 (1971): 599–601.

A. E. Davis and J. A. Wada, "Hemispheric Asymmetry: Frequency Analysis of Visual and Auditory Evoked Responses to Nonverbal Stimuli," *Electroencephalography and Clinical Neurophysiology* 37 (1974): 1–9.

[3]M. Buschbaum and P. Fedio, "Hemispheric Differences in Evoked Potentials to Verbal and Nonverbal Stimuli on the Left and Right Visual Fields," *Physiology and Behavior* 5 (1970): 207–210.

[4]D. L. Molfese, R. B. Freeman, Jr., and D. S. Palermo, "The Ontogeny of the Brain Lateralization for Speech and Nonspeech Stimuli," *Brain and Language* 2 (1975): 356–368.

[5]C. C. Wood, W. R. Goff, and R. S. Day, "Auditory Evoked Potentials During Speech Perception," *Science* 173 (1971): 1248–1251.

[6]D. Galin and R. R. Ellis, "Asymmetry in Evoked Potentials as an Index of Lateralized Cognitive Processes: Relation to EEG Alpha Asymmetry," *Psychophysiology* 13 (1975): 45–50.

[7]A. Mayes and G. Beaumont, "Does Visual Evoked Potential Asymmetry Index Cognitive Activity?" *Neuropsychologia* 15 (1977): 249–256.

[8]E. Donchin, M. Kutas, and G. McCarthy, "Electrocortical Indices of Hemispheric Utilization," in *Lateralization in the Nervous System,* ed. S. Harnad, R. Doty, L. Goldstein, J. Jaynes, and G. Krauthamer (New York: Academic Press, 1977).

[9]N. A. Lassen and D. H. Ingvar, "Radioisotopic Assessment of Regional Cerebral Blood Flows, in *Progress in Nuclear Medicine,* vol. 1 (Baltimore: University Park Press, 1972).

[10]J. Risberg, J. H. Halsey, E. L. Wills, and E. M. Wilson, "Hemispheric Specialization in Normal Man Studied by Bilateral Measurements of the Regional Cerebral Blood Flow: A Study With the 133 Xe Inhalation Technique," *Brain* 98 (1975): 511–524.

[11]N. A. Lassen, D. H. Ingvar, and E. Skinhoj, "Brain Function and Blood Flow," *Scientific American* 239 (1978): 62–71.

[12]F. Plum, A. Gjedde, and F. E. Samson, "Neuroanatomical Functional Mapping by the Radioactive 2-dioxy-d-glucose Method," *Neurosciences Research Program Bulletin* 14 (1976): 457–518.

[13]N. Geschwind and W. Levitsky, "Human Brain: Left-Right Asymmetries in Temporal Speech Region," *Science* 161 (1968): 186–187.

[14]J. A. Wada, R. Clark, and A. Hamm, "Cerebral Hemispheric Asymmetry in Humans," *Archives of Neurology* 32 (1975): 239–246.

S. F. Witelson and W. Pallie, "Left Hemisphere Specialization for Language in the Newborn: Anatomical Evidence of Asymmetry," *Brain* 96 (1973): 641–646.

[15]M. LeMay and A. Culebras, "Human Brain–Morphologic Differences in the Hemisphere Demonstrable by Carotid Anteriography," *The New England Journal of Medicine* 287 (1972): 168–170.

[16]M. LeMay and N. Geschwind, "Asymmetries of the Human Cerebral Hemispheres," in *Language Acquisition and Language Breakdown,* ed. A. Caramazza and E. Zurif (Baltimore: Johns Hopkins University Press, 1978).

[17]A. M. Galaburda, M. LeMay, T. Kemper, and N. Geschwind, "Right-Left Asymmetries in the Brain," *Science* 199 (1978): 852–856.

[18]A. Oke, R. Keller, I. Mefford, and R. N. Adams, "Lateralization of Norepinephrine in Human Thalamus," *Science* 200 (1978): 1411–1413.

## Chapter 5  The Puzzle of the Left-Hander

[1]W. Dennis, "Early Graphic Evidence of Dextrality in Man," *Perceptual and Motor Skills* 8 (1958): 147–149.

R. A. Dart, "The Predatory Implement Technique of Australopithecus," *American Journal of Physical Anthropology* 7 (1949): 1–38.

R. S. Uhrbrock, "Laterality in Art," *Journal of Aesthetics and Art Criticism* 32 (1973): 27–35.

[2]M. Barsley, *Left Handed People* (North Hollywood: Wilshire Book Co., 1979).

[3]C. Sagan, *The Dragons of Eden* (New York: Random House, 1977).

[4]H. D. Chamberlain, "The Inheritance of Left Handedness," *Journal of Heredity* 19 (1928): 557–559.

[5]M. Annett, "A Model of the Inheritance of Handedness and Cerebral Dominance," *Nature* 204 (1964): 59–60.

[6]J. Levy and T. Nagylaki, "A Model for the Genetics of Handedness," *Genetics* 72 (1972): 117–128.

[7]M. Annett, "Handedness in the Children of Two Left Handed Parents," *Quarterly Journal of Psychology* 65 (1974): 129–131.

[8]R. G. Howard and A. M. Brown, "Twinning: A Marker for Biological Insults," *Child Development* 41 (1970): 519–530.

[9]H. Gordon, "Left-Handedness and Mirror Writing Especially Among Defective Children," *Brain* 43 (1920): 313–368.

[10]T. Rasmussen and B. Milner, "The Role of Early Left-Brain Injury in Determining Lateralization of Cerebral Speech Functions," in *Evolution and Lateralization of the Brain,* ed. S. Dimond and D. Blizzard (New York: New York Academy of Sciences, 1977).

[11]P. Bakan, G. Dibb, and P. Reed, "Handedness and Birth Stress," *Neuropsychologia* 11 (1973): 363–366.

[12]P. Satz, "Pathological Left-Handedness: An Explanatory Model," *Cortex* 8 (1972): 121–135.

[13]I. Macgillivray, P. Nylander, and G. Corney, *Human Multiple Reproduction* (London: Saunders, 1975).

[14]T. Nagylaki and J. Levy, "The Sound of One Paw Clapping Is Not Sound," *Behavior Genetics* 3 (1973): 279–292.

[15]C. E. Lauterbach, "Studies in Twin Resemblance," *Genetics* 10 (1925): 525–568.

[16]Rasmussen and Milner, "The Role of Early Left-Brain Injury in Determining Lateralization of Cerebral Speech Functions."

[17]A. R. Luria, *Traumatic Aphasia* (The Hague: Mouton, 1970).

A. Subirana, "The Prognosis in Aphasia in Relation to Cerebral Dominance and Handedness," *Brain* 81 (1958): 415–425.

[18]M. P. Bryden, "Tachistoscopic Recognition, Handedness, and Cerebral Dominance," *Neuropsychologia* 3 (1965): 1–8.

P. Satz, K. Achenbach, E. Patteshall, and E. Fennell, "Order of Report, Ear Asymmetry, and Handedness in Dichotic Listening," *Cortex* 1 (1965): 377–396.

19. H. Hecaen and J. Sauget, "Cerebral Dominance in Left Handed Subjects," *Cortex* 7 (1971): 19–48.

20. E. B. Zurif and M. P. Bryden, "Familial Handedness in Left-Right Differences in Auditory and Visual Perception," *Neuropsychologia* 7 (1969): 179–187.

21. W. F. McKeever and D. VanDeventer, "Visual and Auditory Language Processing Asymmetries: Influences and Handedness, Familial Sensuality, and Sex," *Cortex* 13 (1972): 225–241.

J. A. Higenbottom, "Relationship Between Sets of Lateral and Perceptual Preference Measures," *Cortex* 9 (1973): 402–409.

22. M. P. Bryden, "Perceptual Asymmetry in Vision: Relation to Handedness, Eyedness, and Speech Lateralization," *Cortex* 9 (1973): 418–432.

D. Hines and P. Satz, "Cross-Modal Asymmetries in Perception Related to Asymmetry in Cerebral Function," *Neuropsychologia* 12 (1974): 239–247.

23. J. Levy and M. L. Reid "Variations in Writing Posture and Cerebral Organization," *Science* 194 (1976): 337.

24. L. Smith and M. Moscovitch, "Writing Posture, Hemispheric Control of Movement and Cerebral Dominance in Individuals With Inverted and Noninverted Hand Postures During Writing," *Neuropsychologia* 17 (1979): 637–644.

25. C. Hardyck and L. Petrinovich, "Left Handedness," *Psychological Bulletin* 84 (1977): 385–404.

26. J. Levy, "Possible Basis for the Evolution of Lateral Specialization of the Human Brain," *Nature* 224 (1969): 614–615.

27. E. Miller, "Handedness and the Pattern of Human Ability," *British Journal of Psychology* 62 (1971): 111–112.

F. Newcombe and G. Ratcliff, "Handedness, Speech Lateralization, and Ability," *Neuropsychologia* 11 (1973): 339–407.

## Chapter 6 Sex and Asymmetry

1. M. Coltheart, E. Hull, and D. Slater, "Sex Differences in Imagery and Reading," *Nature* 253 (1975): 438–440.

2. E. Maccoby and C. Jacklin, *The Psychology of Sex Differences* (Stanford, Calif.: Stanford University Press, 1974).

3. H. Lansdell, "A Sex Difference in Effect of Temporal Lobe Neurosurgery on Design Preference," *Nature* 194 (1962): 852–854.

[4]J. McGlone, "Sex Difference in Functional Brain Asymmetry," *Cortex* 14 (1978): 122–128.

[5]D. A. Lake and M. P. Bryden, "Handedness and Sex Differences in Hemispheric Asymmetry," *Brain and Language* 3 (1976): 266–282.

[6]G. G. Briggs and R. D. Nebes, "The Effects of Handedness, Family History, and Sex on Performance of a Dichotic Listening Task," *Neuropsychologia* 14 (1976): 129–134.

B. M. Carr, "Ear Effect Variables and Order of Report in Dichotic Listening," *Cortex* 5 (1969): 63–68.

[7]S. F. Witelson, "Sex and the Single Hemisphere: Specialization of the Right Hemisphere for Spatial Processing," *Science* 193 (1976): 425–427.

[8]J. A. Wada, R. Clark, and A. Hamm, "Cerebral Hemisphere Asymmetry in Humans," *Archives of Neurology* 32 (1975): 239–246.

[9]D. M. Tucker, "Sex Differences in Hemispheric Specialization for Synthetic Visuospatial Functions," *Neuropsychologia* 14 (1976): 447–454.

[10]R. J. Davidson and G. E. Schwartz, "Patterns of Cerebral Lateralization During Cardiac Feedback Versus the Self-Regulation of Emotion: Sex Differences," *Psychophysiology* 13 (1976): 62–68.

[11]D. Waber, "Sex Differences in Cognition: A Function of Maturation Rate?" *Science* 192 (1976): 572–573.

[12]J. Levy, "Lateral Differences in the Human Brain in Cognition and Behavioral Control," in *Cerebral Correlates of Conscious Experience,* ed. P. Buser and A. Rougeul-Buser (New York: North Holland Publishing Co., 1978).

## Chapter 7   The Development of Asymmetry

[1]E. H. Lenneberg, *Biological Foundations of Language* (New York: Wiley, 1967).

[2]L. S. Basser, "Hemiplegia of Early Onset and the Faculty of Speech With Special Reference to the Effects of Hemispherectomy," *Brain* 85 (1962): 427–460.

[3]S. Krashen, "Lateralization, Language Learning, and the Critical Period: Some New Evidence," *Language Learning* 23 (1973): 63–74.

[4]M. Kinsbourne, "The Ontogeny of Cerebral Dominance," in *Developmental Psycholinguistics and Communication Disorders,* ed. D. Aaronson and R. W. Rieber (New York: New York Academy of Sciences, 1975).

[5]M. Nagafuchi, "Development of Dichotic and Monaural Hearing Abilities in Young Children," *Acta Otolaryngologica* 69 (1970): 409–414.

[6]A. K. Entus, "Hemispheric Asymmetry in Processing of Dichotically Presented Speech and Nonspeech Stimuli by Infants," in *Language*

*Development and Neurological Theory,* ed. S. J. Segalowitz and F. Gruber (New York: Academic Press, 1977).

[7]F. Vargha-Khadem and M. C. Corballis, "Cerebral Asymmetry in Infants," *Brain and Language* 8 (1979): 1–9.

[8]C. Berlin, L. Hughes, S. Lowe-Bell, and H. Berlin, "Right Ear Advantage in Children 5 to 13," *Cortex* 9 (1973): 394–402.

  P. Satz, D. J. Bakker, J. Tenunissen, R. Goebel, and H. Van der Vlugt, "Developmental Parameters of the Ear Asymmetry: A Multivariate Approach" *Brain and Language* 2 (1975): 171–185.

[9]D. L. Molfese, R. B. Freeman, Jr., and D. S. Palermo, "The Ontogeny of Brain Lateralization for Speech and Nonspeech Stimuli," *Brain and Language* 2 (1975): 356–368.

[10]J. A. Wada and A. Davis, "Fundamental Nature of Human Infants' Brain Asymmetry," *Canadian Journal of Neurological Sciences* 4 (1977): 203–207.

[11]J. Chi, E. Dooling, and F. Giles, "Left-Right Asymmetries of the Temporal Speech Areas of the Human Fetus," *Archives of Neurology* 34 (1972): 346–348.

[12]J. A. Wada, R. Clark, and A. Hamm, "Cerebral Hemispheric Asymmetry in Humans," *Archives of Neurology* 32 (1975): 239–246.

[13]A. Smith, "Speech and Other Functions After Left (Dominant) Hemispherectomy," *Journal of Neurology, Neurosurgery, and Psychiatry* 29 (1966): 467–471.

  A. Smith, and C. W. Burkland, "Dominant Hemispherectomy," *Science* 153 (1966): 1280–1282.

[14]M. Dennis and H. Whitaker, "Language Acquisition Following Hemidecortication: Linguistic Superiority of the Left Over the Right Hemisphere," *Brain and Language* 3 (1976): 404–433.

[15]C. Trevarthen, "Cerebral Embryology and the Split Brain," in *Hemispheric Disconnection and Cerebral Function,* ed. M. Kinsbourne and W. L. Smith (Springfield, Ill.: Charles C. Thomas, 1974).

[16]Berlin, Hughes, Lowe-Bell, and Berlin, "Right Ear Advantage in Children 5 to 13."

[17]Satz, Bakker, Tenunissen, Goebel, and Van der Vlugt, "Developmental Parameters of the Ear Asymmetry: A Multivariate Approach."

[18]Ibid.

[19]Molfese, Freeman, and Palermo, "The Ontogeny of Brain Lateralization for Speech and Nonspeech Stimuli."

[20]Wada, Clark, and Hamm, "Cerebral Hemispheric Asymmetry in Humans."

[21]M. Morgan, "Embryology and Inheritance of Asymmetry," in *Lateralization in the Nervous System,* ed. S. Harnad, R. Doty, L. Goldstein, J. Jaynes, and G. Krauthamer (New York: Academic Press, 1977).

[22]M. P. Dryden, "Speech Lateralization in Families: A Preliminary Study Using Dichotic Listening," *Brain and Language* 2 (1975): 201–211.

[23]D. S. Geffner and I. Hochberg, "Ear Laterality Performance of Children From Low and Middle Socioeconomic Levels on a Verbal Dichotic Listening Task," *Cortex* 7 (1971): 193–203.

[24]T. Borowy and R. Goebel, "Cerebral Lateralization of Speech: The Effects of Age, Sex, Race, and Socioeconomic Class," *Neuropsychologia* 14 (1976): 363–370.

[25]M. F. Dorman, and D. Geffner, "Hemispheric Specialization for Speech Perception in Six Year Old Black and White Children From Low and Middle Socioeconomic Classes," *Cortex* 10 (1974): 171–176.

[26]S. Krashen, "Lateralization, Language Learning, and the Critical Period: Some New Evidence, *Language Learning* 23 (1973): 63–74.

[27]W. F. McKeever, H. Hoemann, V. Florian, and A. VanDeventer, "Evidence of Minimal Cerebral Asymmetries for the Processing of English Words and American Sign Language in the Congenitally Deaf," *Neuropsychologia* 14 (1976): 413–423.

## Chapter 8    Asymmetries in Animals

[1]C. H. M. Beck and R. L. Barton, "Deviation and Laterality of Hand Preference in Monkeys," *Cortex* 8 (1972): 339–363.

R. L. Collins, "On the Inheritance of Handedness. I: Laterality in Inbred Mice," *Journal of Heredity* 59 (1968): 9–12.

J. M. Warren, J. M. Abplanalp, and H. B. Warren, "The Development of Handedness in Cats and Rhesus Monkeys," in *Early Behavior: Comparative and Developmental Approaches,* ed. H. W. Stevenson, E. H. Hess, and H. L. Reingold (New York: Wiley, 1967).

[2]R. L. Collins, "On the Inheritance of Handedness. II: Selection for Sinistrality in Mice," *Journal of Heredity* 60 (1969): 117–119.

[3]G. Ettlinger and D. Gautrin, "Verbal Discrimination Performance in the Monkey: The Effect of Unilateral Removal of Temporal Cortex," *Cortex* 7 (1971): 315–331.

J. M. Warren and A. J. Nonneman, "The Search for Cerebral Dominance in Monkeys," in *Origins and Evolution of Language and Speech,* ed. S. Harnad, H. Steklis, and J. Lancaster (New York: New York Academy of Sciences, 1976).

[4]J. H. Dewson, A. Cowey, and L. Weiskrantz, "Disruptions of Auditory Sequence Discrimination by Unilateral and Bilateral Cortical Ablations of Superior Temporal Gyrus in the Monkey," *Experimental Neurology* 28 (1970): 529–548.

[5]J. H. Dewson, "Preliminary Evidence of Hemispheric Asymmetry of Auditory Function in Monkeys," in *Lateralization in the Nervous System,* ed. S. Harnad, R. Doty, L. Goldstein, J. Jaynes, and G. Krauthamer (New York: Academic Press, 1977).

[6]C. R. Hamilton, "An Assessment of Hemispheric Specialization in Monkeys," in *Evolution and Lateralization of the Brain,* ed. S. Dimond and D. Blizzard (New York: New York Academy of Sciences, 1977).

[7]F. F. Ebner and R. E. Myers, "The Corpus Callosum and Interhemispheric Transmission of Tactual Learning," *Journal of Neurophysiology* 25 (1962): 380–391.

[8]J. S. Stamm and R. W. Sperry, "Function of Corpus Callosum in Contralateral Transfer of Somesthetic Discrimination in Cats," *Journal of Comparative and Physiological Psychology* 50 (1957): 138–143.

H. Gulliksen and T. Voneida, "An Attempt to Obtain Replicate Learning Curves in the Split Brain Cat," *Physiological Psychology* 3 (1975): 77–85.

J. S. Robinson and T. J. Voneida, "Hemisphere Differences in Cognitive Capacity in the Split Brain Cat," *Experimental Neurology* 38 (1973): 123–134.

[9]Hamilton, "An Assessment of Hemispheric Specialization in Monkeys."

[10]G. H. Yeni-Komshian and D. Benson, "Anatomical Study of Cerebral Asymmetry in the Temporal Lobe of Humans, Chimpanzees, and Rhesus Monkeys," *Science* 192 (1976): 387–389.

[11]M. Lemay and N. Geschwind, "Hemispheric Differences in the Brains of Great Apes," *Brain, Behavior, and Evolution* 11 (1975): 48–52.

[12]C. P. Groves and N. K. Humphrey, "Asymmetry in Gorilla Skulls: Evidence of Lateralized Brain Function?" *Nature* 244 (1973): 53–54.

[13]M. R. Petersen, M. D. Beecher, S. R. Zoloth, D. B. Moody, and W. C. Stebbins, "Neural Lateralization of Species-Specific Vocalizations by Japanese Macaques," *Science* 202 (1978): 324–326.

[14]F. Nottebohm, "Asymmetries in Neural Control of Vocalization in the Canary," *Lateralization in the Nervous System.*

[15]N. G. Lepori (1966), cited in Nottebohm, "Asymmetries in Neural Control of Vocalization in the Canary."

## Chapter 9   Pathology and the Hemispheres

[1]S. T. Orton, *Reading, Writing, and Speech Problems in Children* (New York: Norton, 1937).

[2]E. B. Zurif and G. Carson, "Dyslexia in Relation to Cerebral Dominance and Temporal Analysis," *Neuropsychologia* 8 (1970): 351–361.

[3]M. P. Bryden, "Dichotic Listening—Relations With Handedness and Reading in Children," *Neuropsychologia* 8 (1970): 443–450.

M. E. Thomson, "Comparison of Laterality Effects in Dyslexics and Controls Using Verbal Dichotic Listening Tasks," *Neuropsychologia* 14 (1976): 243–246.

S. F. Witelson and M. Rabinovich, "Hemispheric Speech Lateralization in Children With Auditory-Linguistic Deficits," *Cortex* 8 (1972): 412–426.

[4]T. Marcel, L. Katz, and M. Smith, "Laterality and Reading Proficiency," *Neuropsychologia* 12 (1974): 131–139.

[5]S. F. Witelson, "Abnormal Right Hemispheric Specialization in Developmental Dyslexia," in *The Neuropsychology of Learning Disorders,* ed. R. Knights and D. Bakker (Baltimore: University Park Press, 1976).

[6]G. H. Yeni-Komshian, D. Isenberg, and H. Goldberg, "Cerebral Dominance and Reading Disability: Left Visual Field Deficit in Poor Readers," *Neuropsychologia* 13 (1975): 83–94.

[7]S. F. Witelson, "Developmental Dyslexia: Two Right Hemispheres and None Left," *Science* 195 (1977): 309–311.

[8]F. Pirozzolo and K. Rayner, "Cerebral Organization and Reading Disability," *Neuropsychologia* 17 (1979): 485–491.

[9]D. Hier, M. LeMay, P. Rosenberger, and V. Perlo, "Developmental Dyslexia," *Archives of Neurology* 35 (1978): 90–92.

[10]J. G. Sheenan, *Stuttering: Research and Therapy* (New York: Harper & Row, 1970).

[11]F. K. Curry and H. H. Gregory, "The Performance of Stutterers on Dichotic Listening Tasks Thought to Reflect Cerebral Dominance," *Journal of Speech and Hearing Research* 12 (1969): 73–82.

[12]P. Quinn, "Stuttering, Cerebral Dominance, and the Dichotic Word Test," *Medical Journal of Australia* 2 (1972): 639–643.

N. Slorach and B. Noehr, "Dichotic Listening in Stuttering and Dyslalic Children," *Cortex* 9 (1973): 295–300.

[13]R. K. Jones, "Observations on Stammering After Localized Cerebral Injury," *Journal of Neurology, Neurosurgery, and Psychiatry* 29 (1966): 192–195.

[14]G. Andrews, P. T. Quinn, and W. A. Sorby, "Stuttering: An Investigation Into Verbal Dominance for Speech," *Journal of Neurology, Neurosurgery, and Psychiatry* 35 (1972): 414–418.

[15]R. Heltman, "Contradictory Evidence in Handedness and Stuttering," *Journal of Speech Disorders* 5 (1940): 327–331.

[16]P. Flor-Henry, "Schizophrenic-like Reactions and Affective Psychoses Associated With Temporal Lobe Epilepsy: Etiological Factors," *American Journal of Psychiatry* 26 (1969): 400–403.

[17]A. E. Qalker and S. Jablon, *A Follow-up Study of Head Wounds in World War II* (Washington, D.C.: U.S. Government Printing Office, 1961).

[18]D. Galin, "Implications for Psychiatry of Left and Right Cerebral Specialization," *Archives of General Psychiatry* 31 (1974): 572–583.

[19]J. Gruzelier and N. Hammond, "Schizophrenia—A Dominant Hemisphere Temporal Lobe Disorder?" *Research Communications in Psychology, Psychiatry, and Behavior* 1 (1976): 33–72.

[20]L. Schweitzer, E. Becker, and H. Welsh, "Abnormalities of Cerebral Lateralization in Schizophrenia Patients," *Archives of General Psychiatry* 35 (1978): 982–985.

[21]G. Beaumont and S. Dimond, "Brain Disconnection and Schizophrenia," *British Journal of Psychiatry* 123 (1973): 661–662.

[22]P. Flor-Henry, "Lateralized Temporal-Limbic Dysfunction and Psychopathology," in *Origins and Evolution of Language and Speech,* ed. S. Harnad, H. Steklis, and J. Lancaster (New York: New York Academy of Sciences, 1976).

[23]K. M. Heilman, R. Scholes, and R. T. Watson, "Auditory Affective Agnosia: Disturbed Comprehension of Affective Speech," *Journal of Neurology, Neurosurgery, and Psychiatry* 38 (1975): 69–72.

D. M. Tucker, R. T. Watson, and K. M. Herlman, "Discrimination and Evocation of Affectively Intoned Speech in Patients With Right Parietal Disease," *Neurology* 27 (1977): 947–950.

[24]H. A. Sackheim, R. C. Gur, and M. Saucy, "Emotions Are Expressed More Intensely on the Left Side of the Face," *Science* 202 (1978): 434–436.

[25]K. Heilman and S. Watson, "The Neglect Syndrome—A Unilateral Defect of the Orienting Response," in *Lateralization in the Nervous System,* ed. S. Harnad, R. Doty, L. Goldstein, J. Jaynes, and G. Krauthamer (New York: Academic Press, 1977).

[26]B. T. Volpe, J. E. LeDoux, and M. S. Gazzaniga, "Information Processing of Visual Stimuli in an 'Extinguished' field," *Nature* 282 (1979): 122–124.

[27]G. Deutsch, J. Tweedy, and B. Lorinstein, "Some Temporal and Spatial Factors Affecting Visual Neglect" (Paper presented at the Eighth Annual Meeting of the International Neuropsychological Society, San Francisco, 1980).

## Chapter 10    Beyond the Data: Speculative Issues

[1]R. W. Sperry, "Brain Bisection and Consciousness," in *Brain and Conscious Experience,* ed. J. Eccles (New York: Springer-Verlag, 1966).

[2]J. Eccles, *The Brain and Unity of Conscious Experience: The 19th Arthur Stanley Eddington Memorial Lecture* (Cambridge, England: Cambridge University Press, 1965).

[3]J. E. LeDoux, D. H. Wilson, and M. S. Gazzaniga, "A Divided Mind: Observations on the Conscious Properties of the Separated Hemispheres," *Annals of Neurology* 2 (1977): 417–421.

[4]Ibid.

[5]Sri Aurobindo, quoted in J. E. Bogen, "The Other Side of the Brain. VII: Some Educational Aspects of Hemispheric Specialization," *UCLA Educator* 17 (1975): 24–32.

[6]R. Ornstein, *The Psychology of Consciousness* (New York: Harcourt Brace Jovanovich, 1977).

[7]R. Ornstein, "The Split and Whole Brain," *Human Nature* 1 (1978): 76–83.

[8]H. Gardner, "What We Know (and Don't Know) About the Two Halves of the Brain," *Harvard Magazine* 80 (1978): 24–27.

[9]J. A. Paredes and M. J. Hepburn, "The Split Brain and the Culture-and-Cognition Paradox," *Current Anthropology* 17 (1976):121–127.

[10]J. E. Bogen, R. DeZare, W. D TenHouten, and J. F. Marsh, "The Other Side of the Brain. IV: The A/P Ratio," *Bulletin of the Los Angeles Neurological Societies* 37 (1972): 49–61.

[11]J. A. Zook and J. H. Dwyer, "Cultural Differences in Hemisphericity: A Critique" *Bulletin of the Los Angeles Neurological Societies* 41 (1976): 87–90.

[12]Ornstein, "The Split and Whole Brain."

[13]P. Bakan, "Hypnotizability, Laterality of Eye Movement, and Functional Brain Asymmetry," *Perceptual and Motor Skills* 28 (1969): 927–932.

[14]J. E. Bogen, "The Other Side of the Brain. VII: Some Educational Aspects of Hemispheric Specialization," *UCLA Educator* 17 (1975): 24–32.

[15]G. Prince, "Putting the Other Half of the Brain to Work," *Training: The Magazine of Human Resources Development* 15 (1978): 57–61.

[16]Ibid.

[17]C. Sagan, *The Dragons of Eden*. New York: Random House, 1977.

[18]Ibid.

[19]Ibid.

[20]Ibid.

[21]J. Jaynes, cited in S. Keen, "Reflections on the Dawn of Consciousness," *Psychology Today* 11 (1977): 58.

[22]Ibid.

[23]O. Loewi, *Perspectives in Biology and Medicine, 4* (Chicago: University of Chicago Press, 1960).

[24]A. Koestler, *The Act of Creation* (New York: Dell, 1964).

[25]Ibid.

[26]D. Galin, "Implications for Psychiatry of Left and Right Cerebral Specialization," *Archives of General Psychiatry* 31 (1974): 572–583.

[27] Ibid.

[28] Ibid.

[29] LeDoux, Wilson, and Gazzaniga, "A Divided Mind: Observations on the Conscious Properties of the Separated Hemispheres."

[30] M. S. Gazzaniga and J. E. LeDoux, *The Integrated Mind* (New York: Plenum Press, 1978).

[31] Ibid.

[32] D. Kimura and Y. Archibald, "Motor Functions of the Left Hemisphere," *Brain* 97 (1974): 337–350.

[33] Ibid.

[34] M. Studdert-Kennedy and D. Shankweiler, "Hemispheric Specialization for Speech Perception," *Journal of the Acoustical Society of America* 48 (1970): 579–594.

[35] A. M. Liberman, F. S. Cooper, D. Shankweiler, and M. Studdert-Kennedy, "Perceptions of the Speech Code," *Psychological Review* 74 (1967): 431–461.

# Index